LEGISLATION FOR THE BUILT ENVIRONMENT

LEGISLATION FOR THE BUILT ENVIRONMENT

A concise guide

PENELOPE COOLING
LLB (Hons) Solicitor
Lecturer in Law,
De Montfort University,
Leicester

VINCENT SHACKLOCK
MA DipTP DipLandArch MRTPI
Principal Lecturer in Planning and Conservation,
De Montfort University,
Leicester

DOUGLAS SCARRETT
BSc MA MPhil FRICS
Head of Estate Management,
De Montfort University,
Leicester

DONHEAD

First published in the United Kingdom
in 1993 by
Donhead Publishing Ltd
28 Southdean Gardens
Wimbledon
London SW19 6NU
Tel. 081-789 0138

ISBN 1 873394 03 9

A CIP catalogue record for this book is available from the
British Library.

Typeset by Keyboard Services, Luton
Printed in Great Britain at the Alden Press,
Osney Mead, Oxford

CONTENTS

PREFACE

The legislation which regulates our environment is, today, far-reaching and complex. It seems to cover everything from the amount of exhaust fumes which our vehicles can introduce into the atmosphere to the protection of rare plants in our hedgerows. In writing this book, we intended to produce a guide which would lead the reader through part of this ever-increasing maze of legislation.

Although we are from different professional backgrounds, we have all practised in the area which is loosely termed 'building and development'. This book is aimed at all those practitioners, from whatever discipline, who are called upon to advise in a similar field, and it uses the term 'environment' in that context. The topics covered are limited to those which we believe will be most useful to the practitioner: planning and conservation; pollution of our towns and countryside; regulations relating to building design, as well as some of the statutory responsibilities which particularly affect the builder and his advisers; water services; and compulsory purchase. Additionally, there is an introductory chapter which outlines the fundamental principles on which our legal system is based and the operation within that framework of both the court system and local government in general. We have also included a chapter on financial aid, which should be useful to those seeking funding or grant assistance for development and redevelopment. The book concludes with a series of appendices containing information which we felt would be of particular use to the busy practitioner.

As with any book of this nature, we have had to tread a careful path between including and excluding too much detail. A deviation either way would have defeated the object of the book: to provide the practitioner in this field, not necessarily with the complete answer to a problem, but, at the very least, with a pointer to the answer. For this reason, we have not confined ourselves purely to the statutes. We have included references and, where appropriate, commentary, to regulations and orders, and also circulars and other government advice in the hope that this will provide additional guidance.

This book centres on the *legislation* affecting environmental matters. It does *not*, therefore, deal with any case law, except when absolutely necessary to explain a point or to clarify the way the legislation has been interpreted. This is a simplistic approach as the legislation, as we practise it, has been subjected to the interpretation of the courts, and we apologise to the reader. As justification, we wished to avoid confusing the issues by presenting too much law and not enough practical guidance. For a similar reason, the book does not deal with those areas of law based solely on common law, such as negligence or nuisance.

Legislation changes rapidly. To the best of our ability, and bearing in mind that we have covered a vast range of law, we have presented the law as it stands at October 1992. To keep the book manageable, we have not been able to cover every aspect of the legislation, and we are aware that by the time of publication some further changes will have occurred. The reader is therefore urged at all times to check both that the information in this book is up to date and that it fully deals with the situation in hand before relying in any way upon it.

We have considered only the law of England and Wales, commonly referred to as English law, and on occasion we have confined ourselves to England. This step was taken as a matter of convenience since the legislation is virtually identical, except that the Secretary of State for the principality is the Secretary of State for Wales, and circulars and other government advice is promulgated by the Welsh Office and not the various Departments. This means that circular numbers are different, although the content is the same and, in any event, every circular states both its Departmental number and the corresponding Welsh Office number.

English law does not necessarily apply to Scotland, and much Scottish law is quite different from that in England and Wales. Readers in Scotland are advised to proceed with extreme care.

There is an increasing amount of European Community legislation and we have, of course, covered those areas which now form part of our own statutes. We have not, however, included any detailed commentary on the law of the EC in general or its operation. We would refer the reader to specialised publications on those topics.

We have referred throughout to both the reader and other persons as male: again this is merely for convenience. Lastly, we would like to thank our publisher and especially Jill Pearce for her help and encouragement.

Penelope Cooling
Vincent Shacklock
Douglas Scarrett
October 1992

CHAPTER 1

ADMINISTRATION
AND CONTROL

INTRODUCTION

This book is concerned with the legislation which controls certain aspects of both public and private activity. To enable the operation of the legislation to be understood, it is necessary to have a broad understanding of the framework within which it operates. This chapter aims to provide a guide to that framework, enabling the later chapters to be set in their proper context.

The chapter concentrates on outlining the operation of local government (the controlling body for much of the legislation), and briefly points out the differences between that and other statutory bodies. Firstly, however, it will be helpful to explain and differentiate among some of the classifications of the law which will be met during the course of the book, as well as describing the court system within which the legislative process works.

STATUTE LAW AND DELEGATED LEGISLATION

Statute law comprises that part of the law which has been enacted by Parliament and is embodied in Acts of Parliament. The great majority of Acts are initiated by the government, passing through a fairly complex process before being presented to the monarch for royal assent. At that point the Act will form part of our law. Statutes can also be divided into various types, for example, the Town and Country Planning Act 1990 is a consolidating statute which has, in effect, brought together a number of previous Acts relating to the same subject matter. A codifying statute, on the other hand, is one which takes the existing 'common' or 'judge-made' law on a subject and collates it into one Act, thus forming a written and easily available 'code'.

Parliament is legislatively supreme, but it is impractical for all legislation to pass through the Parliamentary system. This is partly because of the time which would be involved and also because an Act rarely covers all the minutiae of the subject, tending more to be a statement of policy which establishes principles. These principles may involve a technical area which requires considerable expertise and would not be appropriate for debate in Parliament. Detailed provisions are, therefore, more satisfactorily prepared by an expert.

Furthermore, detailed legislative provisions often need updating and, on occasion, emergency provisions are required speedily. Parliament, on the whole, is too unwieldy a body to deal with these problems and a far quicker and more adaptable method is the use of *secondary* or *delegated* legislation. In such instances Parliament delegates its law-making powers to other bodies, usually other government departments, requiring them to produce detailed regulations known as *statutory instruments*. The Building Regulations 1991 were produced in this way in accordance with the delegated powers given to the Secretary of State for the Environment in the Building Act 1984.

In a similar way, local authorities produce delegated legislation in the form of bye-laws. These are for the 'good rule and government' of the local authority area and have to be approved by the Home Secretary. Again, these detailed regulations are produced by the body which is best equipped to recognise the requirements of its area.

STATUTE LAW AND COMMON LAW

Whereas statute law is embodied in Acts of Parliament and statutory instruments, the common law is that part of the law which is found in the decisions of the courts. In the Middle Ages judges travelled the country deciding cases and then pooled their decisions. In this way, a common practice was developed throughout the country. England and Wales are often referred to as common law countries because the legal system was initially derived from judges' decisions. Now, of course, the majority of the law is found in the statutes. In many instances the judge-made law has been codified and the decisions incorporated into statutes, which are more accessible to the public and easier to understand. Furthermore, statutes can more readily adapt to the speed of technological change and cope with the integration of the existing legal system into that of the rest of Europe. It is simply not practical to await the outcome of court decisions (which, by their very nature, depend on one party commencing litigation) for the legal system to develop.

Although much of the law can now be found in statutes, there remain some areas which continue to be governed by past decisions. Two common examples are trespass and negligence. Both of these, along with nuisance, defamation and a variety of other matters, are known as torts. Simply translated, this means a civil wrong for which redress can be sought in the civil courts.

Although this book deals with legislation rather than common law, it must be remembered that statutes need interpretation. The Parliamentary draftsman is trained to anticipate potential loopholes when he is preparing new legislation, but it is only when an Act is put into practice that its inconsistencies and uncertainties become apparent. Interpretation is carried out by the courts and the ingenuity of man provides the judges with a constant source of queries on the construction of statutes. Statutes must be acted upon in the light of the interpretation placed on them by the court, and large bodies of case-law build up in this way. Despite the use of legislation as a means of clarifying the law (and most statutes also have definition sections to assist in their interpretation), it is clear that the role of the court remains fundamental in the application of that law.

CIVIL LAW AND CRIMINAL LAW

The basic distinction between civil law and criminal law is that the former aims to compensate the victim, whereas the latter aims to punish the wrongdoer. The former is usually concerned with disputes between the parties (such as breach of contract) and civil law remedies, the most usual of which is damages, are sought through the civil courts. Criminal matters, on the other hand, are most frequently pursued by the state (in the guise of the Crown Prosecution Service) on behalf of the public in general, and punishment ranges from fines to imprisonment. Criminal offences are tried in the criminal courts.

Local authorities, in their role as protectors of the inhabitants of their area, have many powers to commence criminal proceedings. A district council is able to prosecute a person who is, for example, in breach of an enforcement notice under the Town and Country Planning Act 1990, in contravention of the Health and Safety at Work etc. Act 1974, obstructing a highway under the Highways Act 1980, or creating a noise nuisance in contravention of the Control of Pollution Act 1974.

THE STRUCTURE OF THE COURT SYSTEM

The House of Lords forms the apex of both the civil and criminal court structure, but in the lower tiers there are marked distinctions (see Figures 1 and 2).

Taking the civil court system first: the county court is at the base and is the starting point for the majority of civil actions. These courts are designed to hear disputes or actions which do not involve a complex or controversial area of law and where the remedy sought will, on the whole, be below £50,000. Many minor disagreements are

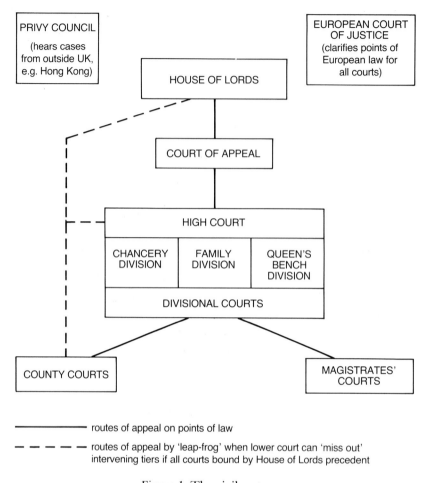

Figure 1 The civil system.

dealt with by these courts by way of arbitration. The jurisdiction of the county courts was extended in July 1991 by the Courts and Legal Services Act 1990 in an attempt to relieve the higher courts of their workload and to streamline the system. The types of action heard before the county courts extend from contract disputes to family and matrimonial matters; unpaid mortgages to negligence claims.

Despite the recent reorganisation of the civil system, there are still some specialised matters which must be brought at first instance before the High Court. These include applications for orders of mandamus or certiorari (see page 12), as well as actions to recover sums in excess of £50,000. The High Court, which sits in London and at specified locations throughout England and Wales, also acts as an appeal court from decisions of the county court.

The High Court itself is split into three divisions. This has the advantage of enabling each division to specialise in a particular area of law. The Family Division, as its name

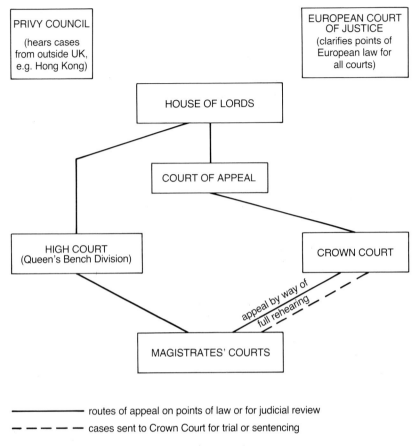

Figure 2 The criminal system.

implies, deals with cases involving the family unit. The Chancery Division mainly concerns itself with trusts, winding up of companies and revenue cases, whilst the Queen's Bench Division hears everything else (largely contract and tort actions).

The decisions of the High Court are also subject to appeal to the Court of Appeal and from there, on points of law only, to the House of Lords. The House of Lords also hears appeals from Scotland on civil matters only.

The criminal court system disposes of almost all (some ninety-five per cent) of its work at the bottom tier, in the magistrates' courts. Unlike the civil courts, which are staffed by legally qualified judges, magistrates are lay people who are guided by a legally trained clerk. All forms of crime, from theft to murder, are initially heard before a magistrates' court, although the more serious offences are passed up to the Crown Court, which has much wider sentencing powers. Cases here are heard by a judge who may be assisted by a jury. The magistrates' courts also have a limited civil jurisdiction relating to family matters, such as child care proceedings.

Criminal offences can be separated into different types. Briefly, some offences, known as *summary* offences, are triable only before a magistrates' court. Other, usually more serious offences, are known as *indictable* offences, and, although they commence their life before the magistrates' court, they can only be tried before a Crown Court. Just to confuse the issue, there is a large group of offences, called *hybrid* offences, which can be tried either before a magistrates' or a Crown Court. With hybrid offences, the defendant may choose in which court he wishes the matter to be heard and will weigh up the possible advantages of a jury trial against the fact that the Crown Court has wider sentencing powers. Even if a defendant requests his case to be heard before the magistrates' court, the magistrates themselves may send the case to the Crown Court if they believe that their own powers are insufficient to deal with the punishment of the offender should the case against him be proved. In addition, the magistrates retain the power to refer a case to the Crown Court for sentencing *after* they have heard all the evidence and found the defendant guilty. Although at first sight this may seem odd, it must be remembered that when initially agreeing to hear a case the magistrates will have only a scanty outline of the facts. Also a person's previous convictions are not made available until after a decision of guilt has been made. The magistrates may feel that they are not equipped to sentence a person suitably if that person has many previous convictions.

Appeals from the decisions of magistrates are usually made to the Crown Court. Appeals from that court are to the Court of Appeal and thence, again on a point of law only, to the House of Lords.

To appreciate fully the hierarchical nature of the court system, it is necessary to understand the *doctrine of precedent*. In short, all this means is that once a decision has been made by a court, all subsequent similar cases before that court or a court lower in the tier structure must be decided in accordance with the precedent case. The lower courts are 'bound' to follow the higher court decisions. If this were not so, it would be impossible to have any certainty in the court system because judges could treat like cases differently on a whim. To prevent courts from becoming hidebound by out-of-date decisions, the House of Lords, is *not* bound by its own previous decisions, nor, of course, by the decisions of the lower courts. Through the appeal mechanism, therefore, higher courts can overturn decisions of lower courts, but only the House of Lords can actually change a precedent which has been set by itself.

The disadvantage of this is that the public's view of what is fair and just changes with the passage of time. A case which became a precedent in 1930 may no longer reflect the feelings of society in 1990 and yet it will remain as a precedent, being followed by all the lower courts, until someone is prepared to take a new case all the way to the House of Lords in an attempt to overturn the earlier decision. This situation can be remedied by Parliament enacting new legislation to deal with the anomaly.

For completeness, it should be pointed out that there are means to short-circuit the usual routes of appeal. The lower courts mainly deal with the facts of a case. Both parties, whether the matter is civil or criminal, put the facts to the court as they see them, the court weighs up the evidence which it is has heard, decides what it thinks really happened and then applies the law to the situation. The losing party can appeal on the basis that the facts have been incorrectly interpreted by the court, but this is usually restricted to a gross error of judgement on the part of the judge or magistrates. As a result, the facts are rarely discussed at a higher level where it is the application and interpretation of the law which is in question. If a precedent has been set by say, the Court of Appeal, then not only the county court, but also the High Court, is bound to follow it. A potential appellant who disagrees with this interpretation knows that he cannot win on appeal to the High Court because of the precedent case. To have a chance he must appeal at the very least to the Court of Appeal, where the judges may be able to distinguish his case from the precedent and apply the law in a different way. This predicament is acknowledged by the court system which endorses a system of 'leap-frog' appeals as shown in Figures 1 and 2. In our example this would enable the appellant to appeal direct to the Court of Appeal from the county court.

In a similar way, an applicant may ask for a case to be 'stated' from the magistrates' court to the High Court. Basically, this means that the facts of the case are referred to the High Court for an opinion on the interpretation of the law in the light of those facts. The case is then returned to the magistrates for a fresh decision with the benefit of the higher court's opinion.

This would not be a complete picture of the court structure unless mention were also made of the Privy Council and the Court of European Justice. The former (which also has administrative functions) is a court made up of judges from the House of Lords which meets infrequently to hear appeals, in the main, from a few countries outside England and Wales. The countries which use the Privy Council as their final court of appeal have diminished significantly over the last few decades. Originally, it was used extensively by commonwealth countries and colonial territories, which, with constitutional independence now have their own final appeal court. Despite this, the Privy Council still hears appeals from Malaysia, some Australian states, New Zealand, Hong Kong, and small islands and colonies such as Gibraltar, Belize and the Isle of Man. Additionally, it has a function as the final appeal court from the ecclesiastical courts and from some professional disciplinary bodies, such as dentists and doctors.

The Court of Justice of the European Community, to give it its full title, sits in Luxembourg. Its major function is to ensure that Community law is observed throughout the EC by interpreting the vast amount of Community legislation which is now in force. It does this by hearing and presiding over appeals from all levels of courts within the member states as to the implementation of Community laws. Despite this, the national courts of the member states are also enabled to interpret Community legislation and will usually refer a matter to the European Court only if it is of particular significance. If this were not so, the European Court would be overloaded. The Court also has the function of enforcing the various European treaties against the member states.

The foregoing is only an outline of the court structure which, in many instances, is rather more complex. It does, however, serve to explain the basic principles and operation of the court system and the hierarchy of the courts within it.

REMEDIES OF THE COURTS

Different courts are designed to achieve different ends: as a result, the remedies available also differ. Taking the civil system first, the majority of actions commenced before the civil courts relate either to breaches of contract or to actions founded on negligence, for example after a car accident. The plaintiff, that is the person bringing the action, almost invariably requires compensation. This is usually an adequate remedy because its aim is to ensure that the plaintiff is financially in the same position as if the breach of contract or accident had not occurred. Compensation awards are referred to as *damages*.

Sometimes damages are not a suitable remedy. When dealing, in particular, with breaches of contract relating to land sales a plaintiff often seeks *specific performance*. He will argue that money alone cannot compensate for the loss of the land which he required and, if satisfied of this, the courts have the power to force the party in default to complete the contract and convey the land. Specific performance is an appropriate remedy whenever the subject of the contract is in some way unique and cannot be replaced purely by money.

Other remedies available in the civil courts include *injunctions* and *mandamus*. The former is an order of the court which requires a person to cease carrying out some kind of activity. For example, a neighbour who is so noisy as to be a nuisance can be restrained by the issue of an injunction. An order of mandamus, on the other hand, enforces the performance of some public duty. This, therefore, is particularly relevant where actions are being taken against statutory bodies in an attempt to force them to comply with their statutory duty. For reasons of enforcement, it is rarely possible or practical to bring a criminal action against a local authority, so these remedies are invaluable. Having said that, neither are issued freely by the courts. A breach of an injunction is treated as a contempt of court, the result of which is a fine or more probably imprisonment. This is viewed as a fairly draconian measure and injunctions are only granted when absolutely necessary. Mandamus is a complex remedy which is expensive to seek and, thus, is used infrequently. (Mandamus is discussed further under 'judicial review' – see page 12.)

Criminal offences are brought by a prosecution service on behalf of the public at large. It is possible for an individual to commence proceedings, but this is rare. The aim is to punish the individual on behalf of the state on the basis that a crime is against society as a whole. Remedies or punishments range from conditional discharges to small fines to imprisonment, through an intermediate series of attendance centre orders, probation and suspended sentences. The only penalties which are likely to be of any concern to us are fines and imprisonment.

Most Acts of Parliament which create criminal offences also state within them the maximum punishment which a court can determine. In an attempt to ensure that levels of fines have some continuing meaning as a punishment, rather than being devalued with inflation, penalties within the more recent statutes are described by reference to a standard scale fixed originally by the Criminal Justice Act 1982. In the Town and Country Planning Act 1990, for example, the maximum penalty for contravention of a tree preservation order at July 1991 is £1000 which is 'in accordance with Level 4 on the Scale'. This scale almost exclusively applies to cases which are heard before a magistrates' court, those which are referred to the Crown Court are subject to an unlimited fine at the discretion of the court. Statutory instruments are issued on a regular basis updating the fines levels across all the statutes where the scale applies (see Appendix 1 for the current scale). This system avoids the problems encountered with older legislation where the maximum amount of the fine was laid down in the Act. The fine inevitably became derisory with the passage of time and lost any deterrent effect.

Additionally, some legislation allows for a daily penalty to be imposed for every day during which the offence continues after conviction. This is the case with planning enforcement notices, the aim being to encourage the wrongdoer to comply with the notice sooner rather than later. Of course, the courts rarely impose the maximum penalty unless the offender has a history of committing the particular crime or has persistently disregarded requests to desist from the offence. In the case of *R.* v. *Chambers and Others* (1988) (unreported) the directors of a company were each personally fined an amount of £34,000 plus £1100 towards the costs of the local authority. They had sanctioned the demolition of a listed building without first obtaining listed building consent. The judge justified the high level of the fine on the basis that the directors knew exactly what they were doing and, furthermore, stood to make considerable financial gains through redevelopment of the site in the absence of the building.

It is also possible, in accordance with some Acts of Parliament, for injunctions to be imposed in the criminal courts. Taking again the breach of an enforcement notice, an offender can be ordered by way of an injunction to comply with the notice by carrying out the required works or desisting from a specified activity. This step would be taken by the court only if it were sure that the offender would comply in no other way. An offender who has been fined on a daily basis, but still refuses to comply with an enforcement notice, may discover that he is punished in this way.

Lastly, compensation orders can be made in the criminal courts as a means of restitution to the victim of the offence.

Where fines and terms of imprisonment are referred to in the body of this book, it must be remembered that these will be the maximum that the court can impose. It will punish the individual or company defendant after taking into account all the circumstances surrounding the commission of the offence, and the penalty will reflect the culpability.

LOCAL GOVERNMENT AND ITS POWERS

In most of England and Wales, local government is split into a two-tier system of county and district councils (sometimes referred to as city or borough councils). The various local authority functions are divided within this basic framework, which is also supplemented in some areas by other statutory bodies, such as the police. This is particularly so in areas which were formerly metropolitan counties. These were abolished in 1985, at which time *metropolitan district councils* took over all the previous county functions. For ease of management after the dissembling of the metropolitan structure, some of the county functions were passed to separate bodies.

Every local authority is recognised by the law as being a *legal person*. This means that it has the ability to enter into agreements and undertake obligations, as well as commence court actions and be sued, in its own right. Natural persons, that is ordinary individuals, have the same ability, but, unlike legal persons, natural persons are limited by the length of their life. In contrast, legal persons, which are created by statute, continue perpetually or until their powers are removed by statute. Thus, the legal capacity of a local authority is not affected by any change in its membership. If this were not so, contracts entered into by one group of councillors could be discarded every time the membership of the council changed.

Local authorities, then, are creatures of statute. They acquire all their powers from statute and cannot act outside those powers. They have the capacity to commence both civil and criminal actions in their own name *where this is authorised by the appropriate Act of Parliament*, but unless they have such authorisation they are powerless. Councils are not as hidebound as may first appear by this. The Local Government Act 1972 (regularising a situation which the courts had recognised for many years) gave them the power to carry out anything else reasonably incidental to what they were expressly authorised to do. This means that a local authority can embark on most ventures as long as these can be justified as a benefit to the administrative area.

A local authority discharges its functions through a system of committees which are made up of elected members, or councillors. The committees are advised by officers, employed by the council, who are skilled in their particular field, but the decision-making powers rest solely with the committee and, ultimately, with the full council. In essence, what happens is that the council delegates most of its powers to the appropriate committee, for example planning applications to the planning committee. Most committee decisions are final and can be acted upon by the officers, but some must be ratified by the full council. The council retains other powers for decision by all its members after discussion in the full council meeting. In a few instances, there may be further delegation of non-controversial matters from the committee to an officer. This may happen with the planning committee which could have a particularly heavy workload if it had to discuss every planning application throughout the council's area. The chief planning officer is therefore sometimes given the power to take certain minor decisions himself which may or may not require ratification by the committee. Irrespective of the practical method of decision-making, the council itself is responsible for the decisions which are made in its name.

LOCAL GOVERNMENT AND ITS DUTIES

Local authorities, like other legal persons, must fulfil their contractual obligations and, also like other legal persons, can be sued for damages in the civil courts if they fail. They are bound to act within the law and can be prosecuted for the commission of a criminal offence. For example, a local authority is obliged to comply with the health and safety regulations in the same way as a company or other person. If an accident occurs and it can be shown that the authority had failed in its obligations, it may be prosecuted and fined for breaches of the regulations. Of course, it would be difficult to imprison a local authority because no one person embodies it. Also, statutes are normally organised in such a way that a local authority is not in a position to try to enforce legislation against itself, the power to do so being given to another body. This is clearly shown in the housing legislation where the power to take action to deal with unfit housing is vested in the housing authority. Council houses are excluded from the provisions as it would be impossible for the authority to look impartially at its own potential offences.

In addition, local authorities are obliged by statute to carry out certain specified duties. If they fail in this, they can themselves be taken to court by those persons who have suffered as a result of the failure. It is important to notice when looking at Acts of Parliament whether the powers given to local authorities are mandatory or discretionary. This is indicated by the wording of the Act, for example:

> . . . the housing authority *shall* . . .

indicates a mandatory duty, whereas,

> . . . the housing authority *may* . . .

indicates that it has a discretionary duty. In the former case, action can be taken by a person aggrieved to force the authority to comply with its duty. In the latter, however, the position is not so clear-cut. Where there is a discretion, the local authority clearly has a choice, however it cannot make decisions based on a whim, but has to show that it has exercised its discretion 'reasonably'. There is a multitude of case law on 'reasonableness' in this context, discussed further under 'Judicial Review' (below).

THE ORGANISATION OF OTHER STATUTORY BODIES

There are, of course, other bodies which were established by statute in the same way as local authorities. Some of these, like the water authorities, have become public limited companies. They are now owned by their shareholders, but their activities are still, to a large extent, governed by the statutes which give them their powers. These bodies are, on the whole, subject to the same controls as local authorities and for the purposes of this book will be treated similarly. It should be borne in mind, however, that because they have a different constitution their internal organisation will be different from a local authority's. Any other fundamental differences will be dealt with in the appropriate chapter.

JUDICIAL REVIEW

Local authorities and, indeed, other public bodies which are established by statute can only act within the powers given to them by the particular statute. Inevitably, from time to time they are perceived by the public to be acting outside those powers. Judicial review is an administrative remedy which can be sought before the High Court by a person who is aggrieved, not by a decision of a public body, but by the decision-making process within that public body. In practice, of course, the person bringing the action is usually aggrieved by the decision, but it is important to remember that the decision itself is not in question. It is the means by which the decision is reached that is subject to the scrutiny of the court, and it follows from this that the court cannot overturn a decision simply because it does not agree with it. It must also be satisfied that the method of arriving at the decision is somehow faulty. Even if the court is satisfied, it has no power to substitute its own decision. What powers, then, does the court have?

The court's powers fall mainly into three categories: an order of certiorari, an order of prohibition and an order of mandamus. Certiorari is available to quash an illegal or unconstitutional decision; prohibition is used to prohibit an illegal or potentially illegal action, and mandamus is available to compel someone to do something. In addition, the court can make a declaration stating or 'declaring' what the law is or grant an injunction. It has already been noted that injunctions can have the same effect as prohibition and mandamus. An order of certiorari is followed by the referral of the original question back to the public body, usually with a statement from the court as to the matters to be taken into account when the item is again on the agenda for a decision.

Despite the availability of this mechanism whereby local authority or other administrative decisions can be challenged, it is one which is sparingly used. There are a number of reasons for this, not least because an applicant has no automatic right to bring an action, having first to obtain the leave of the court. The applicant has, in effect, to 'prove' that he has a legitimate grievance and also that he is personally interested in the outcome of the matter. This system prevents time-wasting actions being commenced by persons who, perhaps, bear a grudge or are not significantly affected by the decision. Secondly, the applicant must, as far as possible, commence proceedings within a very short space of time, preferably before the decision has been acted on by the authority. Applications for judicial review are dealt with speedily by the courts to avoid any lengthy delays in the administrative process, and a tardy litigant will receive little sympathy. Although there is no rigid rule, one would expect such an action to be commenced within three months, and usually far sooner than that. Lastly, as it may not make administrative sense to overthrow a decision, the powers of the court outlined above are discretionary. Therefore, even if the applicant is successful, he has no guarantee that the decision will be quashed or the remedy he requests imposed.

Nevertheless, judicial review is a powerful weapon in the hands of the public which can be used when an individual or a group feel that their local authority has acted unfairly. This then leads to the question of what constitutes such behaviour.

The leading case in the field is *Associated Provincial Picture Houses Ltd* v. *Wednesbury Corporation* (1947) which laid the foundations for the tests which are still applied today. The facts of the case are unimportant as it is the reasoning behind the decision of the Court of Appeal which is significant. (The basic facts are that the Corporation, who were responsible for licensing Sunday entertainments in their area, granted a licence to the company, but imposed a condition that children under the age of 15 could not be admitted. The Corporation justified its decision on the basis that they were entitled to take the moral welfare of children into account. As it happened, the Court of Appeal agreed with the Corporation.) The general principles expounded by Lord Green M.R. in his judgement established the *Wednesbury principle* in this area of administrative law. What he said, in summary, was that local authorities are obliged by statute to exercise discretion. In doing so they must look at the statute conferring the power to see what matters, if any, should be considered when exercising their discretion and also what matters should be disregarded as irrelevant. They must also exercise the discretion reasonably, and he went on to say on the question of unreasonableness:

> . . . there may be something so absurd that no sensible person could ever dream that it lay within the powers of the authority.

The Wednesbury decision establishes that local authorities must act reasonably when making decisions, and take into account all relevant matters and ignore all irrelevant ones. If they fail to do this, then their actions are open to challenge. Despite the somewhat cumbersome process, it must be remembered that judicial review does give individuals an opportunity to question the decisions of the local authority. We live in a democratic society where decisions are taken for us by our elected representatives at either local or national level. It would be inappropriate and impractical for each and every decision to be open to challenge before the courts by a small minority. The remedy of judicial review allows legitimate grievances to be aired and the appropriate sanction imposed when necessary.

THE USE OF TRIBUNALS AND INQUIRIES

The growth of administrative law during this century has meant that many decisions are, of necessity, delegated to local authorities or other statutory bodies. Although it is possible for the local authority decision-making process to be challenged by judicial review, many statutes establish a far quicker and cheaper method of challenge of the actual decision. This is through the use of tribunals or inquiries. The most well known form of tribunal is the industrial tribunal; the public planning inquiry will also be familiar.

Tribunals form an integral part of the court structure with their own system of appeals. However, the majority of statutes covered in this book use the inquiry as the form of administrative control. Inquiries are a type of appeal laid down by statute not to a court but to the appropriate Secretary of State, who discharges his function by appointing an officer to determine the appeal. These appeals are from decisions of local authorities and they can usually be in writing. Frequently, they are by way of a public inquiry, which is commonly a public hearing at which the appellant (the aggrieved party) is able to put his case to an appointed representative of the Secretary of State. The representative, often referred to as an inspector, usually has particular experience in the field in question. For example, inspectors at compulsory purchase inquiries have special expertise in housing or redevelopment problems. The local authority can then respond and explain why it reached its decision. Both parties are normally able to call witnesses to give evidence on their behalf, but the rules of evidence are not as strict as those imposed in a court. The inspector makes a decision based on the evidence produced before him, and that decision, on the facts, is final. The inspector's ruling can be challenged if it errs in law by way of an appeal through the court system. The inspector's decision can also be challenged by way of judicial review if it is unreasonable or does not comply with natural justice. (Natural justice is an unwritten code which says that the arbiter must be impartial, open and fair. If he is seen to be otherwise, perhaps because he allows one party to produce extra evidence without letting the other party comment on it, his decision is open to question.)

Inquiries are less daunting for the public who do not need legal representation, cheaper to administer, far quicker than the more formal court system and use experts as 'judges'. Tribunals have the same advantages, but usually sit with more than one member (three being common – often an expert, a lawyer and a layman). Whereas judicial review only looks at the *method* of reaching a decision, inquiries and tribunals usually have the power to review the decision itself, quash it and impose a new decision with new conditions.

Some statutes also expressly allow certain appeals against local authority decisions direct to the magistrates' court. This is usually when the result of the decision imposes potential penalties on the individual concerned. As an example, the local authority can serve a notice on a person alleging noise nuisance under the Control of Pollution Act 1974. Breach of the notice can lead to prosecution before the magistrates' court and the imposition of a financial penalty. To protect the individual, he is given the right to appeal to the magistrates' court against the service of the notice within a fixed time limit. Failure to appeal means that the individual loses those rights.

This interwoven system of inquiries and appeals protects the public from over-zealous authorities by trying to balance the rights of the individual against the needs of the majority.

PRIVATE LAND LAW

Private land law is a vast and complex area which ranges from landlord and tenant legislation, to easements and restrictive covenants, as well as the more familiar conveyancing aspects. It would be inappropriate in this book, which cannot go into the depth required, to attempt to cover private land law: it is far better dealt with by the wealth of books available on the subject. Suffice it to say that aspects of land law do impinge on the other areas of law which are covered here, and no areas of law can be viewed in isolation. Frequently, remedies available are dependent on the ownership or occupation of land, and this will be explained at the appropriate points.

Public land law, on the other hand, is covered here in part. It is found both in appropriate chapters and in its own right in Chapter 8 which relates to compulsory purchase. This book does not, however, deal with public housing law and other aspects of public land law not strictly relevant to the built environment.

CONCLUSION

This chapter sets the scene for the remainder of the book by providing the framework in which the legislation operates. We have seen that law is classified into different areas and that its administration is divided within the hierarchy of the courts. Furthermore, the delegation of powers means that local authorities and statutory bodies make their own decisions which are subject to challenge through either the courts or administrative tribunals and inquiries. Authorities can be sued for breach of contract or negligence, like any other individual, and can be prosecuted for failing to comply with their duty.

For ease of reference, the current legislation has been divided here into specific areas, each of which is dealt with in a separate chapter. It should be remembered, however, that these areas of law are not mutually exclusive and frequently overlap. Similarly, problems rarely fall neatly into one section. For these reasons, this book can only provide guidance rather than answers.

CHAPTER 2

PLANNING

INTRODUCTION

Legislative commitment to comprehensive controls over land use and development emerged with the Town and Country Planning Act 1947. The essential basis of planning since this time is that 'development', as defined in planning legislation, may not be undertaken without planning permission, and the planning authority in deciding whether to grant permission may be guided by the statutory plans (the 'development plan') prepared by the local planning authority(s). Straightforward though this may seem, the operation of town planning is, in practice, very complex.

The system is designed to regulate the development and use of land in the public interest, and although there is frequently dispute and controversy over individual cases, and between private interests, the system has served the country well. It is one of the important instruments for protecting the environment of town and country, for preserving historic buildings, and for maintaining green belts. It is not designed to prevent change but to control it and to secure economy, efficiency and amenity in the development and use of land. There is a presumption in favour of allowing development which is in accordance with the development plan. An applicant who proposes a development which is clearly in conflict with the development plan would need to produce convincing reasons to demonstrate why the plan should not prevail. The local authority may take into account other material considerations in helping it reach a decision. In principle, any consideration which relates to the use and development of land is capable of being a planning consideration, but whether a particular consideration falling within that broad class is *material* in any given case depends on circumstances and judgement. Material considerations must relate to the purpose of planning legislation (the regulation and use of land in the public interest), and must fairly and reasonably relate to the application under consideration. Any of the fundamental factors involved in land use planning are capable of being material in a given case such as the number, size, layout, siting, design and external appearance of buildings, the proposed means of access, the availability of infrastructure, and the physical or visual impact of the development on a neighbourhood. Where, in addition to the development plan, there are other material considerations the development plan has to be taken as a starting point.

The basic legislation today is the Town and Country Planning Act 1990 (referred to in this chapter as the 1990 Act), the Planning (Listed Buildings and Conservation Areas) Act 1990 (the provisions of which feature mainly in Chapter 3), and the Planning (Hazardous Substances) Act 1990. Each of these Acts has been amended by the Planning and Compensation Act 1991 (referred to in this chapter as the 1991 Act).

Despite the number and length of planning Acts, they still have to be supported by subordinate legislation issued separately by the Secretary of State for the Environment (referred to in this chapter as the Secretary of State). There are two particular subordinate documents to note. The first of these is the Town and Country Planning (Use Classes) Order 1987, usually referred to as the Use Classes Order. Its significance is that where land or buildings are used for one purpose within one of sixteen defined classes, a change to any other use within that class is not taken to involve development. The second document is the Town and Country Planning General Development Order 1988. This deals with procedural matters, such as the action a local planning authority should take when an application is made for planning permission, and, most importantly, sets out types of usually smaller-scale developments which are granted a general planning permission by the Secretary of State and may therefore be undertaken without the need to obtain specific planning permission from the local planning authority.

The main responsibility for planning rests with local planning authorities, which, for most of England and Wales, means the county and district councils acting in a form of partnership. In Greater London and the six metropolitan areas where the county tier of government was abolished in 1986, the planning authorities are the London boroughs and metropolitan districts. In two areas of the country, the Lake District National Park and the Peak District National Park, where park boundaries are wider than any single council's area, the planning authority is a joint board set up by the Secretary of State. In those areas of the country where the Secretary of State has created urban development corporations to secure regeneration, a range of planning authority powers rests with each corporation, some having more powers than others.

The Secretary of State has ample opportunity through the issue of policy guidance, powers of direction, and the appeal system to ensure that local planning authorities of whatever sort or conviction act substantially in accordance with his general policies.

Some key principles will help visualise the planning system in operation:

1. The local authority draws up a development plan which sets out a strategy for an area. The public has the opportunity to be involved in the generation of development plans.
2. Procedures are laid down for planning applications, including who should be consulted. The activity of 'development control' is conducted in an open fashion with opportunities for any interested parties to be involved.
3. Although the development plan must be taken into account in making development control decisions and there must be a presumption in favour of proposals which accord with it, it is not a strict zoning plan and other material considerations can influence the decision.

4. Planning permissions may be granted subject to conditions.
5. If permission is refused or the applicant is unhappy with conditions, there is a right of appeal to the Secretary of State where the planning merits of the whole matter may be considered.
6. Although the courts have no powers to consider policies, they do have a supervisory jurisdiction over procedures and decisions, and any party may seek a judicial review of a local authority's actions in reaching a decision.
7. There is seldom an opportunity for compensation against refusal of planning permission, the right to develop land having, in effect, been nationalised in the Town and Country Planning Act 1947.
8. Enforcing planning control is a discretionary matter in the hands of the local planning authority, although in most cases there is a safeguard for the landowner of appeal against to the Secretary of State.

Even at the small-scale end of development, disputes can be intense between the householder seeking to extend or alter his property, the local authority and other parties, usually a neighbour. Larger-scale development will frequently involve disagreement between the developer and the council but the public image of a local authority regulating the overall development of its area largely by the use of refusals is less justified in recent years. Developers and local authorities working closely together in a form of partnership is increasingly common. Important proposals are usually discussed well in advance of formal application. The process of development plan generation is to a significant extent based on discussion among planners, representatives of the business sector, landowners and developers over objectives, targets and strategies. Most parties, particularly in the urban areas, wish to avoid expensive and time-consuming appeals and seek to find solutions to differences through other means. The actions and decisions of local planning authorities are increasingly conducted in an open manner, and, in any case, the development sector now has its own planning consultants to monitor development plans and promote its own ideas. The traditional conflictual model has been to some extent replaced by a partnership in which the local council and the development industry see their objectives met by co-operation. This is not to say that conflict does not occur, but the successful developer and the skilled council achieve their aims, wherever they can, through an altogether more subtle process.

OVERALL PLANNING POLICIES

White Papers, circulars and planning policy guidance notes

There are a number of ways in which government advice on planning policy is made known but three are particularly important. White Papers have long been the vehicle for expressing the general thrust of government thinking, setting out where policies are to change or emerge, and where legislation of other government action will be initiated. Notwithstanding the retention of the basic structure of the town planning system there have been fundamental changes to government policy in favour of relaxation of controls and the creation of pro-development ideologies in local authorities. The White Papers *Lifting the Burden* (Cmnd.9571, 1985), *Building Businesses, Not Barriers* (Cmnd.9704, 1986), and *Releasing Enterprise* (Cm.512 1988) are the principal such documents to have expressed the theme of deregulation. More recently, *This Common Inheritance* (Cm.120, 1990) projects a commitment to the planned development of environmental policy but in town planning terms contains little new.

Until the late 1980s, circulars had the twin function of giving advice both on legislation and procedures, and on practical planning policies. These days the latter function is being taken over by planning policy guidance notes (PPGs) which will, in time, come to be the main source of practical planning policy guidance to local authorities and developers. Initially, the Secretary of State's regional and strategic planning guidance to local authorities was given in PPGs (nos. 9, 10 and 11), but since 1989 regional planning guidance notes (RPGs) have been issued specifically for this purpose. Minerals planning guidance notes (MPGs) deal specifically with issues relating to mineral extraction. As circumstances and government thinking change, so circulars, PPGs, RPGs and MPGs are revised.

The current PPGs are:

PPG1   (1992)   *General Policy and Principles*
PPG2   (1988)   *Green Belts*
PPG3   (1992)   *Housing*
PPG4   (1988)   *Industrial and Commercial Development and Small Firms*
PPG5   (1988)   *Simplified Planning Zones*
PPG6   (1988)   *Major Retail Development*
PPG7   (1992)   *Rural Enterprise and Development*
PPG8   (1988)   *Telecommunications*
PPG9   (1988)   *Regional Guidance for the South East*
PPG10   (1988)   *Strategic Guidance for the West Midlands*
PPG11   (1988)   *Strategic Guidance for Merseyside*
PPG12   (1992)   *Development Plans and Regional Planning Guidance*
PPG13   (1988)   *Highway Matters*
PPG14   (1990)   *Development on Unstable Land*
PPG15   (1990)   *Regional Planning Guidance, Structure Plans, and the Content of Development Plans* cancelled by PPG12 (1992); issued in Wales as: *Strategic Planning Guidance, Structure Plans and the Content of Development Plans*
PPG16   (1990)   *Archaeology and Planning*
PPG17   (1991)   *Sport and Recreation*
PPG18   (1991)   *Enforcing Planning Control*
PPG19   (1992)   *Outdoor Advertisements*
PPG20   (1992)   *Coastal Planning*

The current MPGs are:

MPG1   (1988)   *General Considerations and the Development Plan System*
MPG2   (1988)   *Applications, Permissions and Conditions*
MPG3   (1988)   *Opencast Coal Mining*
MPG4   (1988)   *The Review of Mineral Working Sites*
MPG5   (1988)   *Minerals Planning and the General Development Order*
MPG6   (1989)   *Guidance for Aggregates Provision in England and Wales*
MPG7   (1989)   *The Reclamation of Mineral Workings*

MPG8   (1991)   *Planning and Compensation Act 1991*
Interim Development Order Permissions
– Statutory Provisions and Proceedings

MPG9   (1992)   *Planning and Compensation Act 1991:*
Interim Development Order Permissions
– Conditions

MPG10   (1992)   *Raw Material for the Cement Industry*

The current RPGs are:

RPG1   (1989)   *Strategic Guidance for Tyne and Wear*
RPG2   (1989)   *Strategic Guidance for West Yorkshire*
RPG3   (1989)   *Strategic Guidance for London*
RPG4   (1989)   *Strategic Guidance for Greater Manchester*
RPG5   (1989)   *Strategic Guidance for South Yorkshire*
RPG6   (1991)   *Regional Planning Guidance for East Anglia*

Ministerial decisions and statements

Government policy can be clarified for local authorities and others through decisions of the Secretary of State or through statements released by him or his ministers. Policy can be clearly demonstrated by a decision on a planning application which has been 'called in' for decision of the Secretary of State, or by a decision taken on appeal against a planning authority decision. A statement in Parliament, a formal press release, or a speech to a suitable audience can make the government position on a planning policy matter clear, and do so quickly.

DEVELOPMENT PLANS

Form of the development plan

The development plan comprises those documents produced by local planning authorities which set out policies for the future development of their areas. In most parts of the country (i.e. outside Greater London and the six metropolitan areas) the development plan is made up of structure plans and local plans. A *structure plan* is prepared by the county council and will usually cover the entire area of a county. The main function of a structure plan is to state in broad terms the general policies and proposals of strategic importance for the development and use of land in the area, taking account of national and regional policies. The plan itself will be a written statement containing policies and general proposals. It will have with it an explanatory memorandum justifying and explaining the overall strategy, and a key diagram. It will deal with the full range of land use issues relevant to topics such as housing, green belt, urban and rural economies, transportation, minerals waste treatment, land reclamation, tourism/leisure, and energy generation. It is not a site-specific document. It may, for instance, identify the amount of housing growth required in the county over the life of the structure plan (usually up to ten years) but it will not identify the detailed sites on which such housing should be provided. It is the job of the *local plan*, usually prepared by the district council, to identify specific parcels of land where development may take place or where individual policies apply. The local plan consists of a written statement and a site-specific proposals map. Local plans have, in the past, usually been prepared for parts of a local authority area, but the 1991 Act has placed a duty on district councils to undertake a single local plan for the entire area within their control. The Secretary of State expects coverage of area-wide local plans to be substantially complete by the end of 1996.

In Greater London and the six metropolitan areas (Tyne and Wear, West Yorkshire, Merseyside, Greater Manchester, South Yorkshire, and the West Midlands) the development plan is the *unitary plan* produced by the various single (or unitary) local authorities responsible. The plan is in two parts. Part 1 deals with the formulation of general policies (rather like a structure plan) and part 2 shows the application of such general policies to specific areas (rather like a local plan).

Local authorities have been given increasing responsibility to adopt plans without the need for the Secretary of State's approval. This began with responsibility for local plan adoption in 1968, and was extended to cover unitary plans in the mid-1980s and, following the 1991 Act, to cover the adoption of structure plans. In all cases it is the authority that prepares the plan which has authority to adopt it. The Secretary of State retains powers to prevent a development plan from being adopted by a local planning authority should he be concerned over its content. This would usually apply where the local authority has not set out policies in accordance with national and regional planning policy.

Importance of development plans

Since the issue of PPG1 in January 1988 it has been clear that where a development plan is up to date and relevant to a particular proposal under consideration, it should be given considerable weight in any decision on a planning application. Under the new s.54A of the 1990 Act, further strength is given to the development plan by requiring that where a planning application decision is being taken and the development plan is relevant to the case, 'the determination shall be in accordance with the plan unless material considerations indicate otherwise'. The critical importance of a development plan policy in helping decide a planning application can be influenced by whether the development plan policies are up to date and apply to current circumstances or whether they have been superseded by events (although the age of the plan is not in itself material). For example, policies and proposals in the plan may have been superseded by more recent planning guidance issued by government, or developments since the plan became operative may have rendered certain policies incapable of implementation or out of date.

THE NEED FOR PLANNING PERMISSION

Basic provisions

Planning permission is needed to undertake development. The 1990 Act defines development as 'the carrying out of building, engineering, mining or other operations in, on, over or under land, or the making of any material change in the use of any buildings or other land' (s.55(1)). Development can therefore be an *operation* (i.e. building something on the land) or can be a *change of use* of land. The Act specifies some changes of use which are material and, therefore, are development; this includes conversion of a single dwelling-house into two or more separate dwelling-houses (s.55(3)(a)). The Act also specifies certain matters which are not development. These include:

1. Repairing, improving, altering a building in such a way that its exterior is not materially affected (s.55(2)(a)).
2. Use of any buildings or land within the curtilage of a dwelling-house for a purpose incidental to its use as a dwelling-house (s.65(2)(d)).
3. Use of land for agriculture or forestry and of buildings on such land for related purposes (s.55(2)(e)).
4. Use of land for any use within the same class in any Use Classes Order issued by the Secretary of State (s.55(2)(f)).
5. The demolition of certain types of building which the Secretary of State may specify in a direction to local planning authorities (s.54(2)(g)).

Use Classes Order

A full understanding of the circumstances in which it is necessary to apply for planning permission depends on understanding two of the most significant statutory instruments issued by the Secretary of State, namely the Use Classes Order and the General Development Order. The current Use Classes Order is the Town and Country Planning (Use Classes) Order 1987 (SI 1987, 764). Its introduction brought the first substantial changes in the arrangement of use classes for town planning purposes since 1948 and full guidance on how it operates is available in circular 13/87. The order identifies sixteen use classes within which uses may change without amounting to development. Briefly the classes comprise:

Class A1. Shops   This covers most shops used by the visiting member of the public including most retail sales shops, travel agencies, hairdressers, funeral directors, post offices and sandwich shops (but not those selling hot food).

Class A2. Financial and Professional Services   This covers banks, building societies and other professional and financial services of the sort usually accommodated in shop-type premises where the intention is to serve visiting members of the public.

Class A3. Food and Drink   This covers restaurants, cafes, hot food take-aways, wine bars, and public houses.

Class B1. Business   This covers all the office-type uses of A2 and the research, development and light industrial processes which do not usually give rise to amenity problems for nearby residential or other sensitive land uses.

Class B2. General Industry   This is the general category of industry covering most types of production.

Classes B3 to B7. Special Industrial Groups A–E   These Special Industrial Groups are divided according to whether they are associated with alkalis, contaminated organic matter, etc. The classes are little changed since

1948 and are increasingly irrelevant as many of these essentially nineteenth century industries die out. There can be few companies today who specialise in breeding maggots, boiling blood or scraping guts.

Class B8. Storage and Distribution This group comprises warehouses and open land used for storage. It does not cover retail warehouses.

Class C1. Hotels and Hostels Use as a hotel, hostel, boarding- or guest-house where no significant element of care is provided.

Class C2. Residential Institutions This covers hospitals, nursing homes, residential schools and colleges, and training centres.

Class C4. Dwelling-houses This covers an ordinary dwelling-house use, and use of a dwelling by up to six persons living together as a single household (such as students).

Class D1. Non-residential Institutions Here are grouped together medical centres (except those attached to a practitioner's house), crêches, nurseries, art galleries, museums, libraries, public halls, exhibition halls, and buildings used for religious instruction or worship.

Class D2. Assembly and Leisure Use as a cinema, concert hall, bingo hall, casino, dance hall, swimming-bath, skating-rink, gymnasium or area for other indoor or outdoor sports or recreation which does not involve motorised vehicles or firearms.

Uses excluded from Use Classes Order's classes

Some uses are specifically excluded from any class, and this includes theatres, amusement arcades, launderettes, petrol filling stations, premises for motor vehicle sales, taxi and car-hire businesses, scrap-yards, vehicle dismantlers and sites containing notifiable quantities of hazardous substances. In these cases any change to these uses will always require permission.

Certain changes within use classes

In addition to the flexibility provided by changes available *within* use classes, the General Development Order makes provision for certain changes *between* groups. These changes are shown in Table 1.

Table 1

From	To
Sale of Cars	A1 (Shop)
A2 (Financial/Professional) if premises have a display window at ground-floor level	A1 (Shop)
A3 (Food and Drink)	A1 (Shop)
A3 (Food and Drink)	A2 (Financial/Professional)
B1 (Business) with less than 235 sq.m building floor area	B8 (Storage/Distribution)
B2 (General Industry)	B1 (Business)
B2 (General Industry) with less than 235 sq.m building floor area	B8 (Storage/Distribution)
B8 (Storage/Distribution)	B1 (Business)

The General Development Order

So wide is the definition of development, notwithstanding the various exclusions, that there would still be the most enormous burden of work on individuals, businesses, the development industry and local planning authorities in dealing with massive numbers of planning applications were it not for the Town and Country Planning General Development Order (often shortened to GDO), the current document being published in 1988 (SI 1988, No. 1813). The effect of the General Development Order is to grant automatic planning permission on a country-wide basis for whole categories of minor development. In the Secretary of State's view, these categories of development are unlikely to have any great impact on the environment and may be lifted out of the focus of local authority concern. The operations and changes of use covered by the blanket planning permissions of the General Development Order are referred to as permitted development, sometimes shortened to PD by town planners and others.

In certain sensitive areas of the country, most notably the national parks, areas of outstanding natural beauty, conservation areas, and the Broads, permitted development rights are reduced to minimise the creeping change which may cause harm to an area's character and appearance. For the rest of the country the following summarised examples of permitted development give some feeling of the opportunities the General Development Order provides.

Dwelling-houses Enlargement, improvement or other alteration of the house by up to 70 cubic metres (or fifteen per cent of its original cubic content) but reduced to 50 cubic metres (and ten per cent) for a terraced house. No house, however large, may be extended by more than 115 cubic metres. Loft conversions are permitted subject to various qualifications including the requirement not to extend the roofspace beyond the plane of an existing roof slope which fronts a highway. Various freestanding buildings and structures within gardens are also permitted subject to limitations including height, location in relation to the house and public highway. This is designed to bring garages, sheds, and similar garden structures out of detailed planning control.

Agricultural buildings The erection and extension of farm buildings (but not farm residential accommodation) is permitted subject to limitations including size, location in relation to any public highway and proximity to residential properties.

Industry and warehousing Extension of factory and warehouse buildings is permitted where it does not exceed twenty-five per cent of the cubic content of the original building subject to an overall limit of 1000 square metres new floor area. There are other limitations affecting this permitted development, including the new development not reducing car parking space, removing areas set aside for turning of vehicles, being within five metres of the curtilage of the site, exceeding the height of the main building, or materially affecting the external appearance of the business (as seen from off the site).

The special case of demolition

Prior to the changes introduced by the 1991 Act there was never any clear statement in the Act or its instruments that demolition was development. The new s.54(2)(g) in the 1990 Act referred to earlier was designed to make the position clear. The direction which has resulted (circular 22/91) has been so worded as to exclude demolition from the working definition of development, specifying only demolition of dwellings and buildings attached to them. Even here the Secretary of State has amended the General Development Order to make such demolition permitted development, although he has required those wishing to demolish a dwelling to give the local authority the opportunity to determine whether they wish to exercise control.

PLANNING APPLICATIONS

Submission of applications

Applications for planning permission are made to the district council. In areas of two-tier local government, applications relating to mineral extraction and waste disposal are made to (and determined by) the county council. The following checklist of material to be sent to the local planning authority may prove useful.

Forms   These are supplied by the local authority and draw from the applicant information which will be useful to the planning officers and to others who may wish to comment on the proposal.

Plans and drawings The applicant must provide a site plan and other plans and drawings necessary to properly identify the site and describe the development.

Ownership certificate (s.66) This tells the local authority that the applicant is the owner of the site, or that he has served notice on the owner(s), or that he cannot trace one or more or all of the owners. Submission of an inaccurate certificate is an offence and, in addition to legal action against the applicant, the courts may quash any permission which has been granted.

Application fee Most categories of planning application must be accompanied by a fee. Fee levels are determined by the Secretary of State and the current charges may be found in the Town and Country Planning (Fees for Applications and Deemed Applications) Regulations 1990 (SI 1990, 2473). Planning officers are usually quite helpful in advising on the appropriate fee. The fee is not refunded in the event of a refusal.

Outline applications

While most applications for building work are for full planning permission, in some circumstances an application for outline permission is more appropriate. The main principle with outline applications is that only a site plan is submitted rather than a full set of drawings and plans. The permission, if granted, will be subject to conditions requiring the subsequent approval of details (usually siting, design, external appearance, means of access, and landscaping) before any development can begin. This form of application is useful where an applicant wishes to establish the principle of a development on a site without going to the expense of preparing detailed plans. A farmer may wish to confirm that his land is capable of development for housing in order to establish its sale value. It is then for the developer who purchases the land to prepare details of estate layout and housing design. In some cases a local planning authority might insist on some element of detail being submitted as part of an outline application. It may, for example, wish to see details of road access to a proposed industrial development from a busy road or complex junction before it commits itself to an outline planning permission. In sensitive locations such as conservation areas, planning authorities may be reluctant to accept an outline application. Applicants can appeal to the Secretary of State if they believe the local planning authority is acting unreasonably in seeking further information.

DETERMINATION OF THE APPLICATION

The statutory period

In most cases the local authority has a statutory period of eight weeks in which to reach a decision on an application. A longer period may be agreed between the parties but the applicant has the right to appeal once the eight weeks are up. Local authorities usually try to deal with applications expeditiously in order to avoid risk of the heavy time burden which an appeal entails. Figures vary considerably throughout the country but most will deal with about seventy-five per cent of applications within eight weeks. A problem for the local authorities is the time-consuming nature of many of the actions necessary before a decision can be made. It is important to find out why an application is taking longer than the statutory period. The delay may be quite justifiable, and even outside the local planning authority's control. It is important to recognise that the appeal process will take several months (or more, depending on the complexity of the case) and the local authority may well have reached a decision well within that period had you agreed to give more time.

Material considerations

The issue of what is material to the determination of a planning application has been covered in principle in the introduction to this chapter. The local planning authority will take into account the development plan and any other material considerations. The importance of the development plan has been strengthened since 1991 with local authorities now required under s.54A of the Act where the development plan is material to the application to determine it in accordance with the development plan unless material considerations indicate otherwise. Therefore, land shown for one use in an up-to-date, adopted local plan is unlikely to receive planning permission for an entirely different sort of development. Material considerations will certainly include government policy as expressed through planning policy guidance notes (PPGs), White Papers and circulars but will also include the range of local amenity and technical considerations which applications frequently raise. In a conservation area, the visual effect of any development by its size, massing, colour, or materials would be a material consideration. A proposal to develop an industrial area will find the authority taking into account the effect of pollution and traffic on any nearby residents. A proposal for a large development placing a severe strain on infrastructure or services could be deemed unacceptable, or at least premature until such time as service or infrastructure provision is improved.

Personal circumstances

The hardship of applicants is often put forward in support of an application but it is unusual, indeed rare, for such circumstances to be taken into account. An example where personal circumstances might be considered would be where a portable building was proposed to provide necessary medical care for a sick or disabled person at his home. It might be unattractive, harmful to the amenities of the area and contrary to established authority policy on house extensions but a personal permission might be granted for the period the person resides at the property.

Processing of applications

Most planning applications are assigned to an individual planning officer to deal with. He visits the site, consults other planning colleagues or other council departments such as environmental health, highways or recreation. He also consults outside the council as necessary. A proposal for a retail development might be sent for comment to the fire officer, police and water company. Objections from the public might be received. A report will be produced describing the development, summarising the comments received and identifying issues. The report will make a recommendation to refuse or grant permission and whether conditions are appropriate. The decision on behalf of the local planning authority is taken by a planning committee comprising elected councillors. In many authorities, applications for developments which are small-scale, in accordance with established policy, and have not attracted objections from consultees or public are determined by a senior planning officer using powers delegated to him by the committee. This arrangement is usually justified by the time it saves for the applicant.

Environmental assessment

European Community Directive 85/337 imposes an obligation to consider likely environmental effects of a development before permission is granted. The Town and Country Planning (Assessment of Effects) Regulations 1988 (1988 No. 1199) makes provision for special consideration of certain types of project by requiring some applications to be accompanied by an Environmental Assessment (EA). Circular 15/88 explains the provisions of the regulations and gives advice on their implementation. The EA must provide data necessary to identify and assess the main effects of the development, a description of likely effects, and a statement of the measures envisaged to combat or avoid significant adverse effects. Projects which definitely require EA (Schedule 1 Projects) include crude oil refineries, thermal power stations, chemical installations, motorways, and waste disposal operations. Other projects which may require an EA (Schedule 2 Projects) depend as much on the size and location of the development as upon the type but might include large industrial, retail or housing projects. Circular 15/88 gives indicative criteria and thresholds to judge whether EA is required. The fundamental test is whether the project will have significant environmental effects. The Secretary of State can arbitrate on whether a developer must provide an EA in any particular case.

PLANNING PERMISSIONS

Notification

The resolution of a planning committee to grant permission does not itself constitute the planning permission. Before starting work or entering into binding contracts, the applicant should await the written decision notice of the local planning authority. This might take a few days or a few weeks, depending on the efficiency of the council.

Conditional permissions

Most permissions are granted subject to conditions. On the surface, local planning authorities appear to have wide powers to impose conditions, but careful examination of government advice and decisions of the courts reveals clear limitations. Nevertheless, many decisions do have conditions imposed more in hope of compliance than with any likelihood of enforcement. Government advice on planning conditions may be found in circular 1/85. Conditions should be imposed only where they are necessary and reasonable. The circular urges planners to consider six matters before any condition is imposed:

1. *Necessity.* Would planning permission have to be refused if the condition were not to be imposed? If it would not be refused then the condition needs special and precise justification.

2. *Relevance to planning.* Does the condition have a planning basis or is its objective more appropriate to other functions of the council? A permission for a private sports centre should not have a condition attached to it requiring some form of access by the general public, however short of public sport facilities the area may be. It is for the council to deal with public facilities from its own means.

3. *Relevance to the development to be permitted.* A condition may serve some useful planning function but nevertheless be invalid because it is not relevant to the development permitted. For example, an existing building may be ugly and visually damaging to an otherwise attractive local area but a condition could not be imposed on a temporary use of the building for storage that it should be demolished at the end of the temporary use. Such a condition arises out of a wish to restore the area not from any need arising from the temporary storage use itself.

4. *Enforceability.* A condition should only be imposed where it can be enforced against the owners or occupiers of the site. A condition imposed on a new restaurant requiring customers to use a particular route having left the site is plainly unenforceable, being beyond the powers of the site owners and operators.

5. *Precision.* A condition should be clear and unambiguous leaving the applicant in no doubt of his obligations.
6. *Reasonableness.* Even where a condition serves some useful planning function it may still be unreasonable. The courts have demonstrated wide interest in the general reasonableness of local planning authority action.

Duration of permission

Before 1968 there was no requirement for permissions to expire after a certain period if they were not implemented, but legislation in that year provided that all new permissions would be time-limited and existing unimplemented permissions should expire, at the latest, by 1974. Permissions usually lapse after five years if they have not been implemented, but the local planning authority can reduce or extend this period where there is justification. A lapsed permission can be renewed using a simpler system than the usual planning application. Local authorities are guided by the Secretary of State (circular 1/85) to grant lapsed permissions unless there has been some material change in planning circumstances since the earlier permission was granted, or where failure to begin the development will contribute to unacceptable uncertainty over the future pattern of development in the wider area.

One way to extend indefinitely the life of a permission is to make a clear start on the development. This can be achieved by simply digging a foundation trench. Section 56(5) of the 1990 Act gives clear guidance on what may be regarded as commencement. The local authority does have the power to serve a completion notice under s.94, but this is a cumbersome process for trying to resolve a slow pace of development and is seldom employed.

Outline permissions The most important thing to note with outline permissions is that reserved matters have to be submitted within three years of the date that the outline permission was granted, and the development must be commenced within five years of the original permission or two years from the date of the last reserved matter approval if this is later. As with detailed planning permissions, the local planning authority can vary these dates.

PLANNING OBLIGATIONS

Background

It has long been the practice of local planning authorities to make use of their powers, where appropriate, to enter into legally binding agreements of one sort or another with developers. For nearly twenty years s.52 of the Town and Country Planning Act 1971 was used to resolve matters between developers and planning authorities which could not be handled through conditions. The local planning authority's requirements were set out in a binding side document signed by all the relevant parties before the permission was issued. Other parties to the agreement agreed to perform certain action, give up rights, pay sums of money, and so on. Sometimes the idea of an agreement came from the developer who saw it as a way of encouraging the authority to grant permission. A typical agreement might, for instance, require the developer to construct a section of public road relevant to the proposed development (or make a financial contribution to it) before the development goes ahead. In some cases, links between planning permission and the provisions of an agreement have been tenuous, and there may have been grounds for challenging the original planning permission through judicial review. Section 106 of the 1990 Act made identical provision for agreements but the 1991 Act has amended s.106 to bring far greater flexibility for the developer, council and Secretary of State.

Planning obligations

The Planning and Compensation Act 1991 has substituted a new s.106, 106A and 106B for the old s.106, introducing the term 'planning obligation' to cover both agreements between parties (which may continue to be used) and a new concept of unilateral undertakings by the developer. The system is intended for far wider use than before. The developer's unilateral undertaking, which may be conditional, becomes a material consideration in the determination of the application. It will be binding on him and on successors in title. The local authority may enforce it, including taking action by way of injunction. If there is a breach of a requirement in the obligation to carry out operations, the local authority may, after a twenty-one day period of notice, enter the land to complete the work itself and recover its expenses from the other party. A planning obligation must be by means of an instrument executed by deed, and will be registered a land charge. The unilateral undertaking allows the developer faced with an unreasonable planning authority to offer an obligation which, if permission is refused and he appeals, will be taken into account by the Secretary of State. Previously, the Secretary of State was unable, in practice, to take account of or enter into any agreements related to planning application decisions. Now, should the application be brought to him or an inspector on appeal the unilateral undertaking can be a legitimate material consideration.

Modification and discharge of obligations

Section 106A provides powers to modify or discharge a planning obligation either by agreement between the parties or, after five years has elapsed, on formal application to the local planning authority. In the event of refusal there is a right of appeal to the Secretary of State. The substantive test for the local authority (or Secretary of State) is whether the obligation no longer serves a useful purpose, or whether such purpose could be equally served by a modified obligation. Planning obligations cannot be modified or discharged by the Lands Tribunal under the Law of Property Act 1925, although existing agreements may still be.

Policy guidance

The Secretary of State's advice lies in circular 16/91. The potential advantages to both parties where planning obligations are involved (be they agreements or unilateral undertakings) are considerable, and the local authority can often stand to achieve objectives out of scale with or even unrelated to the development proposed. Debate about the extent to which authorities should seek, or accept, planning gain has been considerable. Where something necessary in planning terms cannot be achieved through a planning condition, it is reasonable to seek to resolve the matter through a permission and agreement. But the authority is not entitled to use an agreement to extract from the developer a payment simply for the benefit of the community purse. Obligations should not be used to bring about planning permission for schemes which do not justify it just because of attractive side benefits negotiated by the council and offered under s.106. The circular makes it clear that sympathetic consideration will be given to an application for the award of costs following an inquiry where an applicant has appealed against non-determination of his application rather than agree to unreasonable demands put forward as a draft obligation.

ENFORCEMENT

General operation

Town and country planning has had a rather slow system of enforcement. Changes introduced by the 1991 Act, most of which stemmed from the recommendations of the Carnwath Report (*Enforcing Planning Law*, 1989), are designed to simplify and speed up procedures. The effect of new provisions will be to change enforcement from a largely one-weapon system (the enforcement notice) to a more sophisticated system in which a range of devices may be used to suit the case. Planning enforcement, unlike many other fields of environmental law, has usually been a two-stage affair in which an enforcement notice must be issued, and only after it has become effective and has been ignored by the recipients can prosecution commence. It is not the breach of planning control which is the criminal action but the breach of the enforcement notice. The taking of enforcement action by a local authority is entirely discretionary, with authorities advised to consider whether it is 'expedient' to do so having regard to the development plan and other material considerations (s.172). Government advice in circular 22/80 is that enforcement action should only be taken where it is clearly necessary. Some local authorities give formal enforcement action a low priority in their planning activities. Many do not employ a specialist officer in this field, and most prefer to overcome problems caused by unauthorised activities by informal methods including warnings and negotiation. The problems for the local authority have often been related to the time-consuming nature of enforcement action. Added to this has been a certain amount of government discouragement of enforcement action against businesses, the strong chance of enforcement notice appeals to the Secretary of State being upheld (around forty per cent) and usually low levels of fine.

Immunity from enforcement action

Under the 1990 Act, there are a number of circumstances where enforcement action may not be taken, including:

1. Where four years have elapsed from substantial completion of an operational development (s.171B(1)).
2. Where four years have elapsed from a change of use to a dwelling-house (s.171B(2)).
3. Where ten years have elapsed in the case of any other breach of planning control (s.171B(3)).
4. Where there is a Certificate of Lawfulness of Existing Use or Development (CLEUD) under s.191 or a Certificate of Lawfulness of Proposed Use or Development (CLOPUD) under s.192 (both certificates are discussed on pages 45 and 46).

Planning contravention notice

A planning contravention notice is a new provision under s.171C allowing a local authority to serve a notice specifying the breach and requiring information necessary to allow it to take formal action. The notice may require, among other matters, information on the nature of activities being undertaken on the land, details of the parties with interest in the site, and any information which may substantiate the lawfulness of the activity. The notice also gives details of the enforcement action proper which may follow. Failure to comply with the notice can lead to a fine under s.171D at level 3 on the scale of fines. The intention of the planning contravention notice is to clarify the positions of both sides at the earliest opportunity. This may, on many occasions, lead to cessation of the offending activities or some form of compromise which removes the need to take further action.

Enforcement notice

An enforcement notice (s.172) must be served on all owners and occupiers, including licensees. It must specify the breach, the steps required to remedy it, the reasons for issuing the notice and the relevant land. It also identifies a date on which the notice takes effect, allowing at least twenty-eight days from the date of service, and gives a period for full compliance. At the end of this period a failure to comply with the notice's provision will lay the owners or occupiers open to prosecution. The maximum penalty is now £20,000 on summary conviction or an unlimited fine for conviction on indictment. In determining the fine the courts may have regard to any financial benefit accruing to the convicted person. In addition, the local authority also has the right under s.178 to enter the land and put right the breach, recovering its expenses from the wrongdoer.

Appeal against enforcement notice

Any person served with an enforcement notice may appeal to the Secretary of State, but this must be within the period before the notice becomes effective (as little as twenty-eight days). An appeal suspends the operation of the notice until the appeal is finally determined. There are seven grounds of appeal set out in s.174(2)(a–g):

(a) Planning permission ought to be granted or the relevant conditions be discharged.
(b) The alleged breach has not taken place.
(c) The alleged breach in the enforcement notice does not constitute a breach of planning control.
(d) The matters alleged in the notice are immune from enforcement action.
(e) Copies of the notice were not served in accordance with s.172.
(f) The steps required to remedy the breach are excessive.
(g) The period allowed for compliance with the notice is unreasonably short.

The procedures for enforcement appeals are similar to those for ordinary planning appeals and are set out in the Town and Country Planning (Enforcement Notices and Appeals) Regulations 1981 (SI 1981 No.1742) and the Town and Country Planning (Enforcement) (Inquiries) Regulations 1981 (SI 1981 No.1743). The usual choice is available between written representations, informal hearing and public inquiry. The Secretary of State (more usually an inspector acting for him) may uphold, vary, amend or quash the enforcement notice. There is a right of appeal to the High Court on a matter of law.

Stop notice

The enforcement notice may bring to an end an unlawful activity, but not without a period of delay while the notice becomes effective and time is given for compliance. A further substantial delay will occur in the event of an appeal against the enforcement notice. In some circumstances the local authority may consider this delay unacceptable and resort to the service of a stop notice under s.183 at any time between the service of an enforcement notice and the date on which it comes into effect. It may not be used to stop the use of a building as a dwelling-house (except a caravan site) or where an activity has been taking place for more than four years. Stop notices are not as frequently used as might be expected. If the stop notice or enforcement notice is withdrawn, or the recipient appeals and is successful, the planning authority may be required to pay compensation.

Breach of condition notice

The 1991 Act introduced into the 1990 Act (as s.187B) a breach of condition notice which can be an alternative to the enforcement notice. It is a simple summary procedure whereby a local planning authority may serve written notice on a person responsible for non-compliance with a condition. Twenty-eight days must be given for compliance. It is an offence to fail to comply with such a notice, and there is no right of appeal to the Secretary of State. There is a defence on the grounds that the defendant took all reasonable measures to comply with the condition or on the ground that he no longer had control of the land. The legislation does, at first sight, seem to have perfect simplicity but it remains to be seen whether local authorities will use the breach of condition notice as fully as the legislators may have intended. The prospect of defendants challenging the validity of conditions and the likelihood of waters being muddied by the recipient of the notice making applications to discharge the condition may cause too much confusion in the court to secure a clear outcome. Fines are at level 3 on the standard scale and, as with enforcement notices, continuing non-compliance can result in a fine for each day of neglect.

Injunction

Section 187B provides a clear power under which local authorities may act to restrain a breach of planning control through court injunction.

Certificate of lawful existing use or development (CLEUD)

Section 191 of the 1990 Act provides for a certificate to establish beyond question the lawfulness of existing use or development. This replaces the Established Use Certificate (EUC), sweeping aside the limitation of EUCs for dealing with operational development. Lawfulness, as determined by a CLEUD, may be equated with immunity from enforcement action. Evidence for the purpose of substantiating a certificate may include documentary sources and sworn statements. There are penalties for false or misleading statements.

Certificate of lawfulness of proposed use or development (CLOPUD)

The provisions for a certificate of lawfullness of proposed use or development (s.192) have swept away the former 'Section 64 Determination' with its limitation to operational development only. Henceforth it will be possible to establish in advance whether an intended development, be it building or operational use, will be lawful.

PLANNING APPLICATION APPEALS

Right of appeal

The opportunity to appeal to the Secretary of State exists in respect of a number of actions by the local planning authority. The most common appeals to the Secretary of State relate to planning applications where (1) permission has been refused by the local authority; (2) a permission has been granted with a condition thought by the applicant to be unreasonable; or (3) the authority has failed to reach a decision in the statutory period and has failed to secure the applicant's agreement to an extension of time. Section 78 of the Act provides the basis for appeal in each of these cases. Appeals can also be made in respect of other applications to the local authority, such as tree preservation order consent, advertisement consent and listed building consent. Appeals may also be made where an enforcement notice has been served. Appeals are made by the applicant, or, in the case of enforcement action, by any of the parties on whom an enforcement notice has been served. Appeals against enforcement action are considered earlier in this chapter. There is no right of appeal for third parties. The number of appeals each year is around 30,000 with a success rate currently of thirty-four per cent.

Appeal procedure

The general principles and procedures are more or less the same no matter what local authority action has precipitated the appeal. This section summarises the position applying to planning application cases. Notice of appeal must be given within six months of the decision of the local authority and must be in writing on a form obtainable from the Department of the Environment, Tollgate House, Houlton Street, Bristol BS2 9DJ (or in Wales from the Welsh Office, Cathays Park, Cardiff CF1 3NQ). The appellant is required to supply information, including details of the application, copies of correspondence, ownership and other certificates, and the decision of the local planning authority. A fresh ownership certificate must also be supplied (in case circumstances have changed since submission of the application). The local authority must be supplied with a copy of the notice of appeal. The Secretary of State is empowered not to entertain the appeal but the exercise of such power is rare. Since 1991 he has had power summarily to dismiss an appeal where he believes the appellant has been responsible for unreasonable delay. More than ninety per cent of cases are determined by an inspector acting on the Secretary of State's behalf. The appellant, the local authority or the Secretary of State can opt to have a public hearing to air the issues for and against the development. This will mean either a full public local inquiry or an informal hearing. Around ninety per cent of appeals are determined on the basis of evidence provided in writing by the parties involved. This method is referred to as written representations and is normally cheaper and quicker.

Written representations

The Town and Country Planning (Written Representations Procedure) Regulations 1987 (SI 1987 No.701) sets out procedures, and circular 18/86 advises on the format of information to be provided. Although there is no formal hearing of any sort, there are opportunities for members of the public to communicate their views. There is a timetable which all the parties must adhere to in supplying written information. In the event of a delay by one side the appeal may be determined on the basis of the information supplied by the other. The written representations procedure is suitable for straightforward cases where the issues do not require searching questions or cross-examination of witnesses to explore weaknesses or inconsistencies.

Public inquiries

Where the appellant, local authority or Department of the Environment consider it appropriate, a public local inquiry will be held to consider all the evidence. A date, time and place is fixed and the inquiry publicised. The Town and Country Planning (Inquiries Procedure) Rules (SI 1988 No.944) and the Town and Country Planning (Determination by Inspectors) (Inquiries Procedure) Rules (SI 1988 No.945) govern the procedures and circular 10/88 provides explanation. There is a rigorous timetable for the pre-inquiry stages during which statements have to be provided and exchanged. The local authority has six weeks after the announcement of intention to hold a public inquiry to prepare and distribute a statement of case. The appellant then has three weeks to supply his statement. It is clearly important for the case to be adequately prepared from the start and for the parties to have identified the issues they wish to cover and the witnesses they will call. Witnesses will have to produce a proof of evidence containing what they intend to say. Lawyers may be appointed to represent the appellant, local authority and other parties. It is not unusual for an 'expert' town planning witness to be called for the general issues, and for other experts to be called on particular matters. Thus for a large redevelopment scheme, a traffic engineer may deal with highway issues and an architect with design issues. For complicated cases a pre-inquiry meeting may be called to settle procedural and programming matters. Anyone may attend the inquiry and the inspector has wide discretion over how to hear the evidence of the principal parties and private individuals. The appellant and local authority have automatic full participation rights including calling of witnesses and cross-examination. At the close of the inquiry the inspector returns to his office to prepare his written decision or, if the appeal is to be determined by the Secretary of State, to write a report for him, usually with recommendations.

Informal hearing

A quicker, less costly alternative to the public local inquiry is the informal hearing. A hearing is conducted in accordance with a code of practice for hearings issued in annex 2 of circular 10/88. It will not be appropriate where many members of the public are likely to be present, or where complicated matters of policy or law may be raised, or where formal cross-examination is necessary to test the opposing cases. The hearing is conducted in the form of a discussion chaired by the inspector, and the atmosphere is intended to be more relaxed than at an inquiry. The inspector makes his decision known in writing in the following weeks.

Award of costs

Costs are normally borne by the party that incurs them. However, there are circumstances where one party may have to pay some or all the costs of the other. Guidance on the circumstances where this may happen is given in circular 2/87. The award of costs is governed by s.250(5) of the Local Government Act 1972 and is applied to planning appeals by s.320(2) of the 1990 Act. The award of costs does not automatically follow the decision on the planning merits of the appeal. Award of costs may occur when a party has acted unreasonably, vexatiously or frivolously, and where such action has caused the other party to incur unnecessary expense. At the present time the risk of award of costs applies only in cases taking the public local inquiry path and not to written representations or informal hearings.

Appeals to the High Court

For a period of six weeks after an appeal decision the right exists to challenge the decision in the High Court on a point of law only. The Court may not consider the planning merits of the case and its power is restricted to quashing a defective decision and referring the matter back to the Secretary of State so it can be decided again according to law.

DEVELOPMENT BY THE CROWN, LOCAL AUTHORITIES AND STATUTORY UNDERTAKERS

Development by the Crown

Planning legislation does not bind the Crown. However, government departments which carry out development are obliged to consult local authorities. The arrangements for this consultation are set out in circular 18/84. In most respects the procedures to be followed by the Crown department and the local authority are similar to ordinary planning applications. The local authority can object to the development which, if not resolved, may lead to intervention by the Department of the Environment.

Development by local authorities

In many circumstances a local planning authority (county and district) may grant itself a deemed consent for development subject to procedures similar to normal planning applications. As major property owners, developers and organisations responsible for a wide range of services, there is always a danger that a local authority will be unduly influenced in its decision whether to grant consent by matters which are not genuine planning considerations. Regulations issued by the Secretary of State – The Town and Country

Planning General Regulations 1992 (SI 1992 No.1492) – provide safeguards, including decisions being taken by the Secretary of State in certain cases.

Development by statutory undertakers

Statutory undertakers are defined in section 262(1) of the 1990 Act as 'persons authorised by any enactment to carry on any railway, light railway, tramway, road transport, water transport, canal, inland navigation, dock harbour, pier or lighthouse undertaking or any undertaking for the supply of hydraulic power and a relevant airport operator . . .'. In addition, for most purposes, the Act provides for any gas supplier, water or sewerage undertaking, the National Rivers Authority, the Post Office, holders of a licence under the Electricity Act 1989 and the Civil Aviation Authority to be regarded as statutory undertakers. They enjoy extensive permitted development under the General Development Order. Under Section 90(1) of the Act statutory undertakers may be authorised in separate legislation sponsored by the responsible department to undertake their activities without the need for specific planning permission from the local authority.

OTHER TYPES OF APPLICATION

Advertisements

Planning permission is not required for advertisements but, subject to certain exceptions, advertisement consent is. The present regulations are the Town and Country Planning (Control of Advertisements) Regulations 1989 (SI 670) and circular 15/89 explains their effect. Where advertisements may be displayed without consent there are often limitations on size, illumination and location. Such advertisements include election posters, estate agents' sale boards statutory advertisements, traffic signs, name plates, advertisements on business premises. Advertisement consent applications to local authorities are handled in a broadly similar fashion to planning applications. They may be granted, with or without conditions, and may be refused. There is a right of appeal to the Secretary of State. Under s.221 of the Act, local authorities may seek to establish areas of special advertisement control which have the effect of restricting the classes of advertisement which may be displayed without express consent. Such action is more likely in a conservation area than elsewhere. The Secretary of State must approve an area of special advertisement control.

Hazardous substances

In most cases the district planning authority will also be the hazardous substances authority under the terms of the Planning (Hazardous Substances) Act 1990. The Act came into operation in June 1992 and defines types and quantities of substances which are to be controlled. Local authority 'hazardous substances consent' will be required where substances stored on land within 500 metres under the same control exceeds certain limits. The local authority will be required to take into account the current or contemplated use of the land, adjoining land uses (existing or intended), the development plan and the advice of the Health and Safety Executive. Consents may be refused or issued with conditions. There is a right of appeal to the Secretary of State. Contravention of hazardous substances control is an offence punishable in the courts.

Minerals

The control of minerals development is a specialised area of town planning with many legal provisions being peculiar to this field alone. Planning permissions, for instance, usually last sixty years, and the authorities are charged with a responsibility for reviewing past permissions from time to time. The planning authority for the purpose of minerals (and for waste disposal, so often closely related in its activities and interests) is the county council or the unitary district. Minerals operations include all forms of extractive operation and minerals handling. The basic legislation is provided by the Town and Country Planning Act 1990. Government advice is contained in Minerals Policy Guidance Notes (listed earlier in the chapter). The local planning authority has wide powers to review operations, and to impose conditions relating to restoration, after-care and discontinuance. Appeal opportunities to the Secretary of State exist in respect of planning application decisions and enforcement action.

CHAPTER 3

CONSERVATION

INTRODUCTION

The recent history of conservation is one of increasing public, political and legislative support. The 1960s and 1970s saw a re-examination of our architectural heritage, with the result that some buildings thought ordinary or unattractive just a few years earlier came to be classified as examples of period, and have their artistic merits judged against the prevailing philosophies, conventions, materials and technologies of the day. There was no special interest group for the eighteenth century before the Georgian Group was established in 1937 and no society for the study of Victorian and Edwardian architecture and decorative arts until 1958. The legislation to protect areas of townscape, architectural or historic interest emerged only in 1967. In the management of rural areas there has been a matching interest in the identification, assessment and protection of places of one type of importance or another. Today, a reflection of our increased wish to conserve and protect places, features, and qualities is the fact that most planning departments will have one or more conservation officers concerned with built heritage, and many will have other professionals dealing with ecology issues, tree preservation and environmental education.

Despite the deregulatory politics of the 1980s, legislation concerned with conservation was not only shielded from major change but in some cases was strengthened or enhanced. While, as a general rule, local authorities were encouraged to adopt a co-operative position in relation to market-led development, in the field of urban and rural conservation the advice of government was less clear, allowing some councils and groups successfully to oppose destructive or poorly conceived development. With the government increasingly prompted to identify or establish its conservation credentials, neutral or occasionally supportive legislative or policy decisions were made. In conservation areas, for example, controls on development were increased, and recently the government has created a ministry with a specific brief to protect and manage national heritage.

'Greening' of the major political parties now seems to be an irreversible process, and the public's awareness of conservation issues, in the architectural, community and ecological senses, is more substantial than it has ever been. The White Paper *This Common Inheritance* may not have been anticipated in the mid-1980s but can already be criticised for its limited perception and prescription. This chapter looks at legislation to control and protect which, in many cases, has emerged in the past ten or fifteen years. The principle legislation is the Planning (Listed Buildings and Conservation Areas) Act 1990, hereafter in this chapter referred to as 'the 1990 Act'. The next few years should see this legislation tested.

LISTING OF BUILDINGS

The Secretary of State's duty to list

The Secretary of State for National Heritage is obliged under s.1 of the Planning (Listed Buildings and Conservation Areas) Act 1990 ('the 1990 Act') to compile lists of buildings which are of special architectural or historic interest, or approve, with or without modifications, such lists compiled by English Heritage or by other persons or organisations. In considering whether to include a building in such a list, the Secretary of State may also take into account the extent to which its exterior contributes to the architectural or historic interest of any group of buildings of which it forms part. There are now around 475,000 entries on the statutory list, probably amounting to more than a million individual properties. They include large country houses, cottages, farm buildings, churches, town halls, theatres, factories, offices and shops. Almost anything with architectural or historic interest which stands above ground level may be listed, including lamp-posts, milestones, cemetery headstones, telephone boxes, steps, walls and gates.

Principles of selection and grading

The current criteria for listing are contained in Circular 8/87, Appendix 1:

Before 1700: all buildings which survive in anything like their original condition.
1700 to 1840: most buildings although selection is necessary.

1840–1914: only buildings of definite quality and character; the selection is devised to include the principal works of the leading architects of the period.
1914–1939: selected buildings of high quality.

Since April 1987 any buildings over thirty years old have been eligible for listing, and, 'in very exceptional circumstances', buildings as little as ten years old are considered where there is a significant threat, of alteration or demolition.

Not all listed buildings are of equal merit. Approximately two per cent are held to be of exceptional interest and classified Grade I. Another four per cent or so fall into the category Grade II* meaning they have particular importance. The remainder are Grade II. It is important to note that buildings of any grade are protected fully against demolition or alteration. The real significance of the grading system lies in relation to grant aid for repair work covered in Chapter 9 and in the procedures that local authorities must adopt in dealing with listed building consent applications.

Production of the lists

In practice, English Heritage and Department of National Heritage inspectors usually make it known that they are examining an area with a view to listing, but there is no legal requirement to inform owners of buildings or anybody else of such survey work. Only in cases where the inspector wishes to examine a building's interior to help with dating or to establish the nature and quality of internal features will the occupier be sure of listing interest. Locking out the inspector is no safeguard against listing. Inspectors can be authorised by the Secretary of State, giving twenty-four hours' notice, to enter land and buildings at any reasonable time for survey work. In cases where the inspector has grounds to believe that advance knowledge of possible listing may lead to pre-emptive alterations or demolition, it is quite likely that the matter will be conducted in secrecy. Formal listing of the building takes place at the time of signature on the Secretary of State's behalf. The Department will immediately write to the owner/occupier at the property address with a notification. The local authority will advise the (potentially large) number of parties with ownership or occupation interests in the property. Not surprisingly, therefore, in areas where a large number of additions to the list have been made, it may be some weeks or months before all those needing to know are properly informed.

Spot-listing

In most cases listing takes place as a result of a review of the statutory list for an urban or rural area but there is provision for an individual building to be listed separately in response to a request made to the Department by English Heritage, the local authority, a local group or individual. In practice this procedure is often brought into effect where development or demolition threatens a building. These cases are most speedily dealt with if the requesting party supplies photographic, historical and other supporting information.

Building Preservation Notices

For the local planning authority anxious to bring listing protection to a building which it considers worthy of listing, and which is under threat of demolition or unsatisfactory alteration, s.3 of the 1990 Act provides the means to take matters into its own hands by issuing a Building Preservation Notice (BPN). The effect of the notice is to apply immediately most of the provisions of the Act relating to listed buildings. It cannot, therefore, be altered or demolished without listed building consent, and unauthorised work will be liable to criminal prosecution. The BPN lasts for up to six months during which time the Secretary of State must decide whether he wishes to include the building in the statutory list. If he decides not to do so then the owner may be able to claim compensation under s.29 for loss or damage attributed to the effect of the notice. This could include any sum for which the applicant is liable as a result of breach of contract caused by the effect of the notice. The use of BPNs, probably because of the compensation threat, is quite limited although, in practice, the payment of large compensation sums is rare.

Removal of entries from the list

From time to time buildings are removed from the list because they have been altered or demolished since listing, or perhaps the original decision to list in a particular case may have been misjudged. In some cases, buildings have been listed in error. There is no right of appeal against listing but the Department does operate an informal procedure for reviewing cases. Interested parties should write to the Department with a location plan, a copy of the listing, photographs and an explanation of why they consider the listing to be inappropriate. There is no time limit for these informal appeals. If demolition or alteration is con- templated and listed building consent is not granted then a ground of appeal to the Secretary of State may be that the building itself does not merit listing.

Immunity from listing

It is possible to obtain a certificate from the Depart- ment under s.6 of the Act guaranteeing that a building will not be listed for a period of five years. This opportunity exists to protect owners or prospective owners from pursuing plans for alteration or re- development only to find that the property has been suddenly listed. Such an occurrence, though rare, can have extremely damaging effects for the parties concerned. A condition of applying for a certificate is that there must have been a planning permission granted for the property or at least an application for permission submitted. There is no charge for this procedure and no prescribed form.

Extent of listing

The question of the extent of listing has been the subject of much debate in and out of the courts. It is safest to note the general position given below and seek guidance from the local planning authority in individual cases of doubt. It is, after all, the local authority which will decide whether any works undertaken merit enforcement action or prosecution. The entry in the statutory list will usually contain a few sentences of description in which various external and internal features may be mentioned. This description identifies the building but is not intended to be an inventory of features of architectural or historic interest. The listing applies to the whole building in equal measure. It may seem clear that a shop is listed for its particularly fine shopfront, but it is the whole building which is protected and not just the main elevation. Listing also extends to objects or structures fixed to the building such as wall panelling, bathroom furniture, shutters (external or internal), and any lean-to buildings such as a conservatory. Lastly, the listing will usually cover other objects and structures within the curtilage of the property. Protection may extend, therefore, to garden buildings, steps, walls, gates, statues, and so on.

Inspection of lists

Lists may be inspected, free of charge, at the offices of the appropriate local authority, and also, in the case of Greater London, at the offices of English Heritage.

SIGNIFICANCE OF LISTING

Background

The implications of listing for owners, occupiers and developers are considerable. Listed properties are part of the nation's heritage and the local planning authority, English Heritage and public can be expected to show keen interest in their proper use, maintenance and repair. In some cases, listing will be looked upon favourably; perhaps by the small professional practice finding enhanced company image deriving from occupation of a well kept, attractive listed building. Estate agents' sales particulars frequently make a feature out of listing. In other cases, listing can compound the burden of an old building with expensive maintenance, standing on a site which would have greater value if cleared. Of course, listing does not mean that the building must remain but rather that it should not be altered or demolished without careful thought being given to its special qualities. Some listed buildings are demolished, around 150 in 1990, and thousands are altered or extended each year. But with a total number of listed buildings now around 470,000, it is clear that the percentage being lost is not great.

Listed building consent

Listed building consent is required for any demolition, alteration or extension which may affect the character of the building. The need for consent is in addition to any planning permission. Section 8 of the 1990 Act defines listed building consent as being in writing from the local planning authority or the Secretary of State. Consents are frequently granted subject to conditions. In considering whether to grant listed building consent the local authority is required to have special regard to the desirability of preserving the building, its setting, and any features of historic interest. The procedure for securing listed building consent is set out in s.10. Application is to the local planning authority who will supply appropriate forms. The application must be supported by full details to show the nature of work proposed (there is no equivalent of outline planning permission). The local authority will advertise the application in a local newspaper, display a notice on or near the site, and take into account local representations. Within Greater London, the local authority must send a copy of the application to English Heritage although elsewhere this only applies to Grade I and II* buildings. If the application involves full or partial demolition then the local authority must consult six national organisations for their observations; the Ancient Monuments Society, the Council for British Archaeology, the Georgian Group, the Society for the Protection of Ancient Buildings, the Victorian Society, and the Royal Commission on Historical Monuments. The Secretary of State has wide powers requiring local planning authorities to notify him of their intention to grant listed building consent. This allows him the opportunity to 'call-in' applications for his own determination. Currently, this direction applies to all applications affecting a Grade I or II* building, all applications involving demolition, and those applications where the building has previously benefited from certain types of grant aid. Once granted, a consent must normally be implemented within five years. In cases involving any demolition, the Royal Commission has to be given a period of one month after consent to record the building should it wish.

Planning provisions

If a building is of a type which benefits from permitted development (Chapter 2), an immediate effect of listing is to restrict the scale of work which may be undertaken without the need to submit an application. For example, once listed there is little opportunity to undertake work within the curtilage of a listed dwelling-house (extensions, greenhouses, garages, etc.) without specific planning permission. This provision brings greater opportunity for control of works to local planning authorities but it should also be noted that for the listed building there are additional responsibilities for the way in which applications should be administered and determined. Planning applications must be advertised in a local newspaper and a notice posted at or close to the site. The local authority is obliged under the Act to have special regard to the desirability of preserving the building, its setting, and any features of special architectural or historic interest it possesses. The local authority will, quite legitimately, be concerned with aesthetic issues and with details of design. In dealing with new uses for buildings of architectural or historic interest (whether listed or not) local authorities are urged under Circular 8/87 to adopt relaxed controls over such matters as land use allocation, densities, daylighting and to use their powers under the Building Regulations with sensitivity if a new lease of life may be given to a building which might otherwise fall into decline.

Prosecution

Under s.7 of the Act no person may execute or cause to be executed any works for the demolition of a listed building or for its alteration or extension in a manner which would affect its character unless the works are authorised through the granting of Listed Building Consent. Section 9 provides for prosecution. In determining the amount of a fine, the court may have regard to the financial benefit which accrued or is likely to accrue to the defendant in consequence of the offence. The potential scale of punishment is severe, with the magistrates' court having powers to fine up to £20,000 or to imprison up to six months, while in the Crown Court there is no fixed fine limit and the period of custody may be up to two years. Under s.9 of the Act there is, for those cases where something was done to a listed building to deal with a sudden threat, a defence against action if it can be shown that all of the following were applicable:

1. The works were urgently necessary in the interests of safety or health or for the preservation of the building.
2. Providing temporary support or shelter for the building would not have been sufficient action.
3. That the works undertaken were the minimum necessary.
4. Full notice of the actions was given to the local planning authority in writing as soon as was reasonably practicable.

Injunctions

There has long been an opportunity for local authorities to restrain a breach of listed building control through an injunction. Local authorities and English Heritage now have specific authority under s.44A of the Act to pursue such a course, and as a result, such actions may be far more common in future.

Enforcement

As well as taking criminal proceedings for unauthorised work to a listed building, the local planning authority (or the Secretary of State should he be so minded) may issue a listed building enforcement notice (s.38). Such a notice specifies the breach which has occurred and requires steps to be taken to: (1) restore the building to its former state, (2) alleviate the damage caused, or (3) bring the building into the state it would have been had any listed building consent been properly adhered to. The latter category catches the owner who secures a listed building consent and then proceeds to vary from the approved plans or ignore any condition imposed. Unlike ordinary planning enforcement notices there is no sanctuary given by the lapse of time since the breach occurred (the 'four-year rule') but there is a right of appeal to the Secretary of State and the procedures are reasonably similar. One ground of appeal can be that the building does not merit being listed.

Responsibility to maintain a listed building

There are two principal notices relating to the maintenance of listed buildings in poor condition. They are most commonly called the 'urgent works notice' and the 'repairs notice'. Local authorities and English Heritage have power under s.54 to execute any urgent works necessary to preserve an unoccupied listed building or that part of a partially occupied building which is unoccupied. This is essentially for work which will keep the building adequately supported against collapse, weatherproof and resistant to vandalism. The authority can recover the costs of such works through the magistrates' court including the continuing costs of providing, say, prop-scaffolding or sheet roof covering, although the owner can make representations to the Secretary of State over the cost of works. The repairs notice powers available to local authorities (and English Heritage in Greater London) usually has more serious implications for the owner because the result can be that the building is compulsorily purchased. The full powers here lie in ss.47–50. Section 48 is employed first to serve the repairs notice. This specifies in detail the work which should be carried out and warns of the authority's powers under s.47 to take compulsory purchase proceedings. A period of two months is given during which time the owner may carry out the work himself putting an end to the whole matter. There is no right of appeal. If at the end of the two months the work has not been done the authority may commence compulsory purchase. The CPO has to be confirmed by the Secretary of State and the owner may object to the order at this stage, claiming the building does not merit listing or does not require repair. There is also an opportunity for the owners or other party with an interest in the land to apply to the magistrates' court for an order staying further proceedings on the CPO on the grounds that sufficient works have been undertaken to the building to preserve it. The final and perhaps most sobering feature of this area of listed building legislation is the special provisions which can apply for compensation. While this is normally paid on the basis of market value enhanced by a valuation assumption that listed building consent and planning permission would be forthcoming for works of alteration or extension, there is a provision for minimum compensation on the basis that listed building consent would only be available for bringing the building back to a proper state of repair. This may be adopted if the owner can be shown to have deliberately neglected the building for the purposes of justifying its demolition to allow new development on a cleared site. There are several points to note about the way in which Repairs Notice/CPO procedure is used by the authorities. Firstly, the acquiring authority does not have to retain the building but may sell it on to a suitable owner. Often such a new owner will buy it immediately with some form of legal agreement to bring the building back to good condition within a certain period. In these cases the local authority may incur few if any costs in the whole exercise. Secondly, there are English Heritage grant provisions specifically designed to help local authorities and new owners engaged in this sort of 'building rescue'. Lastly, the prominence of building preservation trusts in acquiring properties under these arrangements should be noted. Trusts are usually in the strongest position to draw loans and grants for such schemes. In addition to these specific provisions relating to listed buildings, local planning authorities do have general powers under s.215 of the Town and Country Planning Act 1990 to serve notice on the owner of any land or buildings where the condition adversely affects the amenity of the surrounding area. The notice would require the poor condition to be remedied subject only to the right of appeal to the magistrates' court. Failure to undertake the work could render the owner liable to prosecution and there is, additionally, a provision (s.219) for the local authority to undertake the remedial action itself and reclaim the cost from the owner.

Finance

There are certain financial advantages for owners of listed buildings. Grant aid may be available for repair and restoration. VAT is not payable on alterations provided listed building consent is necessary and has been obtained. Rates are not payable if the building is unoccupied. Chapter 9 contains more detailed information on grant aid.

CONSERVATION AREAS

Background

Under s.69 of the 1990 Act, local authorities are obliged to consider whether parts of their area are of 'special architectural or historic interest the character of which it is desirable to preserve or enhance'. Such areas should be designated 'conservation areas' by the local authority, and to date there have been over six thousand such designations. Every district council in England and Wales has at least one conservation area. There is no standard specification for a conservation area. It may be large or small, taking in a whole town centre or a small group of buildings. It will often be based on listed buildings, but this is not a requirement, and some areas may have no listed buildings at all. A historic street pattern, a village green or features of local historic or archaeological interest may form the foundation for a designation. It is the character of the area, rather than the individual buildings, which s.69 seeks to preserve or enhance.

Designation

The designation process is really quite simple. Once a suitable area has been identified, a report is prepared for the local authority's planning committee which then passes a resolution to designate a conservation area. The local authority should identify the area clearly through a map and a schedule of properties affected. Usually there will have been some form of publicity at the time of the local authority's survey and many authorities will have arranged a public consultation exercise, but there is no formal requirement for publicity before designation and some conservation areas do come into existence without prior public warning. In all cases, however, the authority must advertise the newly designated conservation area in a local newspaper and in the *London Gazette* identifying the land and buildings affected and the significance of designation for owners and occupiers. The Secretary of State and English Heritage must also be advised. Although the designation is registered as a local land charge and most affected parties find out one way or another, the wiser local authorities will advise individual owners/occupiers in writing. There is no appeal against being included in a conservation area and no certificate of immunity. Once the decision has been taken the local authority can reverse its action but this is rare. The Secretary of State does have the power to cancel a designation but he has never done so. English Heritage has its own powers to designate conservation areas in London.

Demolition control in conservation areas

Demolition of unlisted buildings in conservation areas is largely brought within local planning authority control through s.74 of the Act which applies, with modifications, many of the provisions relating to the control of listed buildings found in part 1 of the Act. The demolition consent required is known as 'conservation area consent'. There are exceptions which include any building of less than 115 cubic metres; any agricultural building erected since 1 January 1914; up to ten per cent or 500 square metres (whichever is greater) of an industrial building; any gate, wall or fence erected since 1 July 1948 which is less than one metre high abutting a public highway or public open space, or two metres high elsewhere. In general, the procedure for applying for conservation area consent is similar to that for applying for listed building consent.

Permitted development in conservation areas

To allow greater control over alterations to buildings which may have the effect of harming the character of the conservation area the extent of permitted development in conservation areas is significantly reduced under the *Town and Country Planning General Development Order* 1988 (1988 No.1813). In the case of extensions to dwelling-houses, this means not more than ten per cent or 50 cubic metres (whichever is greater) may be added to the volume of the property without planning permission (elsewhere the figures are fifteen per cent and 75 cubic metres). In addition, specific planning permission is required for cladding of any part of a house with stone, artificial stone, timber, plastic or tiles and for any alterations to a roof (such as dormer windows) which would alter its shape. There is also less opportunity to erect garden buildings and freestanding garages without the local planning authority's specific permission. In the case of warehouse and industrial buildings in conservation areas the size of permitted development extensions is reduced from twenty-five per cent and 100 square metres to ten per cent or 500 square metres floor area.

Felling and pruning of trees

Control over works to trees which are not in a tree preservation order is handled by a system of advance notification. Under s.211 of Town and Country

Planning Act 1990 anyone wishing to cut down, top, lop or uproot a tree must give the local planning authority a period of six weeks in which to consider making a tree preservation order. Work on the tree can only be carried out within this period if the local authority give their specific consent. Under s.212 the Secretary of State has specified five cases to be exempt from this control. The most significant exemption is for felling trees with a trunk diameter not exceeding 75 millimetres, or the felling of a tree having a diameter not exceeding 100 millimetres where the action is to improve growth of other trees. Diameters are measured 1.5 metres above ground level.

General duties of the local planning authority in conservation areas

In a conservation area, the local planning authority has to pay special attention to preserving the character or appearance of the area in any planning decisions. Local authorities have been advised that they 'stand in the vanguard of those protecting historic buildings and areas, and the Secretary of State hopes they will make diligent use of all the powers available to them' (circular 8/87, para. 68). In the field of aesthetic design the local planning authority is under a duty to see that new buildings are designed not as separate entities but as new elements in the conservation area which contribute to its preservation and enhancement. It may therefore legitimately engage in consideration of the development's aesthetic qualities as well as its overall massing and proportion. If the local planning authority considers necessary, it may seek to secure a direction under Article 4 of the General Development Order reducing the permitted development rights for a property, group of properties or for the whole conservation area. Circular 8/87 makes it clear that 'although, in general, the Secretary of State will be favourably disposed toward approving an Article 4 direction relating to land included in a conservation area, it must be emphasised that the existence of a conservation area is not, in itself, automatic justi-fication for a direction.' In the exercise of their conservation area responsibilities, local authorities are recommended by the Secretary of State to consider establishing conservation area advisory committees composed of representatives of professional institutes, amenity societies and local civic groups to provide a source of advice on policies and individual decisions. Probably less than half the country's local authorities have actually done so.

Display of advertisements

Under s.221 of the Town and Country Planning Act 1990 the Secretary of State is empowered to make special controls over advertisements for conservation areas, but little use has been made of this provision. Under the same section there is a general power for the Secretary of State to approve areas of special advertise-ment control. Such areas can be created anywhere, and they are particularly relevant to a conservation area, or part of one, where there are special issues of amenity at stake. A person aggrieved by designation of an area as one of special advertisement control has recourse only to the High Court (s.284(2)(d)).

Buildings in disrepair

The local planing authority may apply to the Secretary of State under s.76 of the 1990 Act to be given the power to treat an unoccupied unlisted building which is in a state of disrepair as if it were listed. This then permits the provisions of s.54 to be used allowing the authority to serve a notice empowering it to undertake urgent works.

Financial assistance to property owners

Financial assistance from local authorities and English Heritage may be payable for repair and enhancement work in some cases in conservation areas. This is dealt with in Chapter 9.

TREE PRESERVATION

General

The protection of trees is secured by two means under the Town and Country Planning Act 1990. Firstly by a special duty on planning authorities under s.97 to ensure they make adequate provision for preserving existing trees by imposing conditions on planning permissions. Secondly, authorities are empowered under s.198 to make tree preservation orders wherever they consider it expedient in the interests of amenity.

Tree preservation orders (TPOs)

The local planning authority may act to preserve a tree, trees, groups of trees or woodlands by making a tree preservation order. Thereafter, consent of the authority is required to cut down, top, lop, uproot, damage or destroy any protected tree. The Town and Country Planning (Tree Preservation Order) Regulations 1969 (SI No.17) sets out the main provisions and a model order. The order and a plan depicting the trees affected must be served on the owners and occupiers of the land, on those known to be entitled to fell trees, and those with mineral rights (if known). There is a period of twenty-eight days during which any objections or representations may be sent to the authority, after which time the authority may confirm the order taking into account any comments received. The order does not come into effect until confirmation, but under s.201 the authority may make a direction giving it provisional effect from a particular date. In practice, most authorities use this direction quite routinely, with the result that most orders provide immediate protection.

Consent to undertake felling, lopping, etc.

The procedure for application and issue of consents is similar to the system for planning permission. Application is made to the local planning authority who have two months to give conditional or unconditional consent or issue a refusal. There is a right of appeal to the Secretary of State who will deal with the matter in the same way as a planning appeal. Consent to fell is usually subject to a requirement to provide a replacement tree.

Works which may be undertaken without consent

Under s.198(6)(a) of the Town and Country Planning Act 1990, trees within an order which are dead, dying or dangerous may be felled without consent, although an obligation to replace them remains. Consent is not required if felling or other work is in compliance with obligations under an Act of Parliament or to prevent or abate a nuisance (s.198(6)). Where planning permission has been granted for a development, the implementation of which necessarily requires felling or other works to a preserved tree, the planning permission is taken to have authorised the work and no further consent is required. Consent is not required where a felling licence has been given by the Forestry Commission under the Forestry Act 1967.

Enforcement of tree preservation orders

Where a tree is uprooted or destroyed in contravention of a tree preservation order or because it is dead, dying or dangerous, there is a duty on the landowner to replace the tree as soon as is reasonable. The local authority may waive such a requirement, but where this is not done, the authority may serve a notice under s.207 of the Act to enforce replacement. Section 210 provides for prosecution of persons felling trees without consent and fines have been increased to a maximum of £20,000. In determining the level of the fine the court may have regard to any financial benefit which has accrued to the defendant in consequence of the offence.

PARKS AND GARDENS OF HISTORIC INTEREST

General

Parks and gardens have in the past ten years begun to receive special notice. Their historical importance has come to be recognised by the government, English Heritage and, more recently, by the majority of local authorities. As settings for listed buildings, as features of conservation areas, and as designs in themselves, historic parks and gardens deserve careful attention. They clearly cannot be preserved in quite the same way as a building, or even an individual tree but, increasingly, there are ways in which they are being protected from damage, neglect, and ill-judged alteration or development. Parks and gardens may be taken to include formal gardens and parklands of large country houses, remnant gardens following loss of primary buildings, cemeteries, and public or private parks. In many cases there are elements which can be specifically protected: trees may be placed in tree preservation orders; garden buildings and structures may be listed; ruins may be scheduled as ancient monuments. In certain cases there is justification for the park or garden being designated a conservation area. The most significant influence on thinking in this field in recent years has emerged with publication of English Heritage's Register of Parks and Gardens of Historic Interest for all counties of England.

Register of parks and gardens

Power to compile a register was given to English Heritage by the National Heritage Act 1983 (amending s.8 of the Historic Buildings and Ancient Monuments Act 1953). The lists applying to all forty-four counties of England were completed by March 1988 with 1200 entries. To a certain extent, coverage is patchy with some counties having far more entries than others with equal or greater richness of garden heritage. More gardens are being added and this will continue. A copy of each entry is to be sent to the owner and occupier of the land concerned and the district and county planning authority. The register, however, does not carry any statutory force. It is an alert mechanism for the owner, developer and planning authority to warn of special importance and the need for care. There are now a number of cases of refusal of planning permission where a major influence on the decision has been an entry on the list.

BUILDINGS IN ECCLESIASTICAL USE

Ecclesiastical buildings generally

Ecclesiastical buildings probably make the single greatest contribution to the country's building heritage. There are 23,150 entries on the statutory list for religious buildings, more than forty-five per cent of which are in the categories I and II*. Many unlisted churches will be in conservation areas. The arrangements for dealing with alterations and demolition of listed and conservation area church buildings are unique and will be described below, but arrangements for planning permission are exactly the same as any other form of property.

Ecclesiastical exemption for churches in use

It may seem surprising in view of their frequent architectural and historic importance that religious buildings, as long as they are in use, are largely outside the scope of listed building and conservation area control. This state of affairs can be traced back to an Act of 1913. The modern provision for 'ecclesiastical exemption', as it is known, lies in s.60(1) of the Planning (Listed Buildings and Conservation Areas) Act 1990. A definition of ecclesiastical building is not provided, but s.60(2) establishes that it should not include the place of residence of a minister from which he performs the duties of his office. Listed ecclesiastical buildings in use by any denomination may be altered without listed building consent. Whole or partial demolition of ecclesiastical property will require listed building consent, except in the case of the Church of England.

Demolition and the Church of England

Under s.60(7), listed building control does not extend to demolition or partial demolition of a Church of England property in pursuance of a pastoral or redundancy scheme under the Pastoral Measure 1983. These exemptions also extend to conservation area control under ss.75(1)(b) and (7). There is an agreement between the government and the Church of England that whole or part demolition of a listed church or one in a conservation area will be preceded by a non-statutory public inquiry if English Heritage, a national amenity society, the local authority or the Advisory Board for Redundant Churches objects to the loss. One justification for the special exemption of the Church of England lies in the Church's own strict ecclesiastical laws and practices concerning alterations and demolition.

ANCIENT MONUMENTS

Background

Scheduling of ancient monuments dates back to the Ancient Monument Act 1882. Today there are over 13,000 scheduled monuments out of a total of 630,000 sites thought to have archaeological interest. English Heritage has embarked on the Monuments Protection Programme which can be expected to raise the number to around sixty thousand by the end of the century. To the uninitiated it may seem odd that we have quite separate protection codes for listed buildings and ancient monuments, but this reflects the incremental way in which heritage legislation has grown. Indeed, some buildings are both listed and scheduled. Government policy on scheduled monuments can be found in planning policy guidance note 16 (PPG16) *Archaeology and Planning*, 1990.

Definition

Section 61(7) of the Ancient Monuments and Archaeological Areas Act 1979 defines a monument to include a building, structure, or work above or below ground, a cave or excavation, or the remains of any of the above or of a vessel, aircraft or other movable structure. Typically, scheduled monuments have archaeological or historic value rather than architectural. Where something is both listed and scheduled, it is the controls relating to the scheduling which prevail.

Production of schedule

The arrangements for scheduling are similar to those for listing. Anybody may put forward a site for scheduling by contacting the Department of the Environment. A good description and photographs will be helpful. English Heritage will investigate and make a recommendation to the Secretary of State. In the event of scheduling, the owners and local authority will be notified and a local land charge registered. Most scheduling in the next few years will occur under more structured survey exercises of the Monuments Protection Programme.

Scheduled Monument Consent

The main consequence of scheduling is the need to secure Scheduled Monument Consent under s.2 of the Act for almost any works including repair, alterations, additions, flooding, tipping, etc. To carry out such work without consent is a criminal offence. The procedure for applications is governed by Schedule 1 of the Act and by the Ancient Monuments (Applications for Scheduled Monument Consent) Regulations 1981 (SI 1301). Applications are to the Secretary of State and arrangements are not unlike those for 'called-in' planning applications. The Secretary of State must hold a public inquiry or allow a hearing to interested parties. The validity of his decision may be challenged in the High Court within six weeks. A blanket consent (under s.3) for works to be undertaken without formal consent has been issued in the Ancient Monuments (Class Consents) Order 1981 (SI 1302) allowing surface ploughing, works by the National Coal Board at depths greater than ten metres, works by English Heritage, routine operations of British Waterways Board and machinery maintenance.

Offences

If unauthorised works are carried out there is no action similar to the planning or listed building enforcement notice. In many cases, a damaged monument by its very nature cannot be restored and the only protection measure possible is to have punishments which will act as a deterrent. Even the use of a metal detector may attract a fine.

Care and maintenance of scheduled monuments

Responsibility for the care and maintenance of a scheduled monument usually lies with the owner. This is not unreasonable given that most monuments require very little work, being not much more than ground-level remains or the lower soil horizons of a field. For more significant sites, however, such as an Iron Age hill fort or a large medieval ruin, there is provision for public ownership or guardianship. In addition, grant aid can be given by English Heritage towards maintenance, preservation, management, or acquisition (grants are dealt with in Chapter 9). Where a private owner is unwilling to co-operate in necessary maintenance, powers of compulsory acquisition under s.10 are available. This can extend to adjoining land or routeways necessary to ensure access and maintenance. It should be noted that guardianship, compulsory acquisition and grant aid can apply to any monuments, not just those which are scheduled. Where a monument in private ownership requires work to be undertaken to preserve it which the owner is unwilling to carry out, there is power under s.5 of the Act for the site to be entered by English Heritage operatives and work undertaken by them. There is no power to charge the owner for the work done and this route is, not surprisingly, seldom pursued.

ARCHAEOLOGICAL AREAS

Background

Arrangements for ancient monuments necessarily deal with known or largely known archaeology. Very often the extent of archaeological interest only becomes apparent as building operations are under way. Work undertaken at this stage is usually termed rescue archaeology. In recent years, well publicised cases in York and the City of London have shown just how important finds can emerge during the development process. Up to 1982 the only controls available to safeguard archaeological interest were conditions attached to planning permissions or consents requiring access to the site during the course of building work for investigations. Such arrangements were often inadequate, not least because of the lack of certainty on anybody's part (with the possible exception of the developer) when the work may begin in the five years opening life of the planning permission. The government's position on the matter of archaeology and development is set out in planning policy guidance note 16 (PPG16) *Archaeology and Planning*, 1990.

Designation of areas of archaeological importance

Under s.33 of the Ancient Monuments and Archaeological Areas Act the Secretary of State may designate areas of archaeological importance. Local authorities are similarly empowered but their action has to be confirmed by the Secretary of State within six months. In either case there must be due publicity and consultation. The effect of designation is to give investigating authorities (probably university archaeological units or similar local authority teams) a period of up to six months to examine and record site archaeology prior to any significant ground disturbance. Designation has been very selective, with only five such areas to date (the centres of Canterbury, Chester, Exeter, Hereford and York); advice in *Archaeology and Planning* states that there will be no further designations until the effectiveness of the PPG has been assessed. The Secretary of State has placed emphasis very much on co-operation among local authorities, archaeological groups, land owners and developers. Voluntary agreements have proved successful in many cases, with some developers not only providing access but financing excavation, analysis, preservation and exhibition of finds.

Offences involving areas of archaeological importance

With the exception of very minor categories set out in the Areas of Archaeological Interest (Notification of Operations) (Exemption) Order 1984 (SI No.1286), it is an offence under s.35(1) for work to go ahead without an operations notice being served. There is a defence on grounds of safety and health, ignorance of the archaeological interest area, or due diligence in the undertaking of work avoiding damage to remains.

RURAL CONSERVATION

Background

Conservation in rural areas is concerned with protection of amenity, landscapes, habitats and wildlife. For the purposes of this book, interest lies mainly in the effects of legislation and practice affecting land rather than the safety and welfare of creatures on or above it. Several pieces of primary legislation cover the field including the National Parks and Access to the Countryside Act 1949, The Countryside Act 1968, The Wildlife and Countryside Act 1981, Town and Country Planning Act 1990, and Environmental Protection Act 1990.

Rural conservation areas

The duty imposed on a local authority to examine its area from time to time to see if some parts ought to be designated conservation areas is as much a responsibility for rural authorities as it is for urban ones. It is often assumed that the character of an area is provided substantially by architectural interest, but this is a misunderstanding and the character of a rural area with its scattered farm buildings, hedgerows, country lanes and groups of trees is as legitimate a basis for a conservation area as a well designed town square with a large proportion of formal historic buildings. Rural conservation areas are increasingly common and it is not unusual for some to cover a thousand or more acres. These conservation areas carry exactly the same controls and responsibilities as their urban counter-parts. Conservation area designation and practice is dealt with earlier in this chapter.

National parks

National Parks, of which there are ten, are designated by the Countryside Commission under s.114(2) of the National Parks and Access to the Countryside Act 1949 to preserve and enhance natural beauty and promote enjoyment by the public. Responsibility for achieving these objectives lies largely with local authorities rather than the Commission and is achieved through three means. Firstly, there is more strict control over development, through reduction in permitted develop-ment rights and the adoption of planning policies geared to careful control of development. Secondly, the local authority may take an active role in providing recreational facilities, including undertaking compul-sory purchase of land for these purposes. Thirdly, positive financial measures exist to permit local authorities to devote financial resources to park objectives. A key requirement in a national park is to understand and protect the local farming, industrial and commercial economies and to safeguard existing communities from being unduly harmed by the recreational and tourist interests. The much smaller and more numerous country parks are distinguished from national parks by being devoted almost entirely to recreation.

Areas of outstanding natural beauty

Areas of outstanding natural beauty (frequently referred to as AONBs) designated by the Countryside

Commission share a high quality of landscape with national parks but are not suitable for such designation because they are too small or for some other reason. The aim of preserving and enhancing natural beauty exists for local authorities but special legal and financial provision for facilities for public enjoyment do not. Careful control of development through suitable development plan and development control policies provide a safeguard for the environment of any AONB.

Green belts

The concept of green belt first emerged for London in the 1920s but it was not until 1955 that it was established as an objective of town and country planning for the capital and other appropriate towns and cities. Green belts are now confirmed around fifteen urban areas and cover a total land area of 5,000,000 acres. Planning policy guidance note 2 (PPG2) *Green Belts* 1988 summarises government policy. Green belts have five purposes: to restrict the sprawl of large built-up areas; to safeguard surrounding countryside from encroachment; to prevent neighbouring towns from merging into one another; to preserve the special character of historic towns; and to assist in urban regeneration. They are created through structure and local plans, and conserved for their strategic value. They do not necessarily have to have an attractive landscape character.

Agricultural land

Since the introduction of modern town planning controls in 1947 successive governments have allowed farming activities and development to remain largely outside the scope of planning control. Under s.55(2)(e) of the Town and Country Planning Act 1990 no development is involved where land or any associated building is used for the purposes of agriculture or forestry. Agricultural land is divided into five grades. Land in grades 1 and 2 is described as highest quality, versatile, and most efficient in response to inputs. Grade 3 is subdivided into 3A, 3B and 3C. In many parts of the country where grades 1 and 2 are in short supply, grade 3A represents the most versatile and will be protected from development. The lower grade 3 land and that graded 4 and 5 would not normally be opposed for development on purely agricultural grounds. Proposals for large-scale development on agricultural land are referred to the Ministry of Agriculture for comment. Government policy is evident in Circular 16/87 *Development Involving Agricultural Land* and PPG7 *Rural Enterprise and Development.*

Sites of special scientific interest

Sites of special scientific interest (SSSIs) currently cover over 3,800,000 acres, or six per cent, of the land area of Great Britain. Selection and designation is undertaken by English Nature, under s.28 of the Wildlife and Countryside Act on scientific rather than amenity grounds. Three months' notice is given of a proposed designation to allow for representations but the designation has interim effect from the date of service. Since English Nature has a *duty* to designate, something which is quite unusual for a largely unaccountable body, objecting to a proposed SSSI is unlikely to have much impact. Once owners and occupiers have been notified they must advise English Nature four months in advance of any works. The purpose of this advance notice is to allow English Nature an opportunity to negotiate a management agreement. It is an offence to fail to notify or to undertake work without specific permission in this four month period. Once the four months has expired the work may go ahead, management agreement or not.

CHAPTER 4   THE CONTROL OF POLLUTION

INTRODUCTION

Pollution is generally defined as something which adversely affects the purity of our natural environment. This includes oil pollution at sea; chemical pollution in rivers; smoke in the atmosphere and, just as harmful but less publicised, unacceptable levels of noise. All of these, and others, are dealt with in either this chapter or, in the case of water pollution, in Chapter 5.

Although it is only comparatively recently that pollution has been controlled by widespread legislation, there has been some form of control for many years. In the past, pollution which affected others was mainly dealt with by the common law as it would constitute an offence of nuisance or trespass. Subsequently, the various Public Health Acts imposed certain controls and, in some instances, criminal sanctions. Legislation today is far more comprehensive, not only because our awareness of the effects of pollution is enhanced, but also because the modern world has a greater capacity to create pollution with potentially far-reaching, long-lasting and highly damaging effects. Controls are, therefore, not confined to England and Wales, but European law attempts to impose high standards across the nations of the EC. Indeed, the Single European Act of 1986 added, by Article 25, the preservation and protection of the environment as a community objective. Furthermore, the European Commission provides a steady flow of directives on environmental protection and these have played a part in shaping our legislation.

In 1990 the Environmental Protection Act was given the royal assent and, as at October 1992, parts of it have come into force. This Act, which covers a wide and varied area, from the control of contaminated land to controls on stray dogs, is the most comprehensive review of our pollution laws. On moving the second reading of the Bill, the then Secretary of State for the Environment, Chris Patten, said:

> Whatever the arguments about the Bill . . . it will surely provide us with the basic framework for much of our pollution control in Britain well into the next century.

It is, however, the new powers to deal with air pollution, statutory nuisances and waste on land which are of major significance in the context of this book.

Pollution does not confine itself to the area in which it was generated. A highly publicised example of far-reaching pollution resulted from the disaster at the Chernobyl nuclear power plant in the Soviet Union in 1986. The cloud of radioactive material released from the damaged reactor crossed Britain and, due to heavy rainfall experienced at the time, some of the material reached the ground. Although it is estimated that the accident will continue to have some effect on the environment for perhaps as long as fifty years, the actual dose of radiation to which people in Britain were or will be exposed is so small as to be negligible. Nevertheless, pollution controls need to contain and prevent such accidents.

THE CONTROLS, THE CONTROLLING AUTHORITIES AND THE ENVIRONMENTAL PROTECTION ACT 1990

For simplicity, this chapter has been divided into four sections, each covering a specific environmental area. These are broadly described as atmospheric pollution, noise pollution, waste disposal problems and statutory nuisances. Water pollution is dealt with in detail in Chapter 5 which looks at the water authorities, their powers and duties.

The powers of the various authorities with responsibility for enforcing the legislation are detailed in the appropriate sections which follow. Before embarking on these specialised topics, and by way of completeness, set out below is a brief resumé of the controls over potentially polluting processes which are now covered by the Environmental Protection Act 1990 (the EPA).

The EPA introduces a system of 'integrated pollution control' which calls on the services of both central government bodies and local authorities. Her Majesty's Inspectorate of Pollution (established in 1987 to deal with industrial air pollution, radioactive substances and hazardous wastes) continues its function of monitoring and controlling the most hazardous pollutants introduced into our environment, whether it be air, land or water. Local authorities have the task of controlling less hazardous pollutants introduced into the atmosphere as well as waste disposal on land, while the National Rivers Authority monitors discharges into 'controlled waters'. These latter include streams, rivers and also sewers.

When fully implemented, the EPA will prevent an unauthorised person (s.6) from carrying out a 'prescribed process' (specified in regulations made under s.2 by the Secretary of State for the Environment, and of which there are over one hundred). Application for authorisation is made to the appropriate body – either HM Inspectorate of Pollution, the local authority or the National Rivers Authority – which is also the enforcing authority for that particular process. Authorisation can be granted subject to conditions (s.7) and the Act envisages that the enforcing body will rigorously monitor the activities of those authorised to ensure that the conditions are complied with. Failure to comply may lead to the service of an *enforcement notice* (s.13) on the person carrying on the prescribed process. Such a notice must state the breach and also the steps required by the controlling authority to remedy the breach. One important point here is that enforcement notices in this context can be used *in anticipation* of a contravention as well as after a condition has been contravened. This highlights the aim of the EPA, which is to control pollution by prevention. Another important distinction, which sets these enforcement notices apart from those issued under the Town and Country Planning Act 1990, is that an appeal against the notice does *not* automatically suspend the notice.

Lastly, the Act provides for the service of prohibition notices (s.14) when the controlling authority believes that there is an imminent risk of serious pollution, regardless of whether there is (or is likely to be) any breach of an authorisation. On the service of a prohibition notice the authorisation is suspended until the steps specified in the notice have been implemented. Again there is a right of appeal against the service of the notice, but again an appeal will not suspend the notice pending the outcome of the appeal.

The conditions which can be attached to an authorisation are limited in that s.7 states that conditions must be imposed to ensure that the 'best available techniques not entailing excessive cost' will be used. This has already come to be known as the BATNEEC test and, on the face of it, one can foresee much litigation to determine such questions as 'what is excessive cost?'. It is anticipated that circulars and other guidelines will be issued to minimise this potential problem area (brief details of those already published are given later) but the government's thinking behind the requirement is clear: persons who wish to engage in prescribed processes must take all reasonable steps to ensure that the environment is not harmed as a result. At the same time, many of these processes are necessary for our daily life to continue and persons must not be discouraged from carrying them on by the inordinately high costs of pollution control.

As well as enforcement and prohibition notices the EPA also lays down criminal sanctions which are particularly stringent. As at October 1992, an offence tried in the magistrates' court could lead to a maximum fine of £20,000 or an unlimited fine if the case is heard in the Crown Court. Both the magistrates' and the Crown Court have the power to sentence a guilty person to up to two years imprisonment in certain circumstances.

Furthermore, under ss.16 and 17 of the Act inspectors can be appointed by both the Secretary of State for the Environment and the various authorities with responsibility for enforcing the legislation. These inspectors have very wide powers of entry and inspection. They are entitled to examine items on the premises, take samples and measurements, and generally to investigate the operation of the prescribed process. Such powers are, of course, necessary if we and our environment are to be satisfactorily protected from the potential pollutants created by the processes.

It is interesting to note that the Crown and Crown land (which includes government departments, their employees and lands) are obliged to comply with the provisions of the EPA unless a matter of national security is involved. It is usual for the Crown (and its land) to be exempted from the requirements of most legislation.

The government has already issued some of the regulations which are required and these are referred to here. The Environmental Protection (Prescribed Processes) Regulations 1991 (SI 1991 No. 472) give a detailed list of the processes covered by the Act. These range from processes involving the production of fuel or power, to the metal and mineral industry, to the chemical industry and a final hotch-potch called 'others'. It should be noted that so far as the prescribed processes are concerned, the legislation is being implemented over a period of time, with some processes unaffected until well into 1995. At October 1992, the requirements with regard to waste disposal, fuel and power production are in force. The anticipated timetable for the remainder is that the mineral industry will also be covered by the end of 1992 with the chemical industry processes following in 1993. Processes relating to the metal industry will be included during 1994 and the 'other processes' will be incorporated before 1 November 1995, which is stated, at this stage, as the final date.

In addition, the Environmental Protection (Applications, Appeals and Registers) Regulations 1991 (SI 1991 No. 507) are now in force. These regulations set out the details required in an application for the authorisation to carry on a prescribed process, as well as the types of condition which the authorising body can impose. They also cover the consultation procedure to be adopted for each application and specify the registers of applications and authorisations which must be maintained. Lastly, the regulations deal in great depth with the appeal process to be implemented in the event that an authorisation is not granted. This can be either by way of written representations or public inquiry before an inspector appointed for that purpose by the Secretary of State.

In an attempt to assist the bodies charged with implementing the Act, guidance has been issued by the Department of the Environment by way of a booklet entitled *Integrated Pollution Control – A Practical Guide*. This document outlines the legislative framework, expands on the standard to be imposed by the BATNEEC test and suggests grounds for refusing authorisations. It also mentions the methods to be used when dealing with appeals. Doubtless, this guide will be expanded considerably as the legislation is brought into force and the areas of difficulty are pinpointed.

ATMOSPHERIC POLLUTION

The Environmental Protection Act 1990 says very little about pollution of the air. What it does do, however, is introduce the integrated pollution control referred to above. Under s.2 of the Act the Secretary of State may by regulations prescribe any description of process as a process for which, after a specified date, authorisation is required from the particular controlling body. This may be HM Inspectorate of Pollution (HMIP) in the case of the most harmful substances, or the local authority. The regulations designate not only controls over the operation of these prescribed processes but also emission limits into the environment. There are limits on the concentration of the pollutant to be emitted and the period of time during which pollutants can be emitted. On top of that, the regulations establish quality standards and quality objectives with regard to the prescribed processes (s.3).

The controls over emissions into the atmosphere by way of prescribed processes are, thus, included in Part I of the Act along with emissions into other environmental media. These controls and the offences associated with them are outlined in the general introduction to this chapter and will not be repeated here.

The older legislation dealing with 'clean air' is continuing to operate along with the new regulations introduced by the EPA. In essence, the position has remained the same, except that controls over prescribed processes have now been removed from the older legislation, as they are dealt with under the EPA. The major legislation is outlined below and, as can be seen, forms a collection of controls which have been generated almost since the beginning of this century.

The Alkali etc. Works Regulations Act 1906

Prevention of noxious gases

Certain industrial and chemical processes result in the emission of hydrochloric acid gas in large quantities. The production of alkali is one such process. The Act, by ss.1 and 2, requires that the owner of any alkali work should use the best practicable means for preventing the escape of noxious and offensive gases to ensure that in each cubic metre of emissions there is only 0.46 grams of hydrochloric acid.

Penalty

Failure to comply with this is an offence punishable before the magistrates' court with a fine of £400 and a daily penalty of £50 for each day the offence is continued.

Registration

Alkali works must be registered with the local authority and failure so to do is also an offence leading to a fine of £400 (s.9).

Inspectors

Inspectors in relation to this Act are appointed under the Health and Safety at Work etc. Act 1974.

Note   The provisions of the Alkali etc. Act will be phased out when the EPA becomes fully effective.

Clean Air Acts 1956 and 1968

These two Acts are designed to be read together and will therefore be treated similarly here.

Duty of local authority

The local authority is under a duty to enforce all the provisions of the Acts. The local authority for the purpose of the Acts is the district council (s.29 1956 Act).

Dark smoke

Under the Acts local authorities must control the emission of 'dark smoke'. This is defined as smoke which is as dark or darker than shade 2 on the Ringelmann chart. It is an offence to discharge dark smoke from:

1. The chimney of *any* building.
2. Industrial or trade premises.
3. Railway locomotive engines.
4. Certain ships.

Chimneys

The offence is committed by the occupier of the building, which can include domestic as well as industrial premises (s.1 1956 Act). It does *not* apply to smoke from bonfires or emitted otherwise than from a chimney. There are four defences available:

1. That the offence resulted from lighting a cold furnace.
2. That the furnace had failed in some way which

could not be reasonably foreseen or prevented.
3. That unsuitable fuel had been unavoidably used.
4. A combination of all these three.

Before prosecuting, the local authority must serve notice of proceedings on the occupier. Failure to do so prevents any legal action being taken.

Penalty

The offence is heard before the magistrates' court. Smoke from a private dwelling has a maximum fine of level 3, and from other premises, level 5.
It is interesting to note that the offence is a daily one. The Act is worded in such a way that a new offence takes place on every day that smoke is emitted.

Industrial or trade premises

The 1968 Act prohibits dark smoke emissions from industrial or trade premises otherwise than through a chimney. Again the occupier of the premises is responsible for ensuring that the offence does not take place. There are some exemptions, subject to conditions, which are laid down in regulations and include, for example, burning waste resulting from demolition (s.1).

Penalty

Again, before the magistrates' court, a maximum of level 4.

Railway engines

In the 1950s railway smoke caused one-seventh of the dark smoke pollution. Despite the changes in propulsion of trains the 1956 Act still retains the old offence which can be applied now to railways run by private groups. The owner of the railway commits the offence although before proceedings can be brought the local authority must notify the owner of its intentions (s.30).

Penalty

Maximum of level 5 before a magistrates' court.

Vessels

The 1956 Act applies the dark smoke principles to vessels in certain waters. Reference should be made to the regulations for details.

New non-domestic furnaces

Section 3 of the 1956 Act states that it is an offence to install a new furnace unless it is capable of continuous operation without emitting smoke (so far as is practicable). Advance notice of installation of a furnace must be given to the local authority, and this includes the removal of an old furnace from one location to another.

Penalty

Installing a furnace which does not comply may lead to a maximum fine of level 5, and failing to notify the local authority, a fine of level 3, before the magistrates' court.

Dust and grit from non-domestic furnaces

Regulations can be prescribed under the 1968 Act to limit the emission of dust and grit from furnaces. Emissions are measured in accordance with the regulations made under s.7 1956 Act, and those which exceed the limit constitute an offence on every day that the emission takes place. The occupier of the premises is responsible for ensuring that the Act is complied with.

Section 3 of the 1968 Act extends the provisions of s.6 of the 1956 Act with regard to the fitting of arrestment plant to contain the dust and grit. The local authority must approve the plant used; if refused, there is a right of appeal to the Secretary of State within twenty-eight days of the refusal. Again it is the occupier of the premises who is liable if these requirements are not met.

There are various specified exemptions from the need to comply, for example if the furnace is mobile or if it can be operated without causing a nuisance or being in any way prejudicial to health.

It is also an offence to fail to supply information requested legitimately by the local authority in connection with the enforcement of the Act (s.8).

Penalty

Before a magistrates' court, a maximum fine of level 5.

Height of chimneys (excluding furnaces)

The height of chimneys is regulated under s.10 of the 1968 Act, although actual control is maintained through the Building Regulations 1991. Chimneys serving dwellings, shops and offices are excluded, as are chimneys which serve furnaces. All other erections or extensions which require Building Regulation consent must show chimneys of a height which satisfactorily prevents the emission of smoke, dust, grit and gases into the atmosphere without being prejudicial to health or a nuisance. The local authority has no discretion in this nor can it specify the height of chimney required. It has a mandatory duty only to approve plans which satisfy the section. The local authority can have regard to the purpose of the chimney, its position and other 'relevant' matters, although the latter are not specified.

An appeal lies to the Secretary of State for the Environment against the rejection of plans.

Height of furnace chimneys

Section 6 of the 1968 Act applies to furnace chimneys. The local authority must approve the height of the chimney, having regard to the smoke, dust, grit, gases and fumes to be emitted, before it can be used. In granting approval the local authority must consider the purpose of the chimney, its position and any other relevant matters. The local authority is also empowered to grant approval subject to conditions as to the emissions from the chimney.

Appeal lies to the Secretary of State if approval is refused, or is granted subject to conditions.

Penalty

Use of a chimney in breach of the section is punishable before the magistrates' court with a maximum fine of level 5.

Smoke nuisance

See 'Statutory nuisances' (page 122) but also note that the Highways Act 1980 prescribes some offences with regard to smoke nuisance which are referred to later in this section.

Smoke Control Orders

Local authorities are empowered to declare part of their area as subject to a Smoke Control Order (s.11 1956 Act). The order can be flexible in that it may relate only to certain specified types of premises or exclude part of the smoke control area from some of the provisions.

The emission of smoke in a smoke control area is an offence, unless it is proved that only 'authorised fuel' was being used. 'Authorised fuel' is specified in regulations made by the Secretary of State, who also has the power to compel a local authority to make smoke control orders if he feels that insufficient progress has been made (s.8 1968 Act).

Fines for breach of an order are at level 3 before a magistrates' court.

Grants

Grants are available, and these are dealt with in Chapter 9.

Sale of smoke-producing fuel

In areas where a Smoke Control Order is in force it is an offence either to acquire fuel which is not 'authorised' for use in a fireplace or boiler or to retail such fuel. The penalty is at level 3 before the magistrates' court.

Health and Safety at Work etc. Act 1974

Noxious substances

Section 5 imposes a duty to use the best practicable means for preventing the emission into the atmosphere of noxious or offensive substances. The duty is imposed on the person having control of premises prescribed in regulations made under s.1 of the Act. The same person is also responsible for rendering those substances harmless. Regulations prescribe such items as ammonia, asbestos, lead and sulphur compounds as 'noxious' under the Act.

Control of Pollution Act 1974

Publicity

Provision is made in s.79 for research into atmospheric pollution and local authorities may provide publicity for the public. Local authorities may also require information (s.80) from occupiers of non-domestic properties with regard to any emissions of potential pollutants into the atmosphere.

Motor vehicle fuel   Section 75 provides that regulations may be made to reduce pollution from motor vehicle emissions by imposing requirements as to the composition of fuel.

Motor vehicles generally   There are many regulations made under a variety of statutes which regulate the construction and use of vehicles and vehicle parts. This is to limit all types of atmospheric pollution, as well as to limit noise. The regulations comply with EC standards and specify rigorous tests of vehicles and their parts, including random road-side tests. The major regulations are set out at the end of this section.

Highways Act 1980

Fires on highways   The discharge of firearms or fireworks or the lighting of bonfires on a highway or within 50 feet of the centre of a highway is an offence under s.161 if a highway user is endangered, injured or interrupted as a result. The penalty is at level 3 on the scale.

Fires near highways   Lighting a fire away from a highway may also be an offence (s.161A) if a highway user is endangered, injured or interrupted as a result. The penalty for this is at level 5.

Defence   There is a defence if it can be proved that the person in control of the fire took all reasonable steps to avoid causing danger or that there was a reasonable excuse for lighting the fire in the circumstances.

Regulations and orders

These are many and detailed. Those covering the most important areas are referred to below and are grouped according to their subject matter.

Smoke, dust and grit   There are a number of Smoke Control Areas (Exempted) Fireplaces Orders dating from 1970 to 1990. These exempt the prescribed fireplaces from compliance with s.11 of the 1956 Act (which relates to smoke control orders), but only on condition that the fireplace is maintained in accordance with the manufacturer's instructions and is operated in such a way as to minimise the emission of smoke.

Smoke Control Areas (Authorised Fuels) Regulations 1991 (SI 1991 No. 1282)   These regulations authorise a long list of specified fuels for use in accordance with the 1956 Act.

The Clean Air (Emission of Dark Smoke) (Exemption) Regulations 1969 (SI 1969 No. 1263)   The effect of these regulations is to exempt certain industrial or trade premises from the requirements of s.1 of the 1968 Act which makes it an offence to emit dark smoke from such premises. The exemptions only apply if certain attached conditions are also complied with, for example the burning of tar from a road surface to enable the road to be resurfaced is exempt as long as there is proper supervision of the operation at all times.

Dark Smoke (Permitted Periods) Regulations 1958 (SI 1958 No. 498), and Dark Smoke (Permitted Periods) (Vessels) Regulations 1958 (SI 1958 No. 878)   Both of these state the periods during which dark smoke can be emitted without contravening the legislation; for example, subject to certain other specified conditions, for an aggregate period of ten minutes in any period of eight hours with no continuous emission for longer than four minutes.

The Clean Air (Emission of Grit and Dust from Furnaces) Regulations 1971 (SI 1971 No. 162)   These regulations prescribe the quantities of grit and dust which may be emitted in a given volume of air. The calculations are complex.

The Clean Air (Measurement of Grit and Dust for Furnaces) Regulations 1971 (SI 1971 No. 161)   These regulations prescribe the detailed method of measurement to be used in relation to the above.

The Clean Air (Height of Chimneys) (Exemptions) Regulations 1969 (SI 1969 No. 411)   These mainly relate to the use of temporary chimneys during the period that the permanent chimney is undergoing repair or maintenance.

The Clean Air (Arrestment Plant) (Exemption) Regulations 1969 (SI 1969 No. 1262)   These regulations prescribe various furnaces in particular specified situations which are exempt from compliance, or total compliance, with s.6 of the 1956 Act.

Motor vehicles

Motor Fuel (Sulphur Content of Gas Oil) Regulations 1976 (SI 1976 No. 1989), and Motor Fuel (Lead Content of Petrol) Regulations 1981 (SI 1981 No. 1523), and Oil Fuel (Sulphur Content of Gas Oil) Regulations 1990 (SI 1990 No. 1096)   All these regulations prescribe the quantities of potential noxious substances which are permitted.

Aircraft

The Air Navigation (Aircraft and Aircraft Engine Emissions) Order 1986 (SI 1986 No. 599), and The Air Navigation (Aeroplane and Aeroplane Engine Emission of Unburned Hydrocarbons) Order 1988 (SI 1988 No. 1994)   These both regulate smoke emissions and fuel venting. They also give power to an authorised person to prevent an aircraft from flying in contravention of these regulations.

General

Control of Atmospheric Pollution (Exempted Premises) Regulations 1977 (SI 1977 No. 18)   Many Crown premises (usually research or defence premises) are exempt from the requirements of the legislation under these regulations.

The Health and Safety (Emissions into the Atmosphere) Regulations 1983 (SI 1983 No. 943)   (Amended by similarly named regulations in 1989.) These prescribe the noxious substances and the types of premises to which s.5 of the Health and Safety at Work etc. Act 1974 applies.

Air Quality Standards Regulations 1989 (SI 1989 No. 317) The Secretary of State for the Environment is given the power here to take any appropriate measures to ensure that the standard of air quality specified in EC regulations can be met.

Circulars

Circular 2/69: The Clean Air Act 1956 This concerns the Clean Air 1956 and, in particular, its application to cold blast cupolas at iron foundries.

Circular 80/69: Asbestos This circular deals with the disposal of asbestos waste and the dangers of its presence in the atmosphere.

Circular 2/77: Control of Pollution Act 1974 This explains the regulations relating to publicity and research under the Control of Pollution Act 1974 and also deals with exempted premises and appeals under the Clean Air Acts.

Circular 24/84: Model Byelaws for Straw and Stubble Burning This is Home Office guidance with regard to model byelaws which a local authority could introduce into its area on stubble and straw burning.

Note See also pp. 117–18 and 122 with regard to additional regulations relating to crops and stubble burning.

NOISE POLLUTION

Our modern environment has greatly increased the noise to which we are subjected, not only in volume but also in type. Statutory regulation tends to be aimed at loud or intense noises, although an incessant low-pitched or even almost inaudible buzz can have equally adverse effects on the listener. The use of instruments to measure the levels of noise are helpful, but one obvious difficulty with this type of pollution is that one man's music is another man's noise. The legislation attempts to deal with this by introducing, wherever possible, an element of subjectivity into the controls, but it remains a fact that measuring devices are at their most efficient when monitoring intense rather than incessant noises. It may be for this reason that the old common law offence of noise nuisance is still used by individuals in bringing actions against their noisy neighbours. However, it is potentially more effective to use the legislation as this imposes sanctions (in the guise of penalties) as well as issuing guidelines by way of controls.

The main statutory provisions are embodied in the Control of Pollution Act 1974 Part III (CPA), which replaced the Noise Abatement Act 1960 and brought up to date the earlier controls available under the Public Health Act 1936. The CPA introduces a basically preventive code which divides noise into five distinct categories: general noise nuisance, construction site noise, street noise, noise abatement zones, and noise from plant and machinery. These will be dealt with in a similar order below and will be followed by a note of the other legislation which imposes noise controls. It will be noted that the CPA is administered by local authorities which have quite onerous responsibilities with regard to inspection, control and enforcement. Rights of appeal are mainly confined to the magistrates' court, where sanctions in the form of financial penalties can be imposed.

Noise nuisance generally

Local authorities are under a duty to inspect and check for noise nuisance in their area and also to decide where in their area noise abatement zones should be designated (s.57).

Penalties

Financial penalties under the Act are in accordance with level 5 of the scale.

Duty of local authority

Once satisfied that a noise nuisance exists, local authorities must serve notice on its perpetrators but only *when the noise emanates from premises* (s.58). (There are different controls when the noise emanates from, for example, the street – see page 100.) The notice may require abatement of the nuisance and either prohibit its recurrence or impose restrictions on further noise. A notice can also be served to prevent the creation of a possible noise nuisance if the local authority is satisfied that such a nuisance is likely. The notice can also require the carrying out of works to prevent the recurrence of the noise nuisance.

It is possible to appeal against a notice served in this

STOP PRESS

Ss.58 and 59 of the CPA have now been replaced by ss.80 and 82 of the Environmental Protection Act 1990 – see also Statutory Nuisances pp. 122–126.   .   .   .

way to the magistrates' court within twenty-one days of receipt. Then the court decides whether or not to uphold, quash or vary the notice.

Contravention of a valid notice without a reasonable excuse is an offence, and the local authority may bring criminal proceedings.

It is a defence to show that the noise is already subject to a notice served under s.60 or s.66 or a consent granted under s.61 or s.65 (see pages 100 and 101). Furthermore, a person who creates the noise in the course of a trade or business has a defence if he can prove that 'the best practicable means' were used to prevent or counteract the noise (see page 102 for definition of best practicable means).

An individual is empowered to bring proceedings himself (s.59) before the magistrates' court if he believes that a noise which affects him *as an occupier of premises* is a nuisance. If he is successful the magistrates will make an order requiring the abatement of the nuisance or imposing restrictions on it. Contravention of the order (as above) is a criminal offence, although the 'best practicable means' defence still applies.

Noise on construction sites

When certain works of construction are to be carried out, the local authority may serve a notice imposing requirements as to the way in which the works are to be done (s.60). The notice may specify:

1. Type of machinery or plant to be used.
2. Hours of working.
3. Level of noise allowable.
4. Other circumstances.

'Works of construction' include demolition, engineering works, maintenance or repair of roads or structures, construction or alteration of buildings (s.60(1)). The notice is served on the person carrying out the works or responsible for them. The recipient has a right of appeal to the magistrates' court within twenty-one days. Contravention of a notice is an offence.

A person who intends to carry out works as detailed above has the right to apply to the local authority for a consent (s.61). An application must give details of the works and method by which they are being carried out and also the steps to be taken to minimise noise levels. The local authority must deal with the application within twenty-eight days of receipt, and may grant or refuse consent or impose conditions. The applicant can appeal to the magistrates' court if consent is refused or the conditions are too onerous.

Noise in streets

Section 62(1) prohibits the operation in a street of a loudspeaker between the hours of 9 p.m. and 8 a.m. and at any other time also if the loudspeaker is to be used to advertise an entertainment, trade or business. Contravention of this section is an offence.

There are exceptions for emergency services, motor horns, telephones, travelling showmen and, between 12 noon and 7 p.m. the advertisement of perishable commodities for sale if the loudspeaker is attached to the vehicle and no annoyance is caused. Election propaganda is also excluded from the provisions.

Noise abatement zones (ss.63–67) (NAZs)

Noise abatement zones may be designated by a local authority which at the same time will specify the premises affected (s.63). The occupiers have six weeks in which to object before the order takes effect. The local authority must consider any objections before confirming the order.

Once an NAZ is designated, the local authority must keep a register of the noise levels recorded and serve a copy on the premises. The occupier can appeal against the recorded level to the Secretary of State within twenty-eight days (s.64). A recorded level must not be exceeded without the local authority's consent, and to do so is an offence. Any consent may be subject to conditions. There is a right of appeal to the Secretary of State for the Environment against refusal of consent (s.65).

If the local authority prosecutes for an offence under s.65, the magistrates may make an order requiring the defendant to carry out works to prevent the noise. Contravention of any order is an offence. The court can require the local authority to do the work if the defendant fails to do so.

The local authority may also require the reduction in a noise level if it believes that it is practicable and can be achieved at reasonable cost (s.66). A noise reduction notice must give at least six months within which the noise level is to be reduced to that specified. It may also state steps to be taken to achieve the reduction and specify days or times when the level should be reduced. A person who receives a notice may appeal to the magistrates' court within three months of receipt.

Note   A noise reduction notice can be served even if consent to exceed a recorded noise level has been granted under s.65 above.

When a new building is being constructed or altered and the local authority believes that a noise abatement order will apply to it, it may, on its own initiative or if the intended occupier requests, determine the noise level which will be acceptable. That level will then be recorded in the register. The occupier may appeal against the decision within three months to the Secretary of State or within two months if the local authority has not reached a decision on the occupier's request.

Noise from plant or machinery

Regulations may be introduced to reduce levels of noise of plant and machinery both inside and outside factories and construction sites. When making regulations the Secretary of State must consult makers and users of the machinery to ensure that the regulations are practicable and can be complied with at reasonable expense.

Additional powers of local authorities

Any notice which requires a person to execute work can specify that the local authority will do the work if the person fails. The local authority may recover its costs from the person against whom the notice was made (s.69).

Supplemental matters

1. Appeals to the magistrates' court are governed by the magistrates' court procedure; those to

the Secretary of State for the Environment are governed by regulations made by the Secretary of State (see Appeal regulations below).

2. Codes of practice may be issued as guidance to minimise noise levels. The following have been issued:

> Code of Practice on Noise from Audible Intruder Alarms (SI 1981 No. 1829)
> Code of Practice on Noise from Model Aircraft (SI 1981 No. 1830)
> Code of Practice on Ice-cream Van Chimes etc. (SI 1981 No. 1828)
> Code of Practice for Construction and Open Sites (SI 1984 No. 1992)

3. 'Best practicable means' is defined in s.72 as being reasonably practicable having regard to local conditions, circumstances, current technical knowledge and cost. Safe working practices are also considered.

Measurement of noise levels and keeping of registers

The recommended method of measurement of noise levels is described in the Control of Noise (Measurements and Registers) Regulations 1976. These regulations also give guidance on the calculation of noise levels when precise measurement is not possible. Lastly, the regulations specify the content of the Noise Level Registers to be kept by the local authority which records the levels from classified premises.

Appeal regulations

The Control of Noise (Appeal) Regulations 1986 specify the grounds and method of appeal to magistrates or the Secretary of State.

Grounds for appeal under s.60:

- Service of notice not justified.
- Informality or defect in notice.
- Local authority unreasonably refused to accept compliance with alternative requirements or the requirements were unreasonable.
- Time given in notice insufficient.
- Notice served on wrong person.

- Notice should have been served on someone else as well, and it would be equitable to do so.
- Local authority had not given due regard to the provisions of s.60.

Grounds for appeal under s.61:

- Conditions not justified.
- The consent granted is defective.
- Conditions unreasonable or unnecessary.
- Time for compliance not sufficient.

Grounds for appeal under s.66:

- Service of notice not justified.
- Informality or defect in notice.
- Local authority unreasonably refused to accept compliance with alternative requirements or the requirements were unreasonable.
- Time given in notice insufficient.
- If the noise is being created in the course of a business, then the 'best practicable means' are already being used.
- Notice served on wrong person.
- Notice should have been served on someone else as well, and it would be equitable to do so.

Note   The magistrates' court has the power to vary, quash or uphold notices and impose fresh conditions.

On an appeal to the Secretary of State for the Environment under ss.64 and 65 the appellant must lodge his notice of appeal in writing, stating clearly the grounds of appeal. The appellant must send with his notice the following:

1. A copy of the application to the local authority.
2. Copies of any plans or details sent to the local authority.
3. Copies of any documents or other items issued by the local authority.
4. Copies of any relevant correspondence with the local authority.
5. A plan of the site.

The Secretary of State may require a further statement to be submitted by the local authority or appellant. If he believes that he is fully informed he may determine the appeal. Otherwise he should hold a local inquiry to determine the issue. The Secretary of State may vary, allow or dismiss the appeal and may direct the local authority to give effect to his determination.

Other applicable legislation

Land Compensation Act 1973

Section 20 states that the Secretary of State may make regulations either imposing a duty or giving powers to local authorities to insulate buildings against noise caused by either the use or the construction of public works. (See the Noise Insulation Regulations 1975 made under this power which include the specifications, noise levels, etc.)

Civil Aviation Act 1982

Provides for the regulation of noise and vibration from aircraft. Operators of aircraft are obliged to comply with notices issued by the Secretary of State regarding limiting or mitigating the effects of noise during take-off and landing. Operators of designated aerodromes are also obliged to comply with notices to a similar effect (s.78). It is an offence to fail to comply with the duty imposed by the notices. There are requirements on some operators to make grants available to persons occupying nearby buildings for insulation purposes.

Motor Cycle Noise Act 1987

The Motor Cycle Noise Act empowers the Secretary of State to make regulations to prevent the supply and fitting of excessively noisy exhaust systems and their components to motor cycles which do not conform to the standard laid down in the regulations.

This Act only applies to a supply in the course of a trade or business and it is an offence (s.1) to make such a supply. The regulations are enforced by the Trading Standards Office.

Note The construction of motor vehicles generally, both domestic and heavy goods, is dealt with under the road traffic legislation. These construction rules are designed to keep noise from vehicles within acceptable limits.

Town and Country Planning Act 1990

Under the Town and Country Planning Act local authorities are able to impose conditions when granting planning consent which enable them to minimise noise levels on certain developments. For example, a condition on a light industrial estate, close to residential development may be used to restrict hours of operation of machinery. (See also Chapter 2.)

Local bye-laws

Many local authorities have local bye-laws or a local Act which imposes restrictions on noise, but these vary from one area to another, and the appropriate bye-laws should be consulted. A common example is a bye-law prohibiting the playing of radios or musical instruments in public parks.

Regulations and orders

Statutory instruments on the subject of noise are varied and, in the main, detailed. They usually list specific requirements to ensure that noise from machinery, vehicles and plant is kept to a minimum. They also usually state that it is an offence to fail to comply with the regulations. Prosecution is before the magistrates' court. The most significant statutory instruments, in brief, are as follows.

The Noise Insulation Regulations 1975 (SI 1975 No. 1763) These regulations impose a duty on the highway authority either to carry out insulation works itself or to make a grant to any person affected by excessive noise from highway works.

Construction Plant and Equipment (Harmonisation of Noise) Regulations 1985 (SI 1985 No. 1968) Components of construction plant are covered by these regulations and must conform to the standard laid down now by the EC. Specific components are listed.

Noise at Work Regulations 1989 (SI 1989 No. 1790 These regulations provide a formula for calculating the level of noise to which employees are exposed. They make it the employer's duty to reduce exposure to a minimum, provide ear protection and maintain plant so that noise is at its minimum.

Road Vehicles (Construction and Use) Regulations 1986 (SI 1986 No. 1078) These regulations deal with vehicles which are adapted to take unleaded petrol. They specify the noise levels which will be accepted in this context.

Lawn Mowers (Harmonisation of Noise) Regulations 1986 (SI 1986 No. 1795) Lawn mowers must also now conform to a standard specified by the EC and set out in these regulations.

Air Navigation (Noise Certification) Order 1990 (SI 1990 No. 1514) Any aircraft which requires a distance of 670 metres or more to take off (which covers all but the lightest aircraft) and all microlights and helicopters must be issued with a noise certificate under this order before landing or taking off from a UK airport. There are some exceptions specified in the order.

The Building Regulations 1991 Sound insulation requirements are to be found in Part E to the regulations.

Relevant circulars

Circular 10/73: Planning and Noise This circular is aimed at the control of development to minimise noise levels.

Circular 2/76: Control of Pollution Act 1974. Implementation of Part III – Noise A circular to assist local authorities in bringing the legislation into operation.

Circular 2/82: Control of Pollution Act 1974. Codes of Practice on Noise from Audible Intruder Alarms; Model

Aircraft and Ice-cream Van Chimes etc.   This explains in more detail how to use the codes of practice.

WASTE DISPOSAL

Historically, waste disposal was treated as a matter of public health and dealt with as a part of the public health legislation. With advances in technology and the increase in industrial waste, the legislation had to be constantly reviewed and updated. In 1974 a comprehensive system of waste management was introduced by the Control of Pollution Act. That Act also required supplementing, and once again there has been a thorough review of the waste disposal legislation with the advent of the Environmental Protection Act 1990 (EPA). Despite this, some of the old statutes continue in existence and are noted after the references to the EPA below.

Waste disposal is dealt with in Part II of the EPA (in ss.29–78) and is divided into provisions relating to controlled waste, which includes 'special waste', and non-controlled waste. Litter is also covered by the EPA in ss.87–99.

The following section numbers all refer to the EPA unless otherwise specified and references to 'waste' should be read in context.

The authorities

Waste regulation authorities

For the purposes of Part II of the EPA waste regulation authorities are county councils, the London Waste Regulation Authority, the Greater Manchester Waste Disposal Authority, the Merseyside Waste Disposal Authority, district councils in Wales and district councils in metropolitan counties.

Waste disposal authorities

Waste disposal authorities are the same as above except in Greater London where the Common Council has responsibility in the City and the borough councils elsewhere.

Waste collection authorities

Responsibility here lies with the district councils outside London and the Common Council, the borough councils and Temple Treasurers within it.

It is clear from the above that, in some instances, the disposal and regulation functions overlap. The Act plainly states that an authority which has a dual function *must* keep its administrative arrangements separate. The importance of this is such that details of the arrangements are to be submitted to the Secretary of State for approval (s.30). The reason for this is that waste disposal operations carried out by a local authority at the time the Act became effective must be transferred to waste disposal contractors. These are either in the public sector or are 'arms length' local authority contractors. The idea is that local authorities should concentrate more on their regulatory function and, at the same time, increasing competition in the waste disposal operations. It is envisaged that in any one local authority area a number of contractors could be operating, some dealing with recycling and others with disposal (s.32).

What is waste?

Waste is defined in s.75 as being 'any substance which constitutes a scrap material or an effluent or other unwanted surplus substance arising from the application of any process and any substance or article which requires to be disposed of as being broken, worn out, contaminated or otherwise spoiled'.

Waste does *not* include explosives, but apart from that, the definition is worded to ensure that it encompasses the widest possible spectrum. Also excluded is waste from mines, quarries and agricultural premises which are dealt with under other legislation.

'Household waste' is described as waste from domestic premises, caravans, schools, hospitals and residential homes, and 'commercial waste' is that produced by premises used wholly or mainly for the purposes of a trade or business. This latter also includes waste from recreational or entertainment premises. 'Industrial waste' means waste from a factory, public transport premises, post and telecommunication premises and premises used in connection with the supply of gas, electricity, water or sewerage services.

'Special waste'

Special waste is defined as waste which is dangerous or difficult to treat or deal with (s.62). The Secretary of State may make regulations with regard to special waste separately from other controlled waste. The regulations can be very wide-ranging, covering everything from treatment to the keeping of appropriate records.

Note   Special waste is included within the definition of controlled waste.

Despite the fairly comprehensive definitions as listed above, the Act also anticipates that other kinds of waste may, at a later date, be brought within its regulations or, indeed, taken outside the ambit of the Act. The Secretary of State retains the right in s.75(8) to alter the designations. In effect this means that waste is whatever the Secretary of State wants it to mean at the time.

Waste management licences (ss.35 and 36)

A waste regulation authority (WRA) can grant licences authorising the treatment, keeping or disposal of controlled waste. A licence can be granted subject to such conditions as are appropriate to the activities to be undertaken. When granting licences WRAs must take account of any guidance which has been issued by the Secretary of State with regard to the particular activities.

In relation to the treatment, keeping or disposal of waste in or on land, an applicant for a licence must be the person in occupation of the land. A licence for treatment or disposal of waste by way of mobile plant must be issued to the plant operator. Once issued, a licence continues in effect. It cannot be surrendered or transferred without the consent of the WRA.

Before granting a licence the WRA must follow a detailed consultation procedure with other potentially interested bodies, such as the National Rivers Authority and the Nature Conservancy Council. It must also ensure that planning permission has been granted for the proposed function.

The variation, surrender, revocation and transfer of licences is covered in ss.37–40 respectively.

Licence fees

Licence fees are payable in accordance with the provisions of s.41 to the WRA and are at a level fixed by the Secretary of State. Fees are charged on the initial application and for the licence to continue in force. It is interesting to note that WRAs must also pay a fee to the National Rivers Authority in accordance with a scheme established by Secretary of State as remuneration for their consultative role.

Supervision

The WRA is under a duty (s.42) to supervise those to whom licences have been granted and to ensure that any conditions have been complied with. If the WRA needs to take any action as a result of its inspection, it may recoup any expenditure incurred from the licence-holder. The WRA may also require that the conditions be complied with and either suspend or revoke the licence if necessary.

Licence appeals

A licence-holder has a right of appeal to the Secretary of State if a licence is refused, revoked, suspended or granted subject to conditions. There is also a right of appeal if the WRA refuses an application for a variation, transfer or surrender of a licence. As with most appeals under similar Acts, the Secretary of State can appoint an inspector to hear the appeal either by way of a formal hearing in private or in public, or by way of written representations. If the applicant is successful on appeal then the WRA is obliged to accept the appeal decision and give effect to it (s.43).

Waste collection

Each waste collection authority (WCA) is under a duty to arrange for the collection of household waste in its area, unless the waste is situated in an inaccessible place. In the latter case, the WCA must still be satisfied that suitable arrangements are being made with regard to the waste. The WCA must also collect commercial waste if requested to do so and it may collect industrial waste. Alternatively, it may arrange for controlled waste to be collected by another body. Household waste is collected free of charge but other waste collection can be charged for at a rate which is deemed to be reasonable (s.45).

Domestic privies must also be emptied under this section at no charge.

Dustbins

The WCA may provide waste receptacles or it may require its inhabitants to use certain specified receptacles. It may also request that different types of household waste are placed in different receptacles for collection, separating, for example, recyclable and non-recyclable items (s.46).

Persons who do not comply with the WCA's requests in this regard can be prosecuted and fined on level 3 on the scale before a magistrates' court. There is a right of appeal to the magistrates' court for an occupier who does not wish to comply with the WCA's requirements.

There are similar provisions in s.47 with regard to receptacles for the collection of commercial and industrial waste where the WCA believe that the waste should be placed in a receptacle to avoid damaging the environment.

Waste disposal

All WCAs are under a duty (s.48) to deliver the waste collected to a place designated by a waste disposal authority (WDA). This duty does not extend to household or commercial waste which the WCA wishes to recycle (see page 112). The WDA may object if it has made its own arrangements for the recycling of the waste.

WRAs are obliged to investigate the disposal of controlled waste in a manner least harmful to the environment or to health. It must then prepare a plan of its proposals which it is under a duty to keep under review. When preparing the plan it must take into account both the costs involved in the proposals and the proposals' likely beneficial effects on the environment, as well as taking into consideration the views of various consultative bodies (s.50).

A further duty is imposed on WDAs by s.51 for both the disposal of controlled waste and the provision of places within their area where persons may deposit waste at all reasonable times. The WDA discharges its duty by arranging for disposal by waste disposal contractors and it has wide powers to enable it to give assistance to contractors, for example by supplying plant or equipment.

Recycling waste

WCAs are under a duty to investigate the possibilities of recycling household and commercial waste and to prepare a plan of its proposals (s.49). A draft of the plan must be sent to the Secretary of State for the Environment who may make further directions with regard to the content of the plan. Once the plan has been approved it must be publicised in the area in which it operates; note, however, that there is no requirement for public consultation at the plan preparation stage.

Recouping costs

When a WCA has successfully made arrangements for recycling of waste, the WDA must pay to the WCA an amount to represent the saving made by the WDA in not having to dispose of the waste. In the same way, the WCA must make payments to the WDA to represent the savings that it makes by not having to collect waste which has been deposited, for example at dumps provided by the WDA (s.52). It is envisaged that private recycling organisations will also be paid by the WDA for savings on the cost of disposal, and that WCAs may make payments to private groups which collect waste which it would otherwise have been under a duty to collect.

The aim of these provisions is to provide the WCAs and WDAs with an incentive to deal with waste efficiently.

Offences

Treatment and disposal

It is prohibited for a person to deposit controlled waste, or allow or cause it to be deposited in or on any land without a waste management licence being in force. Similarly, it is prohibited to treat or dispose of or cause controlled waste to be treated, etc. without a waste management licence being in force; or to treat, keep or dispose of controlled waste in such a way as to be harmful to the environment (s.33).

Exclusions

The above offences do not apply to household waste (in a domestic context) being dealt with on the premises with the consent of the occupier.

Also, the Secretary of State for the Environment can make regulations to exclude certain activities from the offences, for example to permit temporary deposits, treatment of harmless items and situations already covered by other legislation.

Defences

A person has a defence if he can prove either that the action was taken in an emergency and to avoid danger to the public and the WRA was told as soon as practicable; or if he took all reasonable precautions to avoid the offence; or if he acted under instructions and had no means of knowing that he was committing an offence.

Penalties

Before a magistrates' court a fine of £20,000 and/or imprisonment for six months; before a Crown Court unlimited fine and/or imprisonment for two years.

If the waste is 'special waste' then the term of imprisonment before the Crown Court is increased to five years.

Waste management licences

Section 33 also makes it an offence with the same penalties as above to breach a waste management licence.

Duty of care (s.34)

Any person who in any way deals with waste by either producing, keeping, treating, or otherwise controlling it is under a duty to take all reasonable measures to:

1. Avoid a breach of s.33.
2. Prevent the escape of the waste.
3. Ensure that waste is transferred only to an authorised person, and that written details of the waste are passed on at transfer to avoid an

innocent party inadvertently committing an offence.

Penalties

Before a magistrates' court, £2000; before a Crown Court, unlimited.

Code of practice

Under s.34 the Secretary of State for the Environment is obliged to prepare a code of practice to give practical guidance to those who are under a duty of care in accordance with the Act. The initial code must be the subject of appropriate consultation, but any amendments can be initiated by the Secretary of State without reference to others. The aim of the code is to avoid persons unwittingly falling foul of s.33.

False statements

If an applicant for a licence knowingly or recklessly makes a false statement he shall be guilty of an offence (s.44) with a fine in the magistrates' court of £2000, or in the Crown Court unlimited and/or imprisonment for two years.

Other powers

Unlawful deposits

In the event that waste is deposited in breach of s.33 (above) the WRA or WCA may by notice require the occupier of the land to remove it and take any other steps which may be specified. Twenty-one days must be given for compliance (s.59).

The recipient of a notice can appeal to the magistrates' court and the notice is suspended pending the hearing. Failure to comply may lead to a fine on level 5 plus a daily fine equal to one-tenth level 5 for each day the offence continues after conviction. Alternatively the WRA or WCA may do the necessary works and charge their costs to the occupier or person at fault.

Waste sites

It is an offence to 'sort over or disturb' a place where waste is deposited or a receptacle for the collection of waste without authority so to do (s.60). The penalty is a fine on level 3.

Closed landfills (s.61)

The WRA is under a duty to inspect closed landfill sites to ensure that the land remains in a suitable condition to avoid pollution or cause harm to health. If the WRA needs to take any steps to ensure the well-being of the land, it may recover its reasonable costs from the landowner.

Waste which is not controlled

Waste not covered by the Act can also be brought into the ambit of the Environmental Protection Act (EPA) by s.63. This states that the deposit of uncontrolled waste will be treated like the deposit of special waste unless a licence or other authorisation is in force. This will catch any deposits of waste otherwise excluded (e.g. waste from quarries which has its own legislation) unless consent is in existence under the alternative legislation.

Inspectors

The Secretary of State for the Environment and the WRA may appoint inspectors who have powers of entry onto land as well as powers to examine premises, take samples, and so on.

Serious danger

If an inspector has reasonable cause to believe that he has found something which is likely to cause imminent danger of serious pollution, he may render the item harmless.

It is an offence to obstruct an inspector in the exercise of his powers (s.70).

LITTER: PART IV ENVIRONMENTAL PROTECTION ACT 1990

Litter authorities comprise county, district and London borough councils, as well as the Common Council of the City. The Secretary of State for the Environment may also designate other litter authorities (s.86).

Offences

It is an offence to drop litter in a public place or on other designated land (such as Crown land) without consent. The penalty is on level 4 (s.87).

Furthermore, in s.88, a litter officer, that is someone authorised to act on behalf of the litter authority, may issue an offender with a 'fixed penalty ticket' in respect of the offence. This is an alternative to prosecution, but the officer does not have any powers of arrest or means of checking the true identity of the offender.

Litter control areas

Under s.90 the Secretary of State may designate areas as 'litter control areas'. Litter authorities except county councils may also designate such areas but only if they believe that the presence of litter in the area is detrimental to the amenities of that area.

Litter abatement orders and notices

A person aggrieved, which does not include a litter authority, may bring proceedings before a magistrates' court if he believes that a highway, a litter control area, land of the litter authority or other designated land is being defaced by litter and refuse. Five days' notice of the intention to start proceedings must be given to the potential defendant.

The proceedings are to be brought against the person or body which has responsibility for keeping the land in question clear of litter. This section gives individuals an opportunity of enforcing the legislation against public litter authorities and other responsible bodies, such as educational establishments.

At the hearing the magistrates may make a litter abatement order giving the defendant a period of time in which to clear the land. Non-compliance renders the defendant liable to a fine on level 4 with an additional daily fine of one-twentieth the level 4 scale. There is a defence available if it can be shown that all practicable steps were taken to keep the area clear from litter.

The litter authorities themselves may also serve litter abatement notices (s.92) on the bodies responsible for Crown land, educational establishments, land belonging to statutory undertakers and the like. The notices may require both that the land be cleared and also prohibiting a recurrence of the accumulation of litter or defacement. A body served with a notice may appeal to the magistrates' court within twenty-one days. If no appeal is lodged and the notice is not complied with, the litter authority may bring proceedings in the magistrates' court which, if successful, may lead to a fine on level 4, with a daily penalty of one-twentieth the level 4 scale. Again there is a defence available if it can be shown that all reasonable and practicable steps were taken to prevent the litter and defacement.

Street litter control notices

Litter authorities (except county councils) may issue 'street litter control notices'. These can be served on the owner or occupier of commercial or retail premises which have a frontage onto a highway. The notice may require the person served to keep the frontage clear of litter and also to provide such items as suitable litter bins to be placed on the frontage (s.93). The notice does not become effective for at least twenty-one days, during which time there is a right of appeal to the magistrates' court. Failure to comply with the notice means that the litter authority can begin proceedings before the magistrates for a street litter control order (s.94). Breach of the order may lead to a fine before the magistrates' court on level 4.

MISCELLANEOUS

Abandoned shopping trolleys

Under s.99 local authorities can pass a resolution bringing Schedule 4 of the Environmental Protection Act into effect in their area. This Schedule permits local authorities to seize, remove and retain abandoned shopping trolleys. They are to be returned to their owner on the payment of an appropriate fee.

Contaminated land register

Local authorities are obliged to keep a register of any land in their area which may be contaminated with noxious substances, either man-made or occurring naturally after the deposit of items on the land (s.143). Any registers which are kept must be open to public inspection.

Stubble and straw burning

Regulations can be made by the Secretary of State to

prohibit the burning of crop residues by persons engaged in agriculture (s.152). This does not encompass garden bonfires and such like as these are not agriculture. The penalty for non-compliance with the regulations is before the magistrates' court only and on level 5 on the scale.

OTHER APPLICABLE LEGISLATION

Public Health Act 1936

Noxious matter

A district council retains the power to serve a notice on the occupier of premises in an urban area, requiring the removal (within 24 hours) of noxious matter from the premises. If the notice is not complied with, the local authority may carry out the work and charge the occupier the costs of so doing (s.79).

Manure

A district council may request the removal of manure from stables or mews on giving written notice. Failure to comply with the notice is punishable by fine at level 1 on the scale.

Public Health Act 1961

Accumulations of rubbish

When the local authority is of the opinion that an accumulation of rubbish on land in the open air is seriously detrimental to the neighbourhood, it may serve notice on the owner and occupier of the land giving twenty-eight days' notice of the local authority's intention to take steps itself to remove the accumulation (s.34). The owner or occupier can serve a counter-notice agreeing to take the necessary steps himself or he can appeal against the notice within the twenty-eight days to the magistrates' court.

Business or trade waste is not covered by this section.

Refuse Disposal (Amenity) Act 1978

Council dumps

Section 1 imposes a duty on the county council to provide places where non-trade refuse can be dumped free of charge. It may also provide places for trade refuse. The dump must be accessible to the occupants of the area and it must be open at reasonable times.

Abandoned vehicles and other items

A person who abandons a motor vehicle or parts of a motor vehicle or any other item in the open air or on a highway is guilty of an offence. The offence carries a penalty at level 4 on the scale or imprisonment for a maximum of three months or both (s.2).

Abandoned vehicles must be removed by the local authority, which may dispose of them as it thinks fit, within certain guidelines. The local authority must take some steps to trace the owner and cannot dispose of a vehicle while the road fund licence remains current. If the owner collects the vehicle, he can be charged for removal and storage costs, otherwise these costs can be recouped from the person who abandoned the vehicle (ss.3–5).

Other abandoned items can also be removed and disposed of at the local authority's discretion, and again the costs of removal and storage can be collected from the person who abandoned them (s.6).

Highways Act 1980

Litter bins

Highway authorities or other local authorities with the highway authorities' consent may provide and maintain, in or under a street, bins or other receptacles for the collection of street litter (s.185).

Litter Act 1983

Publicity

The Secretary of State is empowered under s.1 to make grants to local authorities for publicity to encourage persons not to drop litter, but to make use of the bins and dumps provided.

Litter bins

County, district and parish councils, as well as just about every other public body, are 'litter authorities' for the purposes of the Act. Any of these authorised bodies may provide and maintain bins in public places and ensure that they are emptied and cleansed regularly (s.5).

It is also an offence, attracting a fine at level 1 on the scale, for a person to 'interfere' with a litter bin.

Airports Act 1986

Abandoned vehicles

The Airports Act 1986 gives airport operators similar powers with regard to the removal and disposal of abandoned vehicles as those given to local authorities under the Refuse Disposal (Amenity) Act 1978.

Control of Pollution (Amendment) Act 1989

Carriage of controlled waste

Section 1 prescribes that only registered carriers can transport controlled waste at a profit, and it is an offence to do so in contravention of the Act.

The carrier may have a defence if he can show that he had no grounds for suspecting that he was carrying controlled waste or if he can prove that he was acting under instructions from his employer. It is also a defence if the carrier can prove that it was an emergency and that he notified the local authority as soon as practicable.

Registration

Carriers must register with the appropriate disposal authority, and the latter has very few grounds on which to refuse to register. One obvious one is where the applicant has previously been convicted of an offence concerning waste disposal. An unsuccessful applicant can appeal to SSE against refusal (ss. 2 and 3).

Local authority powers

Officers of disposal authorities have quite wide-ranging powers with regard to controlled waste. Both the officers and police officers can search vehicles and request sight of the authorisation to carry waste if they suspect that a vehicle is in breach of the Act (s.5). They may also apply to the magistrates' court for a warrant to seize a vehicle suspected of illegally transporting waste if they have reasonable grounds for suspicion and they cannot trace the owner to ascertain the position.

Disposal authority officers cannot stop a vehicle on a road unless they are also accompanied by a police constable (s.6).

The Act makes it an offence for a person to fail to supply information in this connection or to supply false information (s.7).

Relevant regulations and orders

Abandoned vehicles

The Removal and Disposal of Vehicles Regulations 1986 (SI 1986 No. 183)   These regulations were made under the Refuse Disposal Amenity Act 1978 and specify the powers available with regard to the removal and disposal of abandoned vehicles. So far as vehicles abandoned at airports are concerned, these are covered by the Airports (Designation) (Removal and Disposal of Vehicles) Order 1990 (SI 1990 No. 54).

Collection, disposal and carriage of controlled waste

The Controlled Waste (Registration of Carriers and Seizure of Vehicles) Regulations 1991 (SI 1991 No. 1624)   These regulations specify the methods to be adopted on registration and detail the provisions for vehicle seizure.

Litter

The Litter (Fixed Penalty Notices) Regulations 1991 (SI 1991 No. 111), and The Street Litter Control Notices Order 1991 (SI 1991 No. 1324)   This order indicates the premises to which the notices should apply. In particular it states that take-away food premises, service stations, places of entertainment and premises with automated telling machines in the wall would be appropriate for the notices.

The Litter Control Areas Order 1991 (SI 1991 No.

1325) This outlines the type of areas suitable for treatment by the imposition of an order. Amongst others, it suggests car parks, office and business parks, shopping developments, esplanades and inland beaches or seashores.

Crops

The Crop Residues (Restrictions on Burning) (No. 2) Regulations 1991 (SI 1991 No. 1590) These regulations specify the types of crop residue which are to be affected. These are cereal stubble, cereal straw, oil seed rape, linseed, and field beans and peas harvested dry. It also specifies a number of safety matters, for example that there should be no stubble burning within 100 metres of a major road or railway and also that no burning should take place between one hour before sunset and sunrise on a Saturday, Sunday or Bank Holiday.

Circulars and other publications

The Environmental Protection Act 1990: Code of Practice on Litter and Refuse This code advises local authorities on the most suitable means of implementing the litter regulations and the use of litter control areas and street litter control notices.

Circular 11/1991: The Controlled Waste (Registration of Carriers and Seizure of Vehicles) Regulations 1991 Here the local authorities are advised on the granting and refusal of licences, the matters which should be considered when an application is received, and generally on the powers available with regard to controlled waste carriers.

STATUTORY NUISANCES

The Public Health Act 1936 produced the concept of the 'statutory nuisance'. A statutory nuisance was something which was described in a list in that Act as being potentially either 'prejudicial to health or a nuisance' and subsequent Acts added to that list. At the time the 1936 Act was passed, it was principally concerned with matters of health. For this reason the items listed within it and classified as possible statutory nuisances were very clearly matters which could threaten the well-being of the public or an individual rather than simply become an annoyance. It did not, therefore, cover all forms of nuisance, many of which are still dealt with through the common law and not by legislation. In that sense, the phrase 'statutory nuisance' can be misleading and it must be remembered that it only relates to those matters specified within the relevant Act.

Statutory nuisances are now dealt with under the Environmental Protection Act 1990, in Part III (ss.79–85). The EPA has closely followed the old legislation and has re-enacted much of the former Act with some modifications. In particular the list of potential statutory nuisances has been extended, the penalties have been increased and the local authorities enforcing the legislation (in this instance, the district councils) have wider powers. Having said that, it is assumed that for interpretation of the new legislation the courts will lean heavily on the voluminous case law which has been decided over past years.

The most important aspect of the case law, under the 1936 Act, related to the meaning of the words 'prejudicial to health or a nuisance'. It was decided that 'prejudicial to health' meant injurious or likely to cause injury to health: something which was fairly easy to establish factually. The use of the word 'nuisance', however, was more troublesome. It has become settled law that for there to be a 'nuisance' within the meaning of the Act, the action complained of had to constitute either a private nuisance or a public nuisance. A private nuisance is something which causes one person's enjoyment of his property to be affected by the actions of another occupier on adjoining or neighbouring property. A public nuisance is, as it sounds, something which extends to members of the public in general and is so widespread in its effect that any action to stop it should become the responsibility of the community as a whole. It will be seen from this that a nuisance on property which only affects persons *on the same property* is not encompassed as it is not wide enough to be a public nuisance, nor does it affect the enjoyment of neighbouring property and thus fall within the sphere of a private nuisance.

The administrative mechanism with regard to statutory nuisances is to be found in Schedule 3 of the Environmental Protection Act 1990. The Schedule deals with such matters as powers of entry onto land to enable the local authority to ascertain whether or not a statutory nuisance exists. (The following references to section numbers relate to the Environmental Protection Act 1990 unless otherwise stated.)

Statutory nuisances

It is the duty of each local authority to inspect its area for the presence of statutory nuisances, and it must take whatever steps are reasonably practicable to investigate any complaints made by members of the public.

Statutory nuisances are defined in s.79 as being:

(a) any premises in such a state as to be prejudicial to health or a nuisance;

(b) smoke emitted from premises so as to be prejudicial to health or a nuisance;

(c) fumes or gases emitted from premises so as to be prejudicial to health or a nuisance;

(d) any dust, steam, smell or other effluvia arising on industrial, trade or business premises and being prejudicial to health or a nuisance;

(e) any accumulation or deposit which is prejudicial to health or a nuisance;

(f) any animal kept in such a place or manner as to be prejudicial to health or a nuisance;

(g) noise emitted from premises so as to be prejudicial to health or a nuisance;

(h) any other matter declared by any enactment to be a statutory nuisance.

The types of things covered by the definition have been decided by the courts to include the keeping of snakes in unsuitable premises and an accumulation of rubbish which attracts vermin.

Exceptions to the Act

The main exceptions relate to matters which are already adequately covered by other legislation, such as aircraft noise, fumes from industrial premises, and smoke or noise emitted from Crown land (see s.79).

Abatement notices

Once the local authority is satisfied that a statutory nuisance exists or is likely to occur or recur it must serve an abatement notice. The notice will require the abatement of the statutory nuisance or prohibit its occurrence or recurrence. It may also request specified works to be done within a time limit to ensure compliance. The notice must be served on the perpetrator of the nuisance unless it relates to structurally defective premises in which case it is served on the owner. In circumstances where the person responsible cannot be traced or the nuisance has not yet taken place, the notice must be served on the owner or occupier of the premises.

Appeals

A recipient of an abatement notice may appeal against it to the magistrates' court within twenty-one days of receipt. Appeals are covered by the *Statutory Nuisance (Appeal) Regulations 1990 (SI 1991 No. 2276)* which provide that the magistrates may uphold the notice, vary it in the appellant's favour or quash it.

Grounds of appeal are that:

1. The notice is defective.
2. The notice's requirements are unreasonable.
3. The notice's requirements could be replaced by less onerous requirements.
4. The notice was wrongly served or should have been served on some other person also.

During an appeal the provisions of an abatement notice would normally be suspended until the outcome of the hearing. The local authority may prevent this by specifying in the notice that it continues in effect, but this is allowable only if the statutory nuisance is either injurious to health, of limited duration (so delay would render the notice ineffective) or requiring only minor expense to be incurred for compliance.

Penalties

Failure to comply with an abatement notice is an offence (s.80). Maximum penalties are fines of £2000 with a daily penalty of £200 for individuals and £20,000 when the statutory nuisance arises on industrial, trade or business premises. These fines are at level 5 on the scale.

Defences

As well as grounds of appeal, the EPA also specifies one main defence, that 'the best practicable means were used to prevent or counteract the effects of the nuisance' s.80(7). This is limited to business, industrial or trade premises, and guidelines for the interpretation of the phrase are laid down in s.79(9). 'Practicable' means reasonable, so bearing in mind relevant local conditions, financial implications and technical knowledge. The test cannot oust safety factors and other legal requirements but operation of plant and design of buildings can be considered.

Codes of practice under CPA 1974 concerning noise (see page 102) and defences available under that legislation are also relevant s.80(9).

Expenses incurred in abating or preventing the recurrence of a statutory nuisance are recoverable from the perpetrator by the local authority s.81(4).

Local authority's additional powers

Direct action in the High Court for an injunction is permitted where the local authority believes that the usual method of notices, etc. will not be an adequate remedy (s.81(5)). The local authority is granted powers of entry without a warrant for testing, inspecting, sampling and seizure if necessary (see Schedule 3).

Powers of an individual

A 'person aggrieved' is entitled to commence proceedings in their own name in the magistrates' court (s.82), by requesting that the court make an abatement notice. The procedure before the court is similar to on appeal (see page 125).

Before commencing an action, the person must notify the potential defendant of the intention to bring proceedings, giving three days' notice in the case of a noise nuisance and twenty-one days' notice in every other case (s.82(6)).

Penalties for non-compliance are the same, except the higher level of fine for trade, business or industrial premises does not apply. Local authorities can be ordered to abate the nuisance (or prevent its recurrence) if the defendant fails to do this, and they can recoup the costs of so doing.

CONCLUSION

This chapter has highlighted the major areas of legislation which control pollution. It is a subject which provides, however, a rapidly developing source of statute law which will continue to grow as man continues to develop new technical methods and demands a cleaner environment in which to live. The chapter does not cover all types of pollution and there are further controls on a wide range of matters from fouling of footpaths by dogs to specialised industrial pollution and the control of genetically modified organisms.

It should be borne in mind especially that local authorities may well have their own local legislation in the form of a local statute or bye-laws. These can be used to control such diverse topics as stray dogs, use of radios in parks, lighting of bonfires on Sundays, and the disposal of domestic refuse.

CHAPTER 5 WATER AND WATER SERVICES

INTRODUCTION

This book is concerned only with the supply and management of our water services: it does not consider the law relating to the sea or marine pollution, which are topics better dealt with elsewhere.

The internal waters of England and Wales are usually defined as those waters which fall on the landward side of the low-water line around our coast. The areas of local authorities which have a coastal boundary extend up to the low-water line. In addition, the authorities have limited responsibility outside that boundary to the seaward side to enable them to exercise a certain degree of control over the sea for coastal protection and health and safety purposes. The legislation affecting the seashore is largely outside the scope of this book, but reference will be made to it when appropriate.

Surface water comprises all that water which is on or under the surface of the land and is not in a defined watercourse or channel. This includes water which is percolating through topsoil to reach a watercourse, and whilst it remains in this transitory state the owner of the land through which the water is passing has effective rights of ownership. Once water reaches a defined watercourse these rights change dramatically because any ownership of the water itself ceases. Ownership of the bed of the watercourse will be described in title deeds, but, although the owners have the usual rights to utilise their own land as they think fit, they are precluded by both the common law and various different types of legislation from doing anything to the bed which might affect the flow of the water. For example, mooring a platform for use as a helicopter landing stage is classed as development within s.55 of the Town and Country Planning Act 1990 and planning consent is required, thus giving additional control to activities on the water. Many people acquire the right to benefit from flowing water, either by long usage or through the grant of easements. As a result, one person must be prevented from stopping up that flow and affecting the water rights of potentially scores of people situated further down the flow line.

In reality, the position is rather more complex, with much case law dating from the Middle Ages. However, for the purposes of this book the basic statement above serves to explain the general principles upon which the ownership of water are founded. The reader is reminded that the law relating to easements can be found in most textbooks which deal with land law.

This chapter is divided into sections on water authorities and their powers; the supply of water; sewerage, drainage and sewage disposal; and controls over water pollution.

WATER AUTHORITIES AND THEIR POWERS

The Water Act 1989 (WA) introduced a complete restructuring of water and drainage management in England and Wales. The Act established the National Rivers Authority (NRA) and cleared the path to the privatisation of the water industry. Subsequently, parliament enacted the Water Industry Act 1991 (WIA), the Land Drainage Act 1991 (LDA91), the Statutory Water Companies Act 1991 (SWCA) and the Water Resources Act 1991 (WRA), most of the provisions of which came into force on 1 December of the same year. The first three of these Acts deal with the functions of the internal drainage boards and local authorities; the fourth Act covers water resources and the function of the NRA. These Acts consolidate the previously existing water legislation which was spread through a vast array of statutes, although some provisions of the old enactments remain in force and will be referred to where necessary. As with all comparatively new legislation, it is not always possible to see exactly how it will operate in practice, and regulations, circulars, codes of practice and other guidance from the government is awaited in many areas to aid interpretation.

Ultimate control of the industry, despite privatisation, remains with the government and principally with the Secretary of State for the Environment. Other ministers have powers where there is an overlap in function, for example the Secretary of State for Health supervises the fluoridation of water supplies.

Note References in the following sections to undertakers includes both water and sewerage undertakers unless expressly stated otherwise.

National Rivers Authority

The NRA was established under s.1 of the Water Act 1989 (WA) and has been continued under s.1 of the Water Resources Act 1991 (WRA). It has taken over the functions relating to fisheries, flood defences, pollution control, water resources, navigation, conservation and recreation (s.1).

Constitution

The NRA is a corporate body funded, by and large, by the Treasury, but is not an agent of the Crown. It consists of between eight and fifteen members, appointed by the government (none of whom can be MPs), who regulate their own internal procedure through committees or by delegation to officers or employees. This does not apply to flood defence work which must be conducted through regional flood defence committees (Schedule 1 and s.106 WRA). Unlike local authority committee meetings, meetings of the NRA are not open to the public.

Finances

As well as Treasury funding, the NRA is enabled to levy charges for the exercise of its functions (ss.117 and 118 WRA). For example, for providing consultation services to waste disposal authorities.

Functions

The NRAs functions are mainly concerned with the management of water resources. The NRA may take any action necessary to secure the proper use of existing resources, as well as carry out research to ascertain water demand (s.19 WRA). It is responsible for most measures regarding drought and for licensing water abstraction. Most importantly, it has responsibility for control of river water quality and for ensuring that the quality objectives set by the Secretary of State are fulfilled (see further under 'Water pollution', page 155).

Advisory committees

The NRA must set up advisory committees for the different regions of England and Wales (s.7), but it may determine the boundaries of those regions itself. The committee members are appointed by NRA, but they must be independent. Committee meetings are open to the public and consultation with the committees must take place to discuss the carrying out of NRA functions in the region.

Director-General of Water Services

Section 1 of the Water Industry Act 1991 (WIA) established the appointment of the Director-General of Water Services who operates through the Office of Water Services. He has responsibility with regard to charges made to consumers and the protection of consumers' interests. He must resolve disputes between consumers and the industry and set up Customer Services Committees. He also has powers with regard to the appointment of undertakers and may vary areas within which they operate. Conditions and duties imposed on undertakers are enforced by the Director-General who also has the power to refer matters to the Monopolies Commission if he believes that an undertaker is not operating in the best interests of the public (ss.6–18 WIA).

Duties of the Director-General

In exercising his functions the Director-General must consider the duties imposed on him by s.2 WIA. These are to ensure that the undertakers carry out their own functions properly and are suitably financed, achieving an adequate rate of return to allow for capital for future development. He must look into the efficiency of the undertakers and consider the interests of consumers.

Customer Service Committees

Customer Service Committees (CSCs) are established and maintained by the Director-General under s.28 of the WIA to investigate complaints, make recommendations and prepare reports on matters affecting consumer relations with undertakers (s.29). A maximum of ten CSCs can be set up, and each appointed undertaker must be allocated to one of them, thus each consumer will be represented by a CSC.

A CSC may have between ten and twenty members and its meetings are open to the public.

Water Services Plcs

Prior to 1 September 1989, water authorities provided both water and sewerage functions. On that date, by virtue of s.4 of the Water Act (WA), these functions were transferred to the Water Services Plcs (public limited companies), and shares in those companies were sold to the public. The Plcs are, in fact, holding companies for smaller subsidiary companies which carry out the major part of the water authorities' functions. Organisation in this manner enables the water and sewerage functions to be split more easily and each body, theoretically, becomes more accountable. The WA establishes the method by which this was achieved and chapter V of Part II of that Act should be referred to for further details.

Statutory Water Companies

The Statutory Water Companies Act 1991 (SWCA) establishes a procedure whereby the old statutory water companies which were set up during the last century could also adopt company status. For details of this, the SWCA should be referred to. It should be noted that the Secretary of State has the power to approve such a company and an order has to be made by parliament to establish the company formally. The powers necessary for the new companies to carry out their functions are contained in s.1 of the SWCA. As these companies are constitutionally different from those established under the WA, it is likely that in future the Secretary of State will introduce regulations to ensure that both bodies can compete fairly in the same market.

Appointment of undertakers

Once the new format was in place the Secretary of State was under a duty to consider the appointment of water and sewerage undertakers to fulfil the functions of the old statutory bodies and the water authorities. This duty extends to ensuring that there are adequate water and sewerage undertakers to cover every area of the country at all times. These appointments can be varied in the future but the Secretary of State must always maintain a continuous provision of water and sewerage services.

All the appointed companies are obliged to pay a fee to the Director-General as a condition of their appointment (s.11 WIA).

Powers and duties of undertakers

All undertakers must comply with the conditions imposed on their appointment, but, subject to that, they are empowered to carry out any function relating to their appointment (s.6 WIA). This includes functions contained in other Acts which refer to statutory undertakers rather than the new appointees. (Such a provision avoids the difficulties of amending all previous legislation to bring it into line with the new system of Plcs, etc.)

Water undertakers are obliged to provide and develop an efficient and economical water supply for all its users (s.37 WIA). Sewerage undertakers are under a duty to provide and empty public sewers and dispose of the waste (s.94 WIA). All undertakers have a responsibility to prevent pollution (s.217 WIA). The undertakers must also have regard to the environmental and recreational duties imposed by s.13 of the WIA.

Enforcement of undertakers' duties

The Director-General is enabled to enforce the provisions relating to the conditions of an undertakers appointment, whilst the Secretary of State is responsible for ensuring that the environmental and recreational duties are carried out. The enforcement of other duties is split between the two. The enforcement powers are quite stringent and can lead to the service of 'enforcement orders' (s.18 WIA), fines before both the magistrates' and Crown Courts and injunctions.

Special administration orders can also be made by the High Court on the petition of either the Secretary of State or Director-General (s.24 WIA) effectively to wind up the undertaker and transfer its assets to another, or a number of other, companies.

Internal Drainage Boards

Land drainage as envisaged by the Land Drainage Act 1991 (LDA) is basically concerned with flood prevention by the use of efficient drainage systems. Internal Drainage Boards (IDBs) are established in areas where it is believed that the land will benefit from drainage works or where there is a danger from potential flooding. These areas are known as internal drainage districts (s.1 LDA). In urban areas usually only land which falls below the flood levels in an area is included, but in rural areas this general principle is extended to include agricultural land which is up to eight feet above the flood level.

IDBs which were in existence prior to September 1989 have continued in the same form. The NRA has the power to reorganise, abolish or reconstitute them after submitting a scheme to the Ministry of Agriculture, Fisheries and Food which is ultimately responsible for flood defence matters (s.3 LDA). IDBs do not deal with navigable waters or waters or watercourses which are already the responsibility of another undertaker or the NRA (ss.14 and 72). They may, however, carry out works on behalf of these other bodies under an agency arrangement (s.11).

An IDB is composed of elected members and the regulations concerning constitution and administration are contained in Schedule 1 to the LDA. It has the power to acquire land by agreement in connection with its functions or by way of compulsory purchase with the consent of MAFF (s.2 LDA). It is enabled to maintain and improve existing watercourses and drainage works and to construct new watercourses and works where necessary. It may also do any other thing designed to facilitate the performance of its functions (s.14).

Like the NRA and the undertakers, an IDB must further the cause of nature conservation and secure the best use of its land for the benefit of the public (s.12).

THE SUPPLY OF WATER

Before it is possible to discuss the supply of water to the consumer, it is important to consider the water resources from which the supply must be taken. The management of water resources falls mainly to the NRA which is under a duty to take whatever action is necessary to conserve and increase the available water resources (s.19 WRA). It is also obliged to enter into arrangements with other undertakers to ensure that water which is controlled by them is properly managed (s.20 WRA).

Finding water

To enable them to fulfil their functions, the NRA and water undertakers are authorised by s.171 to enter land to survey and search for water. This power is limited to carrying out tests and does not permit engineering works. The Secretary of State may then give authority for further work.

Wells and boreholes

Permission to sink a well or borehole must be obtained from the National Environment Research Council if the intention is to search for water. Failure to do so or failure to comply with any of the requirements imposed is an offence which can lead to a fine on level 3 with a further daily penalty of £20 whilst the offence continues.

Water abstraction licences

Licences to abstract water are granted by the NRA under Part II of the WRA. Any abstraction requires a licence, whether it be from streams or underground sources, and they are required even by those persons who have a right (perhaps by ownership of a river bed) to use the water. Licences which were in force at 1 September 1989 are deemed to have been granted by the NRA. Failure to obtain a licence or to comply with its conditions is an offence which can lead to a fine.

Exceptions (s.27 WRA)

Isolated incidents of abstraction of less than 5 cubic metres, unless the incidents are in fact a series of operations, are exempt.

Minor abstractions up to 20 cubic metres are exempt as long as the NRA gives prior approval. Owners of the land through which the water runs may extract a maximum of 20 cubic metres in any twenty-four hours if the water is to be used for domestic or agricultural purposes.

Various other exemptions apply to persons engaged in land drainage or other works where the abstraction is necessary and is carried out with the consent of the NRA (s.29 WRA).

Licence applications

Under s.35 of the WRA, only occupiers of land are entitled to apply for licences. Application is made in a standard form issued by the NRA and must be accompanied by the appropriate fee and confirmation that notice of the application has been given in the *London Gazette* and a local newspaper.

The NRA must consider any representations made to it either as a result of the publicity or by any of its consultative bodies, such as the Nature Conservancy Council. It must also consider the effect on any existing licence-holders or other users of the supply. The Secretary of State may call in certain classes of application for decision by him and these will be determined after a local inquiry or by an inspector appointed for the purpose.

A licence can be granted subject to conditions or it can be refused. In either case the applicant has the right to appeal in writing to the Secretary of State within one month of being notified of the decision (s.43 WRA). The Secretary of State may refer the appeal to a local inquiry or to an inspector and must hold a local inquiry if requested to do so (s.44 WRA). On appeal, the Secretary of State may grant, refuse or vary the conditions of a licence. The applicant may then appeal to the High Court on a point of law within six weeks of the appeal decision letter date (s.69 WRA).

Charges

The NRA is entitled to charge for the grant of a licence and during its continuance. The charges are levied under a scheme established by s.123 of the WRA. No charge can be made for underground abstractions in connection with agriculture unless the water is needed for spray irrigation. The NRA is empowered (s.126) to exempt certain classes of persons or operations from charges or to reduce the charges levied. Non-payment of the charge may render the licence invalid.

Licence-holders

A licence is issued to the occupier of the land. Once his occupation ceases his entitlement to the licence also ceases. The new occupier, if he notifies the NRA of his occupation, may take over the licence (s.49 WRA).

Variations and revocation

The NRA has the power (s.52) to vary a licence or to revoke it. The holder has the opportunity to object to the variation and his objections must be referred by the NRA to the Secretary of State. Variations can also take place at the instigation of the licence-holder. The Secretary of State may hold an inquiry, and must do so if requested by either party. His decision is final, but compensation may be available to the former holder if the licence is revoked or varied in such a way as to make any expenditure incurred by him on the land abortive (s.61).

Registers

The NRA keep registers of all the licence applications, grants, variations and revocations, which must be open to the public to view (s.189 WRA).

Undertakers

Water undertakers are obliged to apply for a licence in the same way as any other person and are subject to the same provisions.

Licensing of the NRA

The NRA also must acquire a licence for its own abstractions. It advertises its application in the same way and it is empowered to grant itself a licence. Any application must be sent to the Secretary of State and he may call in an application if he so wishes for determination. (See the Water Resources (Licences) Regulations 1965 for further details of the procedures.)

Drought

A water undertaker is able to reduce the supply of water when drought conditions exist (there is no formal definition of drought and the undertaker must rely on its best judgement). Obligations to supply water are therefore not enforceable in these circumstances (s.52 WIA).

Hosepipes

If a water undertaker believes that there is a serious shortage of water it may impose a ban prohibiting the use of hosepipes for private use. Breach of a hosepipe ban is an offence which can be tried before the magistrates' court and may lead to a fine on level 3 (s.76 WIA).

Drought orders

Drought orders can be either 'emergency' or 'ordinary' and are made by the Secretary of State for the Environment at the instigation of NRA or a water undertaker. An ordinary order may impose conditions on the use of water or prohibit its abstraction (s.74 WRA). Consents for the discharge of effluent may also be suspended or varied during the period of the order. Water undertakers may request additional powers to take water from another source or ask for general conditions on usage to be imposed.

Emergency orders are applied for by the NRA when a water shortage is very serious. These orders are more onerous than ordinary orders and can severely limit the use of water or impose a total ban on either a group of consumers or named consumers (s.75 WRA). Standpipes can be set up under an emergency order.

Offences

It is an offence (s.80 WRA) to use water in contravention of a ban or any conditions which have been imposed. There is a defence available if it can be shown that all reasonable steps were taken to avoid committing the offence. There is a maximum penalty of £2000 in the magistrates' court and an unlimited fine before the Crown Court.

Water undertakers

Water undertakers have a duty to supply, develop and maintain an efficient and economical system (s.37 WIA). This duty only extends to the area of the water undertaker, but there are powers for one undertaker to lay pipes in the area of another and to supply water as long as this does not interfere with the other undertaker's activities (Schedule 13 WIA and s.192). A water undertaker has powers of entry on to premises to enable it to carry out its duty (s.170).

Domestic water supply

Any use of water for drinking, washing, cooking, heating or sanitation is classed as domestic use, and this applies even if the supply is to industrial or commercial premises as long as the use is domestic within the above criteria (s.218 WIA). Also a supply to residential premises will cease to be a domestic supply if the use is in fact industrial or commercial, e.g. where an unusually high volume of water is utilised.

A water undertaker has a duty under s.52 of the WIA to supply water for domestic purposes to any premises which were supplied with water prior to September 1989 or are connected to a water main in the future. In the latter case the duty arises when the request for the supply is made (see page 140 for details). The duty only extends to supplying water which is sufficient for the domestic purposes of the occupants, although the water undertaker must also maintain any connections such as stopcocks.

Note Occupiers of caravans are not entitled to request connection as they are not occupiers of 'premises' within the meaning of the Act. (Mobile homes which are in effect permanent fixtures may be regarded as premises, but touring caravans and other temporary accommodation are not.) These occupiers may enter into an agreement under s.55 of the WIA with the water undertaker to ensure their supply.

Requisitions

Under s.41 of the WIA an owner or lawful occupier may require the water undertaker to provide a water main to supply water for domestic purposes. The requisitioner is, however, obliged to enter into an agreement with the undertaker to repay to it over a period of twelve years the effective costs incurred in laying the main (s.43).

A private developer may be required to provide security for the costs to be incurred by the undertaker before the undertaker is obliged to lay the main (s.42 WIA).

In both cases, once the requisition has been made and question of costs resolved, the undertaker must provide the main within three months (s.44 WIA).

Connection notice

An owner, occupier or developer who has provided his own supply pipe may serve notice on the water undertaker requiring that his pipe be connected to the water main. The undertaker is under a duty to comply with such a request but may do so only if certain reasonable conditions are met and the requisitioner is responsible for the undertaker's costs (s.45). The pipe must be laid as soon as is practicable.

Failure by the undertaker

If the water undertaker fails in the duty to supply either a water main or a connection with no reasonable excuse, then it may become liable to pay compensation to anyone who has suffered as a result.

Disconnection

In the event of disconnection of domestic supply to enable works to be carried out, the undertaker must give at least seven days' notice of the impending disconnection. This does not apply in the case of an emergency. If the supply is to be cut off for more than twenty-four hours, then the undertaker must provide an emergency supply (s.60).

Non-domestic supply

Any duties with regard to a non-domestic supply which existed before September 1989 continue in force. New supply is regulated by s.55 of the WIA. This states that the water undertaker must provide a supply (although conditions for the supply can be imposed) once it has been requested so to do, unless the undertaker can show that it would incur unreasonable expenditure or that such a supply would detrimentally affect other parts of its area (ss.55–56 WIA).

Note A supply to industrial or commercial premises will usually consist of both domestic and non-domestic supply, and the former must be provided in accordance with s.52 of the WIA.

Fire-fighting

If the occupier of industrial or commercial premises requests a water undertaker to install fire hydrants, then the undertaker must comply with that request (s.58 WIA). The occupier bears the cost of the installation.

Fire authorities (generally county councils) are under a duty to ensure that adequate water is available for fire-fighting. The authority is governed by the Fire Services Act 1947 and it is empowered to enter into suitable arrangements with a water undertaker for this purpose (s.14 of the 1947 Act). The fire authority bears the cost of the supply (s.57 WIA).

Fire-fighting hydrants must be clearly marked and properly maintained by the water undertaker. If failure to do this leads to delay in the use of the hydrant, the undertaker may be held liable for negligence. The undertaker is also obliged to ensure that there is adequate pressure available to reach all the roofs of the buildings in the area. The Secretary of State has responsibility for enforcing these provisions under s.18 of the WIA.

No charge is levied for the use of water for fire-fighting purposes, although the cost of maintenance of the hydrants can be charged for (s.147 WIA).

Note Fire authorities do not require a licence to abstract water for fire-fighting.

Other duties of a water undertaker

The water undertaker is under a duty to supply water for other public purposes if requested to do so (s.59 WIA) and it may impose reasonable conditions on the supply.

The undertaker is also under a duty to maintain water in its pipes for the purpose of domestic supplies or fire-fighting. Although failure to perform this duty is an offence for which the undertaker can be fined up to £2000 by the magistrates and an unlimited amount in the Crown Court, there is a defence if the undertaker can show that it took all reasonable steps to comply with its duty (ss.65–66 WIA).

Water pipes (s.219 WIA)

The pipes through which water is carried are classified into three types:

1. A *trunk main* is a pipe which carries water from a source of supply to a reservoir or filter. It includes pipes between reservoirs or which are transmitting water in bulk.
2. A *water main* is a pipe which is vested in the water undertaker and is used to make a general supply of water.
3. A *service pipe* may be either a *communication pipe* or a *supply pipe*. The latter is laid by the owner of premises to the street, at which point it is met by the former, with a stopcock marking the boundary between the two.

A main or a pipe is deemed to include all the accessories, such as pumps and manholes, which are necessarily laid with it.

Both a water undertaker and the NRA have the power to lay pipes in public and private streets without the need for planning permission, although they must comply with a code established under the New Roads and Street Works Act 1991. The pipes belong to the water undertaker or the NRA (s.158 WIA). They may also lay pipes elsewhere if it is necessary for the proper performance of their duty (s.159).

Maintenance of pipes (ss.158–159)

It is established that a water undertaker has a duty to maintain its own pipes, but there are a number of grey areas where it is not wholly clear as to whom pipes belong. In these instances, as a general rule, pipes which are under a highway are the responsibility of the water undertaker, and those on private land are the responsibility of the owner or occupier of the land.

The undertaker is empowered to enter land for the purposes of maintenance and to break open streets, but it must cause as little damage as possible and repair that damage which is caused. It may also enter private land to inspect and repair pipes, and may be entitled to recover any costs which it incurs in so doing from the owner or occupier depending on the agreement between them.

Misuses of water supply

A water undertaker has the power under s.75 of the WIA to serve a notice on the owner or occupier of premises to carry out repairs to prevent leakages or excessive consumption. If the notice is not complied with, the undertaker may enter the premises and carry out the work itself and recover the costs which it has incurred from the owner or occupier.

Intentional or negligent misuse of water is an offence under s.73 of the WIA which may lead to a fine on level 3 on the scale. This includes the use of a domestic supply for non-domestic purposes and, under s.174 of the WIA the interference with apparatus which is used to supply water. In addition, the water undertaker can recover the cost of the water which has been wasted or illegally used as a result.

Water charges

A user of water is liable to pay the water undertaker for the supply which is made available to him. Section 142 of the WIA empowers the undertaker to levy charges in respect of the service provided to the consumer, but he will not always be the person actually using the supply. Joint occupiers of property are equally liable, and owners of property may remain liable when they let the property to tenants. To some extent this depends on the method of charging, as unmeasured supplies are charged on the basis of the rateable value whereas measured supplies are metered.

The significant point is that the water undertaker must have in operation a charges scheme to which the consumer of domestic supplies may refer. The charges which are levied are monitored by the Director-General. Any increases in charges are linked to the retail price index, and there are strict limits imposed on the water undertaker. Any consumer with a complaint about charges (or any other aspect of the undertaker) may contact the Customer Service Committee for his area.

A water undertaker can sue for unpaid charges in the county court in accordance with s.142 of the WIA, and may enter into arrangements with local authorities with regard to collection of the charge from council house tenants.

Disconnection

A water undertaker is empowered to cut off a water supply to premises if payment has not been made in accordance with a notice served by it. The notice must give at least seven days for payment, and domestic consumers have various safeguards to be found in the water undertaker's Code of Practice (for example, those on low incomes may obtain assistance from the Department of Social Security). The notice is also held in abeyance if the consumer challenges the amount requested.

Water meters

Since September 1989, a water undertaker is empowered to require that new connections to a domestic supply are metered (s.45 WIA). The undertaker is responsible for the maintenance of the water meter and must test a meter if requested to do so.

It is an offence to tamper or interfere with a meter, and there is a penalty at level 3 on the scale (s.175 WIA).

Water quality

EC regulation

A number of directives have been issued by the EC relating to the quality of water. In particular, the 'Surface Waters' directive (75/440/EEC) and the 'Drinking Water' directive (80/778/EEC). The member states are required to fix standards in accordance with the directives and enforce those standards within their own territory. For details of the provisions, reference should be made to the directives. To some extent the requirements of these directives has passed into our legislation, notably those relating to the quality of domestic water.

Domestic water

The Water Act 1989 established the Drinking Water Inspectorate which now takes its powers from WIA s.86. The inspectorate is able to enter premises to take samples, to investigate any items which may be relevant (e.g. soil), to check records and demand information. A water undertaker is under a duty to provide whatever information an inspector requires, and failure to do so can lead to prosecution in the magistrates' court with a fine on level 5.

The local authority too is under a duty (s.77) to take any steps required to ensure that the water supplied in its area, both from private and public sources, is of a suitable quality. It can appoint its own inspectors who have a power of entry onto premises to investigate (s.84). It may also serve notice on a person or body requesting information; failure to comply with a notice may lead to prosecution before the magistrates' court with a fine on level 5.

Wholesome water

Both water undertakers and private suppliers are under a duty to provide wholesome water (ss.68 and 80) which is defined in the Water Quality Regulations made under s.67 of the WIA. These regulations also specify provisions with regard to the maintenance of water quality standards, sampling procedures and additives which are permitted. It must be remembered that the standard differs depending on the use to which the water is to be put. Drinking water and water for washing and cooking must be to a far higher standard than water for sanitation, for example.

Unfit water

A water undertaker which supplies water which is unfit for human consumption commits an offence which can be heard either in a magistrates' court or in the Crown Court. In the latter there is an unlimited fine and in the former a maximum of £2000 (s.70 WIA). Past case law has shown that unfit water needs to be more than unwholesome but not necessarily dangerous to health.

Water contamination

It is an offence for a person who is responsible for the maintenance of pipes to allow the pipes or other water fittings to get into a condition whereby the water is or is likely to be contaminated (s.73 WIA). The maximum penalty is a fine on level 3.

Under s.75 of the WIA the water undertaker may serve notice on the responsible person requiring that works be undertaken to rectify the situation. At least seven days must be allowed for the work to be done and, if it is not, the water undertaker has the power to enter and carry out the work itself. It may then recoup its costs from that person. There is no right of appeal against a notice, but the undertaker is responsible for any unnecessary costs which the person incurs and if it carries out work itself which is not required it will have to bear its own expenses.

Fluoridation

A District Health Authority is empowered to produce a scheme for the fluoridation of water in its area (ss.85–87). Once the scheme is prepared it must submit a formal application to the water undertaker for its implementation. The Health Authority and the water undertaker are able to enter into an agreement specifying their various responsibilities with regard to the monitoring etc. of such a scheme. The health of any person which is damaged as a result of such a scheme will have an initial claim for liability against the water undertaker. It, in turn, is indemnified by the Secretary of State for Health.

SEWERAGE, DRAINAGE AND SEWAGE DISPOSAL

Drains and sewers

Section 219 of the WIA defines a 'drain' as a drain used for the drainage of *one building* or a *number of buildings within the same curtilage* and will include drains from yards or outbuildings. On the other hand, a 'sewer' includes any drain or sewer (except those defined as drains above) which is used for the drainage of *buildings* and their appurtenances (s.219). In essence, the difference between them is that a drain serves a single unit and a sewer serves a combination of units, the latter usually being vested in the sewerage undertaker and the former being the responsibility of the building owner or occupier. A sewer and a drain can be used for the passage of either sewage or surface water, although the main function of a sewer is to carry sewage. The definitions of both these include any manholes or other accessories required for their use.

Sewerage undertakers' duties

A sewerage undertaker must provide sewerage services within the Sewerage Service Area allocated to it (s.219 WIA). Under s.18 of the WIA the sewerage undertaker is under a duty to cleanse and maintain the sewerage system, make provision for the disposal of the effluent and improve the system. It may appoint a local authority to act as its agent for this purpose, although local authorities are not authorised to deal with sewage disposal or the discharge of trade effluent (s.97 WIA).

Public sewers

The ownership of sewers is a complex and confusing area of law. As a general rule, sewers which are used for the purpose of carrying out the functions of a sewerage undertaker are public sewers and are vested in the undertakers. Other sewers are private sewers and include those which are used to drain the sewerage undertaker's own land as this is not for the purpose of the undertaker, but for private purposes (s.219 WIA). Although this covers by far the majority of sewers, there are some which were constructed before 1937 which have never been formally vested in the sewerage undertaker and remain as private sewers despite having a public function.

Adoption

A sewerage undertaker has the power to adopt sewers which were constructed after 1937 under s.102 WIA and may do so after receiving a request from the owner. This is done by way of a vesting declaration and can only be used in respect of sewers which serve the undertaker's area and are not already vested in another sewerage undertaker'. An aggrieved owner, in either situation, has a right of appeal to the Secretary of State for the Environment within two months of the undertaker's decision. The appeal will be determined by the Secretary of State after taking into consideration all relevant matters, including the position of the sewer, its state of repair and the number of buildings which it serves. He has the power to make any order which the undertaker could have made. Once the sewer is adopted, all those who used it prior to adoption retain the right to continue to use the sewer.

Sewer requisitions

Property developers and the owners or occupiers of premises have a right to requisition the sewerage undertaker under s.98 of the WIA. Such a requisition can only relate to drainage for domestic purposes, that is, washing, cooking and sanitary uses (excluding commercial cooking and washing), and the removal of surface water from those premises. A requisition notice must be served on the undertaker together with a financial commitment on the part of the requisitioner to pay to the undertaker over a period of twelve years the costs incurred by the undertaker (s.99 WIA). These costs will include the provision of any necessary apparatus, such as pumps. A requisitioner may also be asked to provide security for the costs, usually in the form of a guarantee or bond. Once the financial provisions have been complied with and any other necessary work has been undertaken, the undertaker has a period of six months in which to supply the sewer.

Laying sewers

A sewerage undertaker has the power under ss.158 and 159 of the WIA to lay sewers and carry out other ancillary work in any street, whether public or private. If it causes damage whilst carrying out its work it is liable to compensate any person who suffers loss as a result. It must obtain the consent of any railway or navigation body before carrying out such work on its land. A sewerage undertaker also has the power to lay a sewer in any other land if it is expedient to do so and, again, compensation may be payable. Notice of the intended works must be given to those affected by it: three months for a new sewer and forty-two days for any others. In case of an emergency, no time limit applies.

Sewer maintenance

There is a duty on an undertaker to ensure that its area is effectively drained and sewage disposed of. To enable it to comply with this duty, an undertaker has the power under ss.158 and 159 to enter any land for the purpose of inspecting, maintaining, cleansing and repairing any sewer. This will include relaying a sewer if necessary. Regulations can be made under s.94 of the WIA to prescribe standards of performance for sewerage undertakers.

Damage to sewers (Building Act 1984, s.18)

To avoid any damage to sewers, the sewerage undertaker is empowered to supervise any works which are being carried out and which require the opening of a sewer. Also, a local authority must notify an undertaker of any applications received by it for building regulation consent which affect a sewer or a drain (including all the associated manholes, pumps, etc.) which is vested in the undertaker. A local authority must also reject any application for building regulation consent which it believes will adversely affect a private sewer or drain. Conditions may be imposed by the sewerage undertaker on any consent and there is a right of appeal to the magistrates' court.

**Construction of
private sewers
by developers**

A developer of either a housing or industrial estate will need to construct adequate sewers, to comply with both the Building Act 1984 and the Town and Country Planning Act 1990. A sewerage undertaker may require the developer to construct the sewer to its own specifications if it believes that the sewer might be needed to supplement the general sewage system (s.112 WIA). In this case the undertaker must pay any additional costs incurred by the developer as a result.

Adoption agreements

It is more common for the developer and the sewerage undertaker to enter into an agreement under s.104 of the WIA that the sewers will be built to the undertaker's specifications and then adopted by the undertaker as part of the public sewage network. This relieves the developer from any continuing liability in respect of the sewers after completion of the development.

A developer may request the sewerage undertaker to enter into such an agreement; if the undertaker refuses, does not reply within two months of the request, or agrees subject to unduly onerous conditions, the developer may appeal to the Secretary of State for the Environment. He must take into consideration all the relevant factors, such as position, number of premises served, suitability for general use (s.102 WIA) and may then make any decision which the undertaker could have made. If the Secretary of State makes an agreement it is enforceable against the sewerage undertaker.

**Private connections
to sewers**

An owner or occupier of premises may serve a notice on a sewerage undertaker stating that he wishes to connect into the public sewerage system. The undertaker has twenty-one days in which to refuse to allow connection if it believes that to grant consent would prejudicially affect the system (s.106 WIA). Any dispute concerning the suitability of the connection is determined by the magistrates' court.

If connection is permitted, it may be carried out either by the applicant or by the sewerage undertaker.

In the former case, the undertaker has the right to supervise the works, and in the latter, its reasonable costs must be paid. Even if the applicant wants to carry out the work himself, the sewerage undertaker can insist that it does it on his behalf (s.107). An applicant who continues with the work, despite receiving notification under s.107, is guilty of an offence and may be fined on level 4 in the magistrates' court. A similar penalty is imposed on those who connect into the system without first obtaining the sewerage undertaker's consent.

Repairs and alterations to private drains and sewers

Private drains and sewers are the responsibility of their owner or the occupier of the premises in question. Any works must be carried out in accordance with the Building Act 1984 (with respect to giving notice to the local authority) and the Public Health Act 1961 (which enables local authorities to require owners and occupiers to repair drains which are defective).

Discharges into sewers

Of necessity, there are limits imposed on the type of effluent which can be discharged into the sewerage system, although surface water has no restrictions as long as it discharges into the allocated sewer. (In some instances, but not always, there are separate sewers for foul and surface water drainage.)

Domestic premises

Generally, and subject to the above comment, the owners and occupiers of domestic premises are entitled to discharge both foul and surface water into the allocated public sewer.

Highway authorities

Under s.115 of the WIA the sewerage undertaker and highway authority may enter into an agreement that the public system may be used for the discharge of surface water from roads and other highways. In the same way, the highway authority may agree to permit the sewerage undertaker to utilise highway drains for the purpose of draining premises. Any dispute between the parties can be referred to the Secretary of State who has the power to force the parties to enter into an acceptable agreement.

Trade premises

Trade effluent is defined in s.141 of the WIA as any liquid produced in the course of a trade or industry carried on at trade premises. Domestic sewage is expressly excluded, unless it is produced as a result of a trade, such as a laundry or restaurant. Surface water is also excluded.

Any other discharge must be with the consent of the sewerage undertaker under s.118 of the WIA.

Consents

The consents procedure requires that an applicant (i.e. the owner or occupier of the premises) make a written application to the sewerage undertaker, stating the type of effluent, the maximum quantity to be discharged in any twenty-four hour period and the highest anticipated rate of discharge. The undertaker may request further information, and unreasonable failure to supply this is an offence leading to a fine on level 3. If the undertaker grants consent, it is for the benefit of the premises and not the applicant. This means that the consent can continue in force if the ownership changes or the sewers and drains themselves have been changed. It does not continue if the quantity or type of effluent changes.

If the sewerage undertaker fails to respond to the application within two months, refuses to grant consent or imposes unacceptable conditions, the applicant has a right of appeal to the Director-General. The Director-General may hold a local inquiry into the application (s.122).

Note   There may still be in existence agreements relating to the discharge of trade effluent which have not yet been brought into line with the consent system now imposed. These agreements were made under s.7 of the Public Health (Drainage of Trade Premises) Act 1937 and can continue in force for an indefinite period.

Conditions

Any consent can be subject to conditions imposed by the sewerage undertaker under s.121 of the WIA. These may cover such matters as the times of discharge, the maximum rate of discharge and type of effluent. Conditions can be varied without the applicant's consent, unless the variation is within the first two years. In that case, variation would rarely be approved and the undertaker would be liable to compensate the applicant (ss.124–126). There is a right of appeal against any proposed variation to the Director-General within two months of receipt of the notification.

Offences

The discharge of trade effluent without the required consent is an offence under ss.118 and 121 which can lead to the imposition of a fine of £2000 in the magistrates' court or an unlimited fine in the Crown Court. There is no defence unless the sewerage undertaker had agreed to the discharge.

Special consents

Some types of discharge are known as special category effluent and require a special consent (s.138 WIA). These substances are potentially harmful and are the responsibility of HM Inspectorate of Pollution (HMIP). An application for a special consent which the sewerage undertaker is minded to grant, must be referred to the Secretary of State for his approval. He may refuse or impose conditions or agree to the application as it stands. The applicant has a right of appeal to the Director-General in the usual way and he will refer it to the Secretary of State if he has not already been consulted. Variations of consents which relate to an increase in special category effluent must also be referred to the Secretary of State before the sewerage undertaker can grant the variation. Special consents are also subject to review (usually no more than once every two years) and, if a consent is revoked as a result of a review, the applicant may claim compensation. This will not be payable if the review has the result of a change of circumstances or due to the availability of new information (s.134 WIA).

The substances which are classified as special category effluent are listed in Schedule 1 of the Trade Effluents (Prescribed Processes and Substances) Regulations 1989 as amended by SI 1990 No.1629.

Sewage disposal

Standards have been imposed by the EC with regard to the treatment required for acceptable sewage disposal. The EC directive 91/271 EEC, concerning waste water treatment sets out the time-scale within which the member states should achieve the minimum standards. Under s.94 of the WIA, a sewerage undertaker has a duty to deal with the effluent in its sewers and may not delegate this duty to others. It may also deal with the contents of cesspools or this can be left to the waste collection authority.

A sewerage undertaker must not discharge foul water (as opposed to surface water) into any watercourse, unless the foul water has first been treated to ensure that it will not prejudicially affect the purity of the watercourse (s.117 WIA). This includes discharges into a lake or pond. Section 159 does permit the disposal of sewage at sea through the use of outfall pipes which have been approved by the Secretary of State for the Environment. It should be remembered that there are a number of international agreements which prohibit or restrict matter which can be disposed of in this way and it is not possible to give a comprehensive review here. Disposal of sewage on land is controlled by the Environmental Protection Act 1990 (see 'Waste disposal', Chapter 4).

Sewerage charges

A sewerage undertaker is empowered to fix charges for all its activities in accordance with a 'sewerage charges scheme' established under s.143 of the WIA. It may then recover its costs from the consumer to whom it has made the supply (s.142 WIA). In general, it is the occupier of premises who is liable to pay. In some instances, responsibility may lie with the owner even if he is not the occupier (e.g. where the premises are let to tenants) or where there are joint owners and only one is the occupier.

The charges can be either based on the rateable

value of the premises or fixed by reference to a metered quantity of effluent. Alternatively, the sewerage undertaker can base its charge on the volume of water supplied to premises and measured by a meter by a water undertaker (s.205 WIA). If it takes this option, the sewerage undertaker is liable to pay to the water undertaker a proportion of its costs in collecting the readings and processing them.

Charges can be increased in accordance with the retail price index, but must not exceed that amount.

Sewerage meters

A sewerage undertaker has the power to install meters at its own cost, unless the consumer has requested that a meter be supplied: then the cost is borne by the consumer. The sewerage undertaker must maintain the meter together with any other apparatus which is required by it (s.148 WIA).

Trade effluent charges

Charges for trade effluent are levied either under a scheme for charging or by agreement. The former become payable by the person who has the benefit of a trade effluent discharge consent. As with domestic sewerage, the charge may be calculated on a measured or unmeasured basis (s.143 WIA).

Unpaid charges

The sewerage undertaker is empowered to recover its charges from the consumer of the supply or other person responsible in the county court.

WATER POLLUTION

The principal functions of the National Rivers Authority (NRA) are to control pollution and generally to enhance and improve the quality of our inland, coastal and underground waters. Together with the Secretary of State for the Environment, the NRA has a statutory duty to take all practicable steps to achieve water quality objectives. These are set by the Secretary of State, but are heavily influenced by EC directives, in particular the 'Aquatic Environment Directive' (No. 76/464/EEC), which have been promulgated during the past fifteen years or so. In addition, international conventions, such as the 'London Convention on the Prevention of Marine Pollution by Dumping of Wastes and Other Matters 1972' which has been accepted by the majority of countries throughout the world, play a vital part in shaping the water pollution laws of the British Isles. Although the international dimension is outside the scope of this book, the wide-reaching and potentially disastrous effects of inland water pollution should always be considered.

The Water Act 1989 introduced comprehensive legislative controls to protect our water, and this Act has been superseded by the Water Resources Act 1991 (WRA). The Act applies to 'controlled waters', which are defined in s.104 as falling into four classes: territorial waters, coastal waters, inland waters, and ground waters. The first two are only of passing interest and briefly comprise the area from the low water mark extending seaward for three nautical miles and inland from that mark to the high water mark, including, in the case of rivers, inland to the freshwater limit. Inland waters are the waters of any river or watercourse (above the freshwater limit) and any lake or pond which discharges into such a river or watercourse. The definition expressly excludes public sewers or sewers or drains which discharge into public sewers. Ground waters comprise any waters which are contained in underground strata, wells, boreholes or other works designed to facilitate the collection of water. The Secretary of State does have wide powers which enable him to amend these definitions by making an order to exclude or include specified waters.

The Water Resources Act 1991 does *not* apply to any radioactive substances, unless the Secretary of State makes regulations to bring these, or some of them, under control. Radioactive wastes are controlled by the Radioactive Substances Act 1960. (References to 'waters' in the following sections relate to controlled waters as defined in the WRA.)

Water quality

The Secretary of State for the Environment has made regulations, the Surface Waters (Classification) Regulations 1989, to classify waters according to their suitability for use (after appropriate treatment) as drinking water. He is empowered under s.82 of the WRA to make further regulations and introduce a more general system of classification. This will take into account the use to which the water is put and the substances and the concentration of them contained within it. From this it will be possible to assess the quality of water and take steps to maintain and improve that quality. This will be achieved by serving on the NRA a notice under s.83 classifying the waters which are specified in the notice. The notice must give the NRA and any other interested parties at least three months within which to make representations. Once classified, the quality of the waters must be maintained at that level or improved. The Secretary of State may review the classification after five years or on the request of the NRA.

Water protection zones

Despite the creation of criminal offences to deter pollution (see page 159), it is inevitable that some water pollution will occur. Additional protection is given to some areas by creating water protection zones in accordance with s.93 of the WRA. These are designated by the Secretary of State with a view to preventing or limiting the entry of pollutants into the zone. The NRA is responsible for determining activities which can be undertaken in the zone and those which are to be prohibited or restricted. It may also permit certain, otherwise restricted, activities as long as they are pursued with its consent. Lastly, the NRA may prosecute persons contravening the restrictions, and offenders may be liable to a fine before the magistrates' court of £2000 and/or three months' imprisonment, or an unlimited fine in the Crown Court and/or two years imprisonment.

When designating a water protection zone the Secretary of State is to be guided by the NRA. It is envisaged that zones will be designated specifically to protect sources of drinking water, fisheries and waters which are used for recreational purposes. Before zones can be formally designated, notice must be given publicly and also to any local authority or water undertaker which is likely to be affected. A local inquiry may be held to consider any representations made.

Note Nitrate pollution as a result of agricultural activities cannot be controlled by the use of water protection zones.

Nitrate sensitive areas (NSAs)

Where it is deemed desirable to control or prevent the entry of nitrate into controlled waters, a nitrate sensitive area may be designated (s.94 WRA). Within the NSA the use of nitrates can be either prohibited or restricted, the aim being to achieve the EC standard with regard to nitrate levels in water. A person who suffers as a result of a designation may be entitled to compensation, although any compensation will be repayable if it is proved that the person has not complied with the provisions (s.94). It is also possible for owners of the land affected to enter into voluntary arrangements in consideration of payments made by the Ministry of Agriculture, Fisheries and Food (MAFF). Pilot schemes were established in accordance with the Water Act 1989 under the Nitrate Sensitive Areas (Designation) Order 1990 which placed detailed restrictions on the use of fertilisers on agricultural land.

To implement an NSA, notice must be given publicly and served on all those likely to be affected, including the NRA and any water undertaker. Representations may be made and a local inquiry held before the order is passed.

The contravention of any of the requirements imposed within an NSA is an offence which is punishable by a fine up to £2000 and/or three months imprisonment before the magistrates' court, or an unlimited fine and/or two years imprisonment in the Crown Court.

Other anti-pollution measures

Regulations can be made by the Secretary of State for the Environment to prescribe works and precautions which must be taken by a person who is in control of pollutants to prevent or limit the entry of the pollutants into controlled waters (s.92 WRA). Regulations relating to the storage of silage have been made under this provision.

The NRA is empowered by Schedule 26 of the WRA to make bye-laws. These can prohibit or control the washing or cleansing of any article as specified in the bye-laws in controlled waters and also prohibit or regulate the use of vessels which are supplied with sanitary facilities on controlled waters. Any bye-laws which cover these matters and were in force before the WRA will remain in force until superseded.

The NRA has the power to take steps to prevent any pollutants from entering or being present in waters where it believes that its intervention is necessary (s.161 WRA). It may enter onto any land for this purpose and carry out works or operations. In most cases, it may recover the costs it incurs from any person who knowingly permitted the pollutant to enter the waters or allowed it to remain present in the waters. The NRA is expected to consult water undertakers to ensure that they are working together and that any inadvertent pollution is caused by lack of communication.

The Secretary of State together with MAFF, may make Codes of Good Agricultural Practice to give practical guidance and promote desirable practices to those engaged in agriculture. Codes have been made under the Control of Pollution Act 1974 and these will remain in force until new codes are implemented.

Control of discharges and consents

It is an offence for any person to cause or knowingly permit poisonous, noxious or polluting matter, solid waste, trade or sewage effluent or anything likely to impede the flow of controlled waters to enter the waters (s.85). A person guilty of an offence may be liable on conviction before a magistrates' court to a fine up to £2000 and/or three months' imprisonment. Before the Crown Court the fine is unlimited and imprisonment can be for a maximum of two years. (The 'polluting matter' referred to in the section will include anything which might affect the quality of the water.)

The only defences to a charge under this section are if the person carrying out the activity has an appropriate consent; acts in an emergency; or takes all reasonably practicable steps to minimise the damage and notifies the NRA as soon as possible (s.88 WRA). Consents can, of course, be granted, not only under the WRA, but also under other legislation such as the Environmental Protection Act 1990 or the Control of Pollution Act 1974. The provisions for the grant of consents under the WRA is found in Schedule 10. Application for a consent must be in writing to the NRA, and the applicant must supply any additional information that the NRA reasonably requires. The NRA is under a duty to publicise the application locally and in the *London Gazette*. Any proposed discharges into the sea must be referred to the Secretary of State. Local authorities and water undertakers must also be notified. Representations can be made within six weeks of the notices to the NRA which must take them into account when determining the application. Where the NRA proposes to grant consent and it has received firm objections, it must give the objector the chance to ask the Secretary of State to call the application in for decision. It may not grant consent until any called-in determination has been concluded. It may grant consent subject to conditions, these could require, for example, pre-treatment of the pollutant, a limit on the quantity permitted or requirements as to the place of discharge.

Appeals

The NRA has four months in which to make its decision, and failure to do so will be deemed a refusal. An applicant may appeal against a refusal or against the imposition of any conditions. Appeal is to the Secretary of State, unless he made the initial determination, and he must hold a local inquiry if one of the parties requests him to do so. He may then direct the NRA to grant consent, modify its conditions, etc. There is no appeal against the Secretary of State's decision.

NRA discharges

Discharges by the NRA must also be in accordance with consents. These are granted by the Secretary of State and the method of application and publicity is basically the same as above.

Reviews   Both the Secretary of State and the NRA have the power to review the consents granted, and they may modify, revoke or impose fresh conditions. Compensation may be payable as a result.

Charges   The NRA may implement a charging scheme which must first be approved by Secretary of State and the Treasury to cover its costs in considering consent applications (s.132 WRA).

Registers

The NRA is under a duty to maintain registers which must contain all relevant particulars regarding:

1. Notices of water quality.
2. Applications for consents.
3. Consents and any conditions imposed.
4. Water and effluent sample analyses.

The registers must be available for public inspection at all reasonable times (s.190 WRA).

Miscellaneous matters under the 1991 legislation

Flood defence   Flood defence is a function of the NRA which discharges its responsibility through a number of regional flood defence committees. Further details of the composition of the committees and their activities can be found in the Water Resources Act 1991.

Access for works   Both the NRA and water undertakers can apply to the Secretary of State for the Environment for an order to enable it to gain access to land and premises to carry out necessary works and, if need be, to compulsorily purchase the land in question (s.168 WRA). The NRA has a general right to do whatever work is needed to fulfil its functions.

Recreation   The NRA and the water undertakers have a general duty which was imposed by s.8 of the WA to make the best use of their lands and waters for recreational purposes, and this duty has been continued by Schedule 2 of the Water Consolidation (Consequential Provisions) Act 1991. To achieve this end they should consult with the Sports Council and any other interested bodies. The Secretary of State may authorise the use of reservoirs for leisure purposes and may make provision for the construction of other facilities, such as community centres, on any available land (s.184 WRA). The NRA can make charges for any facilities which it provides under s.16 of the WRA and water undertakers have a similar power under s.3 of the WIA.

Conservation

Under s.16 of the WRA the NRA is under a duty to have due regard when carrying out its functions of the need to conserve and, if possible, enhance flora and fauna and geographical and physical features. This duty is extended to water undertakers under s.3 of the WIA.

OTHER APPLICABLE LEGISLATION, REGULATIONS AND ADVICE

Agriculture pesticides

The Food and Environment Protection Act 1985 imposes controls upon the use of pesticides. The Control of Pesticides Regulations 1986 specifies detailed provisions and also states that all reasonable precautions must be taken in the use of pesticides, not only to avoid danger to health, but in particular to avoid the pollution of water. Failure to comply with the regulations constitutes an offence under the 1985 Act.

The use of aircraft for the administration of pesticides is governed by the Air Navigation Order 1989, but the duties are as detailed under the 1986 regulations above. Before any spraying operations can be carried out near to waters, the NRA must be consulted.

Silage

The Control of Pollution (Silage, Slurry and Agricultural Fuel Oil) Regulations 1991 (SI 1991 No.324) provide that the storage of crops being made into silage or slurry, or the storage of fuel oil for the operation of a farm must be kept in the manner prescribed to avoid pollution of land and, ultimately, pollution of water. An offence under these regulations can lead to a fine of £2000 in the magistrates' court or an unlimited fine in the Crown Court.

Building and development

Provision of water

Any plans which are submitted in accordance with the Building Act 1984 to the local authority and which relate to a dwelling-house must be rejected by the local authority unless satisfactory proposals are included with regard to the supply of 'wholesome water' (s.25). In addition, the house must not be occupied until the water supply is in proper working order. Failure to comply with this is an offence at level 1 on the scale and a daily penalty of £2 can also be imposed by the magistrates.

Building over sewers, etc.

Plans for the erection of a building or an extension to a building over a sewer or drain must also be rejected unless the LA believes that the proposal can proceed satisfactorily. If the sewer or drain belongs to a water undertaker, it must consult with that undertaker before reaching its decision (s.18 Building Act 1984).

Drainage

The local authority is not entitled to approve plans for any building or extension unless it is first satisfied that adequate provision has been made in respect of drainage, which includes both waste and storm water (s.21). Under s.22 the local authority may require that buildings are drained in combination, that is, into one private, jointly owned drain leading into the main sewer. A request can be made when the local authority is satisfied that it would be more economical or in some other way advantageous to use combined drainage. The expenses of construction and maintenance of the combined drains will be borne by the owners in the proportions specified by the local authority. An aggrieved owner has the right of appeal to the magistrates' court against the proportion allocated to him. An appeal lies to the Crown Court if the owner is not satisfied (s.41).

Building Regulations 1991

The Building Regulations 1991 (SI 1991 No.2768), which are made under the 1984 Act, contain detailed provisions with regard to drainage and waste disposal in Part H, as well as dealing with subsoil drainage and moisture exclusion in Part C. Breaches of the Building Regulations are punishable before the magistrates' court by a fine on level 5 of the scale with a further daily fine of a maximum of £50 (see also Chapter 6.)

Defective water supply or sanitation

Under s.76 of the Building Act 1984 the local authority may serve an abatement notice on the owner and occupier of premises if it believes that the premises are in such a state as to be prejudicial to health or a nuisance. A defective water supply or inadequate sanitation may led to the service of such a notice. The notice must give nine days' warning that the local authority will enter to execute the works itself and recover its costs from the responsible person *unless* that person serves a counter-notice within seven days confirming that he will be doing the work himself. If he fails to carry out the work satisfactorily within a reasonable time, then the local authority may enter for that purpose. This procedure is similar to that prescribed by the Environmental Protection Act 1990 in relation to statutory nuisances (covered in detail in Chapter 4). In normal circumstances, the statutory nuisance procedure would be used by a local authority but it is more time-consuming and this section gives emergency powers.

Notification to fire authority

Any person who intends to connect into a water supply must give six weeks' notice of that intention to the fire authority under s.16 of Fire Service Act 1947. Failure to give the required notice is an offence on level 5 of the scale.

Water pollution

The EC

Circular 7/89, *Water and the Environment* gives guidance on the EC directive 76/464/EEC, the Aquatic Environment Directive. It gives a detailed explanation of the water pollution which may result from the discharge into waters of various potentially dangerous substances and guidance on the standards to be applied.

Statutory nuisances

Under the Environmental Protection Act 1990, a water course which is foul or in a state such as to be prejudicial to health or a nuisance may comprise a statutory nuisance. These are dealt with in Chapter 4.

Water contamination

The Public Order Act 1986, makes it an offence under s.38 for any person to contaminate or interfere with water. This includes doing anything to make the water *appear* contaminated, with the intention of causing injury or alarm. The penalty in the Crown Court could be as great as ten years' imprisonment and/or an unlimited fine, or six months' imprisonment and/or £2000 fine before the magistrates' court.

Any act or neglect which leads to the contamination of a spring, well, borehole or adit, the water from which is used for human consumption, constitutes an offence under s.21 of the Water Act 1945. This includes water which is to be used in a food or drink manufacturing process or for other domestic purposes. Punishment is on level 5 of the scale with the possibility of an additional daily penalty of £50. In the Crown Court the penalty is an unlimited fine and/or two years' imprisonment. There is a defence if the activity complained of was the result of cultivating the land in accordance with the principles of good husbandry, or the reasonable use of oil or tar on a highway by a highway authority.

Water, water supply and drainage

Private works to rivers, etc.

Landowners or occupiers are responsible for ensuring that rivers and other waters crossing their land are able to flow unimpeded and that the banks are in a satisfactory condition. If they wish to carry out works, such as culverting, however, they must first obtain the consent of the local authority under s.263 of the Public Health Act 1936. Any works can only be performed in accordance with plans approved by the local authority for this purpose.

Unfit houses

If the water supply to a dwelling-house is not adequate or wholesome, the house is not deemed to be fit for habitation and the local authority can take steps to close the property under s.604 of the Housing Act 1985.

CONCLUSION

The new regime with regard to the management of our water resources is still in its infancy. The streamlining of the administration and the allocation of responsibility among the various bodies should, theoretically, lead to greater efficiency and closer control over these limited resources.

The legislation surrounding water usage is far more extensive than depicted by this chapter. It includes navigation on our inland waterways, controls over canals and tidal rivers, as well as a wealth of statute law concerning freshwater fisheries and the conservation of wildlife. These have all been ignored for the purposes of this book as they do not fall within its scope: however, their existence should not be forgotten.

CHAPTER 6

THE SYSTEM OF BUILDING CONTROL

HISTORICAL DEVELOPMENT

Although the forerunners of local authorities had influence over buildings as early as the twelfth century, it was not until the last half of the nineteenth century that controls over construction practices and materials really began to have wide effect. Certain towns and cities voluntarily adopted limited powers under private Acts of Parliament. Most notable of these was London, which, since the Building Act of 1774, had controlled the construction of party walls and other matters by establishing four classes of house based on size and value (so-called first, second, third and fourth rate housing). Acts in 1855 and 1878 regulated, in theory if not entirely in practice, the construction of foundations, the quality of materials and the height of ceilings. Other cities followed this example, either through private Acts or through the production of bye-laws under existing legislation such as the Public Health Act 1858.

Much early legislation was concerned with banning, or at least regulating, back-to-back housing. This form of development was prohibited in Manchester in 1844 and in Liverpool in 1861, while in Bradford an 1860 bye-law restricted back-to-back housing to a maximum of two pairs by specifying open space at the side or rear of every house. Typical of a period in which local government was influenced by strongly held notions of *laissez faire* and by powerful lobbyists on behalf of property and building interests, some bye-laws were seldom enforced. In Leeds, the City's Improvement Act of 1842 allowed the council to require a proper privy for each property, but few summons were ever issued, and in 1866 a new bye-law allowed development with shared facilities once more. Leeds allowed back-to-back housing longer than anywhere else in England and Wales, with the last such houses being put up in the 1930s.

Important powers of building control emerged in the last quarter of the nineteenth century still under the aegis of 'public health', partly because the matters at issue were in a broad sense related to health, but more importantly because the extension of sanitary laws was politically an easier way of dealing with housing quality than a full frontal attack on the rights of property. The Sanitary Law Amendment Act 1874 allowed local authorities to regulate drainage of premises and ventilation of rooms. The Public Health Act 1875 was the most important of the Acts in its effects. Almost all of the legislation up to then had been permissive rather than mandatory, allowing local authorities discretion whether to make use of the powers being made available. The 1875 Act remained permissive in most respects, but it did give clear and strong powers to those authorities who wished to use them and, with model bye-laws available, most came to decide in favour. They took on powers to require developers to give notice of their activities, to deposit plans, and to make their building work open to inspection. The Act set in motion the local regulatory controls which gave rise to much of the late-nineteenth-century, low income housing we see today: rows of usually robust terraced properties, each giving reasonable family accommodation, receiving adequate light, with flushing outside toilets, small backyards and rear access. In 1890 the Public Health Amendment Act at last gave improved control over the structure of floors, hearths, staircases and heights of rooms, and prohibited building over land filled with offensive matter. Some towns and cities continued to avoid full use of powers but the basis of modern statutory controls over building were set out to be strengthened and improved with each passing decade.

Twentieth century developments in building control

By 1936, local authorities were required to have bye-laws specifically for the regulation of building. Although there was some similarity among most of the bye-laws produced, there were enough differences to make it necessary for architects and builders to review the particular local requirements every time. A break-through came in 1952 with the issue of model bye-laws which were so useful they were adopted by every local authority in England and Wales (except by the London County Council). The most significant feature of the new bye-laws was the adoption of a different control technique whereby standards of performance were stated. Descriptions of structural minima, which previously had been mandatory, were now contained in 'deemed to satisfy provisions', leaving the way open for newer methods and materials to be adopted, provided their performance could be established. Advisory publications, such as British Standard specifications and codes of practice, could be increasingly referred to, allowing designers and developers to operate in different areas with greater confidence in the acceptability of their methods.

The Public Health Act 1961 provided for the preparation of a national set of building regulations for England and Wales (again excluding London), introduced as the Building Regulations 1965 and revised in 1972 and 1976.

Recent developments in building control

The building control system for England and Wales was radically revised with the passing of the Building Act 1984. This Act consolidated most of the primary legislation relating to building which was formerly divided between various Acts of Parliament. Part I of the Act deals with the building regulations, Part II with the system of private certification as an alternative to the local authority, and Part III deals, amongst other matters, with local authority powers in respect of dangerous buildings, defective premises and demolition. The first regulations under this legislation were made in 1985. The latest are the Building Regulations 1991 which came into effect on 1 June 1992 consolidating earlier provisions, setting out certain new technical requirements, and laying down new procedures. The major difference between the Building Regulations 1991 (and those in 1985) and the earlier ones they replaced lies in the entirely non-prescriptive approach adopted.

THE BASIC BUILDING CONTROL SYSTEM

The Secretary of State is empowered under s.1 of the Building Act 1984 to make building regulations with respect to the design and construction of buildings for three purposes:

1. To secure the health, safety, welfare and convenience of people in or about buildings.
2. To further the conservation of fuel and power.
3. To prevent waste, undue consumption, misuse or contamination of water.

With the objective of making the system flexible and easy to use, the Building Regulations 1991 themselves are short and do not cover technical detail. This is found in the Approved Documents which give 'practical guidance'. Other non-statutory documents such as British standards and codes of practice are also relevant. This can include European standards bearing the CE mark in accordance with the Construction Producers Directive (89/106/EEC), those which conform to an appropriate harmonised standard issued by the European Committee for Standardisation (CEN), or have undergone a European Technical Approval (ETA), and those which conform to some other national technical approval of a member state provided it gives protection equivalent to a British standard or *agrément* certificate.

Current regulations

The Act provides for regulations on a number of procedural and technical matters. Those currently in force are:

1. The Building Regulations 1991.
2. The Building (Approved Inspectors, etc.) Regulations 1985.
3. The Building (Prescribed Fees) Regulations 1985 (as amended).
4. The Building (Inner London) Regulations 1985 (as amended).
5. The Building (Disabled People) Regulations 1987 (as amended).

Application to new building

The Act defines 'building' in the widest of terms so that even movable objects such as vehicles and aircraft can be covered, but the building regulations provide a more restrictive definition omitting boundary walls, silos, air-supported structures and the like and, in addition, a number of buildings and structures are, subject to certain safeguards, exempted from the regulations, including:

1. Buildings subject to the Explosives Acts of 1875 and 1923, Nuclear Installations Act 1965, and scheduled monuments under the Ancient Monuments and Archaeological Areas Act 1979.
2. Detached buildings into which people do not normally go or where they go only intermittently for the purpose of inspecting or maintaining plant.
3. Greenhouses and agricultural buildings.
4. Temporary buildings in place for less than twenty-eight days.
5. Ancillary buildings associated with construction, quarrying and mining or used to sell plots or houses on a new estate.

6. Small detached buildings of less than 30 square metres with no sleeping accommodation.
7. Ground-level extensions of less than 30 square metres floor area used as greenhouses, conservatories, porches, covered yards or a carport open on at least two sides.

Application to existing buildings

In many circumstances the regulations can apply to existing buildings. Thus, for example, material alteration of a building which might affect its structural stability, means of access, means of escape, or resistance to the spread of fire is likely to be covered, as will the substantial rebuilding of a property. The change of use of a building will always be covered if:

1. It is changed to a dwelling from another use.
2. It will contain a flat or a maisonette for the first time.
3. The building becomes a hotel or boarding house or institution when it was previously not.
4. The building becomes one intended for public use.
5. An exempted building is changed to a use that is no longer exempt.

The insertion of cavity insulation in existing buildings must comply with specific regulations related to the passage of moisture across the cavity and the control of toxic substances which can be given off by certain insulation material. In certain cases the alteration of a building will bring the entire structure within control, such as where a floor is being added to an existing building imposing additional load. Finally, the insertion or alteration of certain building services and fittings are controlled, including the provision of bathrooms, certain hot water storage systems, drainage and waste disposal.

THE BUILDING REGULATIONS 1991

There are twenty-one regulations arranged in five parts:

Part I: General
    Reg. 1   Citation and application
    Reg. 2   Interpretation

Part II: Control of building work
    Reg. 3   Meaning of building work
    Reg. 4   Requirements relating to building work
    Reg. 5   Meaning of material change of use
    Reg. 6   Requirements relating to change of use
    Reg. 7   Material and workmanship
    Reg. 8   Limitation on requirements
    Reg. 9   Exempt buildings and work

Part III: Relaxation of requirements
    Reg. 10 Power to dispense with or relax requirements

Part IV: Notices and plans
    Reg. 11 Giving of a building notice or deposit of plans
    Reg. 12 Particulars and plans where a building notice is given
    Reg. 13 Full plans
    Reg. 15 Completion certificate

Part V: Miscellaneous
    Reg. 16 Testing of drains and private sewers
    Reg. 17 Sampling of material
    Reg. 18 Supervision of building work otherwise than by local authorities
    Reg. 19 Revocations
    Reg. 20 Transitional provisions
    Reg. 21 Contravention of certain regulations not to be an offence

There are three schedules:

Schedule 1:   Requirements
Schedule 2:   Exempt buildings and work
Schedule 3:   Revocation of regulations

It is Schedule 1 which contains the thirteen areas of technical requirements listed A–N (omitting I). In contrast to the earlier 1985 regulations, almost all requirements are now expressed in functional terms. The summary of Parts A–N below will provide a useful overview of the scope of the building regulations.

Part A: Structure   Covers the strength and stability of buildings to sustain and transfer loading safely to the ground and measures to be taken to resist collapse of a building disproportionate to the cause of the damage.

Part B: Fire safety   Covers prevention of internal and external fire spread, facilities for the fire service and the provision of adequate means of escape.

Part C: Site preparation and resistance to moisture   Covers preparation of the site, protection against dangerous and offensive substances which may be present in the ground (such as radon and landfill gases), subsoil drainage, and resistance to weather and ground moisture.

Part D: Toxic substances   Deals with cavity insulation.

Part E: Resistance to passage of sound   Covers measures to control airborne and impact sound within dwellings to avoid disturbance to occupiers.

Part F: Ventilation   Covers means of ventilation, and applies generally to dwellings, and specifically to sanitary conveniences and bathrooms in any building and the roofs of all classes of building to prevent condensation.

Part G: Hygiene   Deals with provision, adequacy and safety of sanitary conveniences, washing facilities and hot water supply from systems which are not ventilated to the atmosphere.

Part H: Drainage and waste disposal Deals with foul water drainage, cesspools, septic tanks and settlement tanks, rainwater drainage and solid waste storage.

Part J: Heat producing appliances Covers the safe installation of heat producing appliances burning solid fuel, oil or gas and deals with the provision of an adequate supply of air, proper discharge of combustion products and protection of the building from heat or fire.

Part K: Stairs, ramps and guards Covers the suitable design and construction of stairways and ramps.

Part L: Conservation of fuel and power Provides that reasonable provision must be made for conservation of fuel and power through providing appropriate heating controls, insulation and other measures to conserve energy.

Part M: Access and facilities for disabled people Deals with the provision of access and facilities for the disabled, sanitary conveniences and audience seating.

Part N: Glazing – material and protection Deals with reducing the risks associated with glazing at critical locations in buildings. In particular, it deals with the need for glass in certain locations to break in such a way that injury is not caused, and for transparent glazing to be made apparent where there may be a risk of a building user walking into it (the last requirement does not apply to dwellings).

Significance of the Approved Documents

The fourteen Approved Documents give practical guidance on how the technical requirements of Schedule 1 may be complied with. They are written in an easy-to-follow technical style and are expected to be updated regularly.

Section 6 of the Act gives the Secretary of State power to issue these documents and in their text to refer to other non-statutory publications (e.g. codes of practice and standards produced by the BSI). Failure to comply with an Approved Document does not in itself involve any criminal or civil liability but the document can be used by a party in proceedings relating to an alleged contravention. If the applicant can show he has complied with the detail of an Approved Document he can rely upon this 'as tending to negative liability'. A local authority may attempt to show failure to comply with an Approved Document 'as tending to establish liability'. In other words, the onus will be upon the designer or contractor to establish he has met the performance requirements in some other way.

'Linked powers'

Although many construction-related public health controls have been brought under the remit of building regulations in recent years, local authorities still have certain health responsibilities to operate alongside building control. They are known as 'linked powers' and in practice are operated within the building control administrative system. The most significant of these linked powers are controls over construction above drains and sewers, adequacy of drainage provision for a development, adequacy of access and exit in public buildings, and provision of fresh water supply to any new residence. In cases where the local authority is not satisfied with provision made to meet one of these requirements it may reject plans (or the building notice) submitted under the building regulations.

Local legislation

Despite attempts in recent years to rationalise the main controls over building, there remain a host of local Acts giving councils special powers over building and related activity. The building regulations make it clear that local enactments must be taken into account. The most common local provisions cover special fire precautions for garages and tall buildings, provisions for access by the fire brigade, requirements for separate drainage from individual buildings, and controls over the design of retaining walls.

Inner London

With its own particular urban history and building traditions, London developed a separate system of building controls from the eighteenth century. Since the mid-1980s this system has gradually been brought into line with national regulations but there remain some local peculiarities in both requirements and enforcement. The main fields in which London Building Acts still apply include uniting of buildings, temporary structures, means of escape from fire, rights of adjoining owners, and dangerous and neglected structures.

Application of building regulations to Crown and United Kingdom Atomic Energy Authority property

Section 44 applies the substantive provisions of the regulations to Crown property but the procedural arrangements do not apply. Section 45 provides similar immunity from procedural compliance for the United Kingdom Atomic Energy Authority.

Defective premises

Under s.76 of the Act, if the local authority believes that any premises are in such a state as to be prejudicial to health or a nuisance, it may serve a notice stating that it intends to remedy the defect(s). The owner of the property may act quickly to undertake the work himself if he so wishes, but if he does not then the local authority may complete the work and seek to recover its costs through the court.

Dangerous buildings

Where a building or structure is in such a condition, or is carrying such loads, that a local authority considers it dangerous, the authority may apply to a magistrates' court under s.77 of the 1984 Act to require the owner to execute works to obviate the danger. If the owner does not comply, the local authority may execute the work itself and this can include restricting the use of a building. The local authority can seek to recover its costs from the owner through the magistrates' court. The owner may also be prosecuted for his failure to obviate the danger and, if found guilty, fined at level 1 on the standard scale.

Where a local authority believes the dangerous condition of a property necessitates immediate steps, it may act without delay. Cost again may, at the discretion of the court, be charged to the owner.

Ruinous and dilapidated buildings and neglected sites

The most wide-ranging power is available under s.79 of the 1984 Act where the local authority believes a site or building is sufficiently ruinous or dilapidated as to seriously affect the amenities of the area. The unusual feature of this section of the Building Act is the extent to which it allows the authority to concern itself with amenity as opposed to safety. Like earlier sections referred to above, the owner is first given the opportunity to rectify the ruinous or dilapidated appearance himself.

Demolition

Demolition is subject to control under s.80 of the Act. A person intending to demolish the whole or part of a building must notify the local authority, the occupier of any adjacent building, and the gas and electricity companies. He must also comply with any requirements of the local authority under s.82, which might include:

1. Taking steps to protect the public and to preserve public amenity.
2. Shoring up adjacent property, making good any damage and weatherproofing exposed surfaces.
3. Removing demolition waste from the site and making good the ground surface.
4. Sealing off or removing any sewers or drains in or under the building.
5. Making arrangements for disconnection of gas, electricity and water supplies.
6. Making suitable arrangements with the fire brigade with regard to any burning of demolition waste on the site.

Demolition notice procedure does not apply to certain minor demolition work, including:

1. Where the work is internal to an occupied building and the building is intended to remain in occupation.
2. Where the building has cubic content ascertained by external measurement not more than 1750 cubic feet (approximately 50 cubic metres).
3. Where the building is a greenhouse, conservatory, shed or prefabricated garage forming part of a larger building.

It should be noted that there are controls under the Planning Acts covering demolition in certain cases. These are covered, as appropriate, in Chapters 2 and 3.

CONTROL OF BUILDING WORKS

The regulations make provision for building works to be controlled either by a system of private certification or by the local authority.

Private certification

Under Part II of the Building Act 1984, provisions were set down for a 'private' system of building control to be available as an alternative to that offered by the local authority. This private system of certification relies on 'approved inspectors' operating under The Building (Approved Inspectors, etc.) Regulations 1985. Although the system was created to allow corporate bodies (such as the National House Building Council – NHBC) and individuals (such as architects, chartered building surveyors, etc.) to be approved as inspectors under the private system, to date only the NHBCs subsidiary company, NHBC Building Control Service Ltd, has been approved for house-building work only. There are still no individuals approved, and this seems likely to be the case for some time yet. The full operation of private certification is held up on the questions of insurance cover and agreement on the qualifications of individual inspectors. The Secretary of State has designated a number of professional bodies (such as RIBA, RICS, CIOB) to approve persons to certify plans and has designated certain public bodies and (since) privatised organisations to do likewise in respect of their own development only.

In cases where private certification is intended, the local authority still has to be advised through the service of an Initial Notice and give its consent.

Control of building work by local authorities

For reasons explained above it is the local authorities which are likely to handle the vast majority of building control work for the foreseeable future. Part IV of the Building Regulations contains the procedural arrangements which should be observed where a builder wishes to undertake work under local authority control. In the main, two procedural routes are open to the person undertaking the building work:

1. Control based on service of a building notice.
2. Control based on the deposit of full plans.

There is no local authority involvement where the building work comprises installation of gas heating appliances by British Gas-approved installers.

Building notice procedure

A person intending to undertake building works or make a material change of use may give a notice to the local authority indicating his intention. The local authority may ask for plans and other information but usually will not do so. Building notice procedure is not intended to be used for buildings designated under the Fire Precautions Act 1971 or for factories, offices, shops or railways premises.

Deposit of plans

The traditional mechanism for building control has been the deposit of full plans with the local authority in accordance with s.16 of the Building Act 1984 in advance of work commencing. The authority then has the duty to pass or reject the plans within a period of five weeks or two months should the applicant agree to this extension. The advantage of deposit of plans over the building notice is that once the plans have been passed by the authority, and as long as the work is implemented as set out in the deposited plans, there is no risk of any action in respect of an alleged contravention under s.36 of the Act. The authority may, with the applicant's agreement, pass the plans in stages, imposing conditions on the deposit of further plans as necessary. Should the local authority believe the plans are defective or show that the work would contravene the regulations, it may reject the plans but must specify the defects or non-conformities. There is an 'appeal' procedure which is outlined below.

Regulation 13 requires that the plans must be in

duplicate and that the local authority may retain one set. Two additional copies must be submitted where the building is to be put to a designated use under the Fire Precautions Act 1971. Along with the deposited plans, the applicant must submit an estimate of the cost of the works and pay the prescribed fee. Work may be commenced as soon as plans have been deposited, although the local authority must be given two working days' notice to arrange for site inspection.

Should the applicant wish the authority to issue a completion certificate in due course, a request to that effect must be submitted with the deposited plans (except in the case of works to which Part B, Fire Safety, applies, where the authority must give a completion notice anyway).

Reference to the Secretary of State

Under s.16 a joint approach may be made to the Secretary of State to determine cases of conflict between the parties over application of the Regulations. Cases before the Secretary of State are usually dealt with on the basis of written representations from the two sides, but the Secretary of State may, if he considers it appropriate, appoint a person to hear representations.

Site inspections

All persons undertaking work, whether adopting the building notice or deposit of plans procedure, must give certain notices to the local authority during the execution of the work. The notices required are for:

1. Start of work (two days' notice).
2. Covering up of any foundation excavation, foundation, damp-proof course, concrete or other material laid over the site (one day).
3. Covering up of any drain or private sewer subject to the regulations (one day).
4. Completion of any drain or private sewer (five days).
5. Erection of a building (five days).
6. Completion of any other work (five days).

Failure to provide notice of intended work is a criminal offence punishable on conviction by a fine. In practice, however, most local authorities require the builder to expose or partially demolish work undertaken to establish that it does comply with the regulations.

Prescribed fees

The Building (Prescribed Fees) Regulations 1985 (as amended) lay down fees for dealing with:

1. Development handled through the building notice arrangement.
2. Plans deposited with the local authority.
3. Inspection of work on site.
4. Work reverting to the local authority where private certification is intended but the initial notice is cancelled.

A flat rate applies for small domestic buildings, extensions and garages, etc. up to 40 square metres. All other work is subject to a variable fee related to the value of the work. The current prescribed fees are set out in the Building (Amendment of Prescribed Fees) Regulations 1989.

Testing and sampling

In addition to visual inspection of works made at site visits, local authority building control officers regularly undertake physical test of drains to ensure their watertightness. The building regulations permit this under regulations 16 and 17, making provision for tests to be undertaken by the person responsible for carrying out the building work and for the results and, where appropriate, samples to be passed to the authority. Testing of soil, subsoil, materials, fittings, services or equipment may be undertaken under this procedure. In all cases the local authority may expect the builder to carry the costs of these tests, although the authority is given the discretion to bear the whole or part of the cost itself. The courts may be asked to determine the reasonableness of any tests required and any decision of the authority to charge costs to the builder.

Contravening works

In order for the building regulations to be effective they must be given teeth; this is done through ss.35–36 of the Building Act. Where a building is put up, or building work is implemented contrary to the regulations, the local authority may serve a notice on the owner of the building requiring removal or alteration as appropriate. Where the owner fails to comply within twenty-eight days the local authority may execute the necessary works itself, recovering expenses from the owner. There are, however, certain controls on the exercise of this power:

1. The local authority must serve the notice within twelve months of the offending work being completed.
2. A notice may not be served where deposited plans have been passed and the work has been carried out in accordance with the plans.
3. The recipient of a notice has a right to appeal to the magistrates' court.

In court, the burden of proof will lie with the local authority if the works have been executed in accordance with the Approved Documents, and will lie with the recipient of the notice if they have not. Section 37 provides a useful method of resolving any difference of professional opinion. The recipient of a notice may notify the local authority that he intends to obtain a report on the alleged contravention from a 'suitably qualified person'. This action extends the period for appeal to the magistrates' court from twenty-eight to seventy days – long enough for a report to be made available to the local authority and, if the local authority concedes, for the contravention notice to be withdrawn. If the authority does not, then the case will go to court in due course, where, among other matters, the issue of which side pays the cost of the expert report will be determined.

Relaxation and dispensation of regulation requirements

Under s.8 of the Act, the Secretary of State may relax or dispense with a requirement of the regulations on the basis that it is unreasonable in relation to the particular case in question. Power under this section has been delegated by the Secretary of State to local authorities (but not to approved inspectors). The application procedure is set out in ss.9–10. There is no prescribed application form. The local authority is under certain obligations to advertise the application before taking a decision. Where the application is refused, there is a right of appeal to the Secretary of State within one month. A failure to make a decision within two months is interpreted as a refusal and activates the right of appeal. The use of relaxation or dispensation in the context of the 1991 regulations will be interesting to follow. With the majority of regulations requiring work to be 'adequate' or 'satisfactory', the granting of a relaxation implies acceptance of the inadequate or unsatisfactory. Dispensations are the more likely outcome where conformity cannot be achieved.

Building regulations and fire safety

The Department of the Environment, the Welsh Office, the Home Office and the Deregulation Unit of the Department of Transport have given advice on the interaction of fire and building regulations (The Buildings Regulations and Fire Safety: Procedural Guidance, June 1992). The intention is to help architects, developers and occupiers of buildings to understand the steps necessary to obtain approvals for fire safety aspects of building work. Much of the guide is concerned with co-operation and conflict resolution between the fire authorities and building control, but a number of points are useful to note for other interested parties. It is made clear that the building control authority (or the approved inspector) is the lead authority with a responsibility to consult the fire authority as appropriate. The need to prepare plans carefully and with fire safety in mind *before* submission is emphasised. Preliminary advice should be obtained by approaching the building control authority (or approved inspector). Approaches to the fire authority are likely to meet only with advice on non-building regulation fire precautions which the completed building must comply with. A joint meeting with fire and building regulations officers may be appropriate where the building is one which will require a certificate under the Fire Precautions Act 1971 and the building control authority is willing to host such a discussion.

CHAPTER 7

STATUTORY RESPONSIBILITIES OF THE BUILDER

INTRODUCTION

Obligations on the builder, his advisers and others involved in the construction industry continue throughout the building process, and may not cease even after completion of the project. Some of these obligations are founded in common law rather than in legislation, and thus do not form a separate topic for this book. However, it would be foolish to ignore the existence of the fundamental concepts of trespass, nuisance and negligence which are briefly explained below. The remainder of the builder's responsibilities are imposed by statute; some of these have already been covered in other chapters and the balance are dealt with here. Firstly, however, tortious liability can be quickly summarised.

TRESPASS AND NUISANCE

Trespass to land (there is also trespass to the person) occurs when one person enters onto the land of another without consent. Furthermore, a person legally entering land, perhaps to use a public right of way, becomes a trespasser if he exceeds or abuses the privilege granted to him, in this example, by stepping off the footpath. A landowner is entitled to sue for compensation in the county court for any damage caused by the trespasser. It is clearly important that all necessary rights of entry to land are obtained and defined by the builder before construction work begins, for example to ensure that scaffolding can be erected on adjoining land.

Private nuisance is a tort which consists of any wrongful interference with a person's use or enjoyment of his land. The nuisance may result from smoke or noxious fumes escaping from one property onto another, it may arise from excessive noise preventing the reasonable use of neighbouring land, and many other similar incidents. Much of this is also controlled by legislation, and that aspect is discussed in Chapter 4. Suffice it to say that a person who suffers in this way also has a remedy at common law in the county court for either damages, abatement or an injunction against the perpetrator of the nuisance. One important point to note about private nuisance is that only owners or occupiers of land can bring an action, and the action must relate to the enjoyment of that land. In addition, the plaintiff must demonstrate to the court some form of actual damage, although physical damage to the land is not necessary and a deterioration in health of the occupiers would be classed as damage in this context.

The Attorney-General can be asked by the public to take steps to prevent a *public nuisance*. This is an act which interferes with the rights of a body of people or a community as a whole and may lead to action before the criminal courts.

NEGLIGENCE

The final tort with which the builder and his professional team must be concerned is that of *negligence*. Negligence, at its simplest, is the failure of a person to exercise care towards another person. In many instances of negligence the plaintiff is protected not by the law of tort, but by the law of contract. Although contract has also developed through the common law, legislation imposes statutory duties (in particular a duty of care) on the parties, whether or not these have been specifically agreed between them. Some of these duties will be looked at in detail below. Problems arise when there is no contract between the parties, frequently because the person who suffers is a third party with no direct relationship with the perpetrator of the negligence.

It is plain to see that if we drive carelessly and knock over a child, we should be liable to compensate that child for his injuries. But should we also compensate the mother who suffers shock as a result of seeing the accident? Every careless act does not lead to a successful action for negligence, and the difficulties surrounding the concept of negligence, therefore, hinge on when and the extent to which we should be liable for our actions.

As negligence is a product of our common law system, it has developed this century to reflect our growing demands on society. In the celebrated case in 1932 of *Donoghue* v. *Stevenson* which was heard before the House of Lords, Lord Atkin, in an attempt to define when one's careless actions became legally defined as negligent, said:

> You must take reasonable care to avoid acts or omissions which you can reasonably foresee would be likely to injure your neighbour. Who then in law is my neighbour? The answer seems to be – persons who are so closely and directly

affected by my act that I ought reasonably to have them in contemplation as being so affected when I am directing my mind to the acts or omissions which are called in question.

This 'neighbour principle' put forward by Lord Atkin is still used as the starting point from which claims for negligence are viewed today. This particular case took the unprecedented step of finding a manufacturer liable for injury suffered by the ultimate consumer of his goods, a person completely unknown to him. The House of Lords decided that the manufacturer did know that there would be a consumer and he should have directed his mind to any injury which that person might suffer as a result of his carelessness in production.

Until *Hedley Byrne & Co. Ltd* v. *Heller & Partners Ltd* in 1964, the law did not compensate the third-party victims of negligent advice, damages being limited to those who had suffered some form of immediate physical injury, either to their person or their property. Having been asked increasingly to decide cases where the plaintiff suffered by relying on advice passed on by an intermediary, the court initially took the view that such claims were untenable. It was feared that once the floodgates had been opened, claims would be impossible to resist and, at the same time, it would be unreasonable for a man to be liable for every piece of advice handed on to unknown third parties. In fact, Hedley Byrne opened the floodgates a little and also achieved a restriction on the number of potential claims by making an adviser liable only to those he knew or ought to know would rely on his advice. In this way, a building society surveyor is held liable to a purchaser who relies on his survey, even though the surveyor has no immediate contact with the purchaser and may not even know his name. What the surveyor does know is that if the building society grants the mortgage, someone will have reasonable grounds for assuming that the survey was satisfactory. Similarly, solicitors have been held liable to beneficiaries of wills when poor draftsmanship or inadequate execution has rendered the wills ineffective. The solicitor has no direct relationship with the beneficiary, but the beneficiary falls within the 'neighbour principle' evinced by Lord Atkin.

However, for reasons of public policy, the court has always imposed its own limits on one person's liability. If it did not do so, the potential consequences of an unintentioned, but careless, act could be so far-reaching as to be financially crippling. It has remained a principle in negligence that the victim cannot recover damages (except in the 'professional advice' and a few other isolated situations) for 'economic loss'. Basically, what this means is that the plaintiff can be compensated for his injuries and for damage to other property, but he receives nothing for any ensuing loss. As an example, in the case of *Spartan Steel & Alloys Ltd* v. *Martin & Co. Ltd* in 1972 an employee of the defendant dug up a cable which cut the supply of electricity to the plaintiff's factory. It was decided that the plaintiff could recover damages for the immediate loss of molten material in its furnaces, but could not recover for the loss of profit sustained until the electricity supply was reconnected.

Negligence has developed in this way to encompass new situations until limits of liability, in particular, for professional advisors, were extended quite widely. Then, in 1988, the courts began to cut back. In the case of *D & F Estates Limited* v. *Church Commissioners of England* (1988) the House of Lords decided that the cost of repairing property (in this case, a building) was not recoverable because it was 'economic loss'. This was reiterated by the House of Lords in *Murphy* v. *Brentwood District Council* (1990). All that is now recoverable is damages for loss caused to other property and persons by the negligent act.

Again, in the field of professional advice, the House of Lords has limited the liability of auditors of companies by restricting their responsibility to the existing shareholders and have excluded members of the public who rely on the auditors' report when purchasing shares. (See *Caparo Industries Plc* v. *Dickman* (1990).) It seems likely, from this recent trend, that there will be similar constraints placed on claims in the future.

These examples barely scratch the surface of the law relating to negligence, which is complex and ever-changing. The reader is advised to consult specialist books on this topic for a more thorough treatment. The remainder of this chapter deals with the obligations imposed by statute during and after the building process.

STATUTORY LIABILITY

It has been demonstrated in previous chapters that the builder and others involved with him in development projects are constrained in their activities by a multitude of statutes. The planning legislation dictates *where* he may develop land; the building regulations and environmental protection legislation *how* he may do it. In addition to these controls, other statutory obligations are designed to protect the people who are directly or indirectly affected by the project.

The builder's remaining statutory obligations, and those of others involved in the construction industry, can be subdivided into three categories: obligations to employees; obligations to other persons on the site, and obligations to members of the public. However, the legislation is not neatly packaged in this way and, for ease of reference, is classified below in accordance with the appropriate statute and its subsidiary legislation. It begins by looking at the effect of statutes on the general law of contract and is followed by the Health and Safety at Work etc. Act 1974. This imposes obligations on an employer (and an employee) not only with regard to his own workforce, but also to others who may be affected by the work process. It continues with the legislation that deals with premises or land that are in some way defective or dangerous, and finishes with the Highways Act 1980 and the responsibilities generated by that Act.

The use of the term 'builder' includes, where appropriate, the other persons involved in the development team, such as architects, surveyors, engineers and lawyers, all of whom are subject to the same statutory regulation.

Contractual responsibility

Building and development contracts are usually in one of the standard forms, either that produced by the Joint Contracts Tribunal (JCT) or the Institution of Civil Engineers depending on the type of project. The JCT produces a variety of standard forms to cope with the requirements of different employers. These range from minor works contracts to contracts for nominated subcontractors. The contents of the contract between the parties is a matter for those parties, but statute does intervene by imposing clauses which were not expressed in the contract or by refusing to exclude certain types of liability.

The Supply of Goods and Services Act 1982 implies terms into a variety of contracts, including contracts for work and materials. In particular, ss.13–15 imply that the supplier will use reasonable care and skill, will carry out the contract within a reasonable time and for a reasonable fee. These two latter terms can be overridden by express terms in the contract, but a supplier can never exclude or restrict his liability to use reasonable care and skill. Similarly, the Sale of Goods Act 1979 implies terms as to the fitness for purpose of goods sold. These terms are mandatory in consumer sales, but will also be implied into commercial contracts when it is fair and reasonable to do so.

The Unfair Contracts Terms Act 1977 deals specifically with contracts between parties with unequal bargaining power – the dealer and the consumer. The Act prohibits the enforcement of exclusion clauses which are unreasonable in the circumstances. For these purposes, the employer/client in a building contract may be classed as a consumer if he has no specialist knowledge and, thus, given the protection of the Act, even though it will be a commercial transaction. As a result, it is almost impossible to exclude liability for negligence or for breach of contract because such clauses would be patently unfair and unlikely to be enforced by the courts.

The Act also states that, with regard to business premises, liability can never be excluded for death or personal injury and, again on business premises, any other loss can only be excluded where it is 'reasonable' to do so.

Health and Safety at Work etc. Act 1974 (H&SWA)

Employees

Every employer must, as far as is reasonably practicable, ensure the health, safety and welfare of his employees whilst they are in course of their employment (s.2 H&SWA). This includes the provision of adequate training and supervision, safe plant and machinery and a system of work which minimises risks to health.

Employees also have a duty towards their fellow employees whilst in the course of their employment to take reasonable care, not only for their own safety, but also that of others who may be affected by their acts or omissions (s.7). They must also co-operate with the employer in implementing safe systems of work.

Other persons

Employers must also, as far as is reasonably practicable, ensure that other persons in the working environment are not exposed to risks to their health safety or welfare (s.3 H&SWA).

Premises

Those in control of premises within or upon which persons are employed must, as far as is reasonably practicable, ensure that the premises are safe and without any risk to health (s.4 H&SWA).

All the above sections of the H&SWA are written very generally, giving the court scope for interpretation, in particular, with regard to the meaning of the words 'reasonably practicable'.

Enforcement

The Health and Safety Executive, established under the H&SWA, is responsible for the enforcement of the

Act. It is directly answerable to the Health and Safety Commission, a body given the task of achieving the purpose of the Act, namely to secure the reasonable health, safety and welfare of persons at work and those affected by the activities of persons at work (ss.11 and 1). The Commission has the administrative control of the operation of the Act and provides information and advice on safe practices. It also issues and approves codes of practice (see below) and it has the power to order investigations into accidents. The Executive employs inspectors, although local authorities also have some enforcement functions mainly limited to activities on trade premises, such as in shops.

Inspectors can issue improvement notices (s.21) where the legislation is being contravened and prohibition notices (s.22) where it is believed that the contravention may lead to personal injury. The latter may have immediate effect, but will usually come into force at a time specified in the notice. Appeals against both notices can be made within twenty-one days of service to an industrial tribunal. An improvement notice is suspended during this time, but a prohibition notice remains in force unless the tribunal directs that it be suspended pending the hearing.

Inspectors also have the power to seize items which are believed to be a cause of 'imminent danger' (s.25), and render them harmless by either destruction or other means.

Offences

The Act provides that it is an offence:

1. To fail to discharge a duty.
2. To contravene the health and safety regulations.
3. To contravene the requirements of an improvement notice.
4. To fail to comply with a prohibition notice.

   Fines for all these are at the statutory maximum in the magistrates' court or, on indictment in the Crown Court, are unlimited. Contravention of a prohibition notice can lead to imprisonment by the Crown Court for a maximum of two years. There are also daily penalties of £200 per day.

Note An employee who is injured at work may be able to take action against his employer for compensation on the basis that the employer was in breach of his statutory duty under the H&SWA.

Codes of practice

The codes are not statutorily enforceable, but in the event of an accident or the service of a notice on the employer, the inspector can use the codes to demonstrate a safe system. Breach of them is *prima facie* evidence that the employer was not operating in accordance with the legislation. There are a number of codes covering safety in general, but none specifically relating to the construction industry.

Regulations

The Construction (General Provision) Regulations 1961 (SI 1961 No. 1580)   These regulations relate primarily to safe systems of work with excavations, shafts, tunnels, etc. and the supply of adequate ventilation. Also they prescribe precautions to be taken when dealing with demolition, dangerous machinery and falling materials. Employers with twenty or more employees must appoint a safety supervisor.

Construction (Lifting Operations) Regulations 1961 (SI 1961 No. 1581) Safety in connection with lifting appliances, chains, hoists and ropes is covered by these regulations. Secureness of loads being lifted and carried is also dealt with.

The Construction (Working Places) Regulations 1966 (SI 1966 No. 94) These regulations state that, as far as is reasonably practicable, suitable safe access and egress should be provided to all areas of work. The regulations provide for the construction and maintenance of scaffolds, widths of working platforms, use of guard rails, and methods of work on sloping roofs.

The Construction (Health and Welfare) Regulations 1966 (SI 1966 No. 95) These regulations deal with the provision of washing and toilet facilities, the supply of protective clothing, and adequate shelter from inclement weather.

The Construction (Head Protection) Regulations 1989 (SI 1989 No. 2209) These regulations make it the responsibility of the employer to ensure that, as far as is reasonably practicable, each employee wears suitable head protection when there is any danger of damage to the head. The employee is under a duty to wear the protection supplied. Other appropriate regulations include Protection of Eyes Regulations 1974 (SI 1974 No. 1681) and Health and Safety (First Aid) Regulations 1981 (SI 1981 No. 917).

EC directive

The Construction Sites Directive (92/57/EEC) is due to come into force at the end of 1993 and will be incorporated into UK law at that time. The contents of the directive, which imposes liability on the employer/client or instigator of the development project for health and safety, will have to be taken into account when interpreting our own law. This will have a potentially dramatic impact on the employer as historically the responsibility for safety, etc. 'on site' has been with the main contractor. The employer/client may well have little or no knowledge of the site conditions and will usually have handed over control of the day-to-day management to his professional team or the main contractor.

Occupier's liability

The liability of occupiers of premises is imposed by two statutes: The Occupier's Liability Acts 1957 and 1984. In this context 'premises' includes building and construction sites, as well as movable structures like scaffolding, lifts and ladders. The occupier need not be the owner or anyone with a legal interest in the land, but will encompass all those having some degree of control over the premises. As a result, there may be more than one occupier for the purposes of the Acts.

Act of 1957

A statutory duty of care is imposed by this Act on an occupier, the duty being owed to all lawful visitors on the premises (s.1). 'Visitor' includes those with specific permission and also persons with deemed or implied permission, for example persons who deliver to premises or inspectors with a legal right to enter. The duty extends to taking such care as is necessary to ensure that the visitor is reasonably safe in using the premises for the purpose for which he is permitted to be there. Thus, a visitor who exceeds the permission given to him will not be able to rely on the statutory duty if he is injured.

Exclusion of liability

The occupier is able to exclude his liability or restrict it by giving to the visitor adequate warning of any danger, usually in the form of warning notices or by contract (s.2). Any attempted exclusion has to be read in the light of the Unfair Contracts Terms Act 1977 (see page 190).

Independent contractors

An occupier who takes reasonable steps to rectify any defect in the premises, by employing a suitable independent contractor to do the work, is not liable if those repair works are themselves defective and lead to injury. Furthermore, the occupier is not under the same duty of care to the independent contractor who is on his premises to carry out such work. Whilst he is doing the work the contractor is responsible for his own and his employees' system of working because he has the required knowledge and expertise to deal with the problem. The occupier will be liable if the contractor is unaware of another defect and is subsequently injured as a result of that.

Defence

The occupier has a defence under the Act of *volenti non fit injuria* which basically means that the injured party assented to undergoing the risk. For this defence to succeed, the visitor must voluntarily consent and simply pointing out to him the defect is not sufficient.

Act of 1984

It has been seen that the 1957 Act only imposed a duty in respect of lawful visitors. This duty was extended by the 1984 Act, in a limited way, to trespassers. The Act states that an occupier owes a duty to take such care as is reasonable in all the circumstances to see that the trespasser does not suffer injury. For the Act to apply, the occupier must know or have reasonable grounds for knowing first, that a danger exists on his land; secondly, that the trespasser is in the vicinity of the danger and likely to be injured by it, and thirdly, that it is reasonable for the occupier to take steps to protect the trespasser in all the circumstances of the case (s.1). This section applies equally to persons who are using a public right of way across private land.

Discharge of duty

The occupier can discharge his duty under s.2 of the Act (as long as the premises are not used as part of a business) by giving adequate warning of the danger.

The 1984 Act was passed to protect persons, in particular children, who used private land to the knowledge, albeit without the consent, of the occupier. A building site, for example, unless properly fenced may be used as a playground by children or a short-cut by others. If the occupier knows of its use but does not take reasonable steps to secure such a site, he would be liable for any injury suffered by a person whilst on the site.

At the same time, the legislators wanted to encourage occupiers to allow the public access to the countryside. As long as no charge is made for the grant of access, the occupier is deemed not to be running a business and may successfully exclude liability for the dangerous state of the land, for example the presence of unfenced cliffs or old quarries.

Defective Premises Act 1972

The construction of dwellings is subject to the provisions of the Defective Premises Act 1972. This

Act states in s.1 that any person taking on work for or in connection with the provision of a dwelling owes a duty to ensure that the work is done in a workmanlike manner, with proper materials and so as to be fit for the purpose required.

Other persons, as well as builders, who are involved in the construction are affected by the Act and can be liable for any breach. This will include architects, quantity surveyors, site managers and the like.

The Act does not apply to dwellings which are covered by an 'approved scheme', such as the National House Building Council guarantee scheme, as this already provides protection. Commercial properties are outside the scope of the Act, as are the majority of new dwellings (which are invariably covered by the NHBC), but any conversions of properties to dwellings will be included.

Finally, it is not possible to exclude or limit the operation of the Act by means of a contractual exclusion clause.

Dangerous structures

Liability in respect of dangerous structures can arise under a number of different statutes. Clearly, the Defective Premises Act 1972 and the Occupiers Liability Acts 1957 and 1984 (above) may be relevant for persons who have suffered injury, but the most significant powers lie with the local authority under the Building Act 1984.

Building Act 1984

Where the local authority believes that a building or other structure (perhaps, a wall) is in such a condition or carrying such loads as to be dangerous, it may apply to the magistrates' court for an order (s.77). The order may require the owner to carry out remedial works or to demolish the structure. Failure to comply within the time period specified in the order empowers the local authority to do the work itself and to charge the owner its costs. The owner is also liable to a fine for failing to comply with the order. Alternatively, if the danger results from overloading, the court may restrict the use of the building or structure to obviate the danger.

Urgent action can be taken by the local authority in an emergency (s.78) although, if possible, the owner and occupier should be notified of the local authority's intentions. The local authority can recover its costs in carrying out the work, but the owner or occupier may challenge those costs before the magistrates' court. Also, the owner or occupier may be entitled to compensation under s.106 if the local authority's actions were not justified and the s.77 procedure would have been adequate.

Defective premises which are prejudicial to health or a nuisance can be dealt with by s.76 if the statutory nuisance procedure under the Environmental Protection Act 1990 would be too time-consuming (see Chapter 4). Here, a notice is served on the appropriate person with control of the premises stating that the local authority intends to do certain works and giving the person an opportunity to serve a counter-notice within seven days stating that they will do the work themselves. If no counter-notice is served, the local authority may enter after nine days, do the work and recover its costs. Where the appropriate person does serve a counter-notice, the local authority must wait a reasonable time to allow work to be done, failing which it may enter itself.

If the local authority applies to court to recover its costs, the appropriate person has the right to object on the grounds that the local authority was not justified in taking the action or should have proceeded in a different way.

A building or structure which is so dilapidated as to be detrimental to the amenities of the area may be subject to a notice under s.79. This requires the owner to restore the structure or to demolish it and clear the site. Again, the local authority has the power to enter, do the work and recoup its costs from the owner. The owner has the right to appeal to the magistrates' court against the notice.

Demolition

The Building Act 1984 imposes controls over demolition, although small buildings of less than 1750 cubic feet, agricultural buildings unless they are contiguous to non-agricultural buildings and buildings which are subject to demolition orders under the Housing Act 1985 are not affected. Nor is demolition of an internal part of an occupied building affected if the intention is for the building to remain occupied. In all other circumstances, the person who intends to demolish must notify the local authority under s.80 and must also notify any adjoining occupiers and the gas and electricity authorities. The local authority has six weeks within which to respond by serving a notice under s.81, otherwise the demolition work can proceed. The local authority can impose conditions with regard to the demolition by a notice (s.82) which may require certain works, namely:

1. To shore up adjacent buildings.
2. To weatherproof any exposed surfaces.
3. To make good any damage to adjacent buildings.
4. To remove rubbish and clear the site.
5. To disconnect and seal any sewers or drains.
6. To make good the ground surface.
7. To arrange for disconnection of supplies of gas, electricity and water.
8. To make suitable arrangements with the fire authority (if appropriate).
9. To take such steps as are necessary to protect the public during the work.

Failure of the person undertaking the work to serve the initial notice is an offence and may lead to a fine in the magistrates' court of £2500. It is possible to appeal against the local authority's requirements to the magistrates' court, and one ground of appeal is that the adjoining owner should bear a proportion of the costs.

Town and Country Planning Act 1990

It must be remembered that planning consent is now needed in respect of demolition which is classed as development under s.55 (see Chapter 2 for a full explanation).

Highways Act 1980

Creation and adoption

It was established by case law and is now confirmed by statute that a 'highway' is a way over which there exists a public right of passage. This means that the way must be available for use by all members of the public. Highways were historically created at common law simply by long use, but are now more likely to be created in accordance with statute. The Highways Act 1980 s.24 empowers the Secretary of State for Transport and local highway authorities to create highways to serve their areas and also to acquire land for that purpose. The majority of highways are adopted by the highway authority and are maintained by them at public expense.

For the builder, the most significant section of the Act is s.38 under which the highway authority is empowered to enter into an agreement with the builder to adopt a new road after its construction. A s.38 agreement requires the builder to construct the road in accordance with the standards laid down by the highway authority and to maintain the road for a fixed period after construction. If the highway authority is satisfied with the condition of the road it will automatically adopt it at this time. Most highway authorities require the builder to enter into a 'bond' to support the s.38 agreement. This is usually provided by a bank and ensures that if the builder does not construct the new road adequately then the highway authority can call upon the funds of the bondsman to enable it to carry out the work at no extra cost to itself.

Diversion

It may be necessary for highways to be diverted or stopped up to permit development to proceed. This may only be done by the highway authority, although any person may ask the authority to initiate action (at the cost of the applicant). The highway authority must apply to the magistrates' court for an order for the stopping up or diversion under ss.116 and 117. It must show to the magistrates that the highway is unnecessary or it would be more advantageous to the public to have its route altered.

Note   Public paths can be extinguished by order by the highway authority or the district council if they are proved to be unnecessary under s.118. They can also be diverted (s.119) if it is in the public interest to do so. Either order must be confirmed by the Secretary of State for the Environment after publicity. See the Public Paths Orders and Extinguishment of Public Right of Way Orders Regulations 1983 (SI 1983 No. 23).

Nuisance and obstruction

Although the public have unlimited rights of way on a highway, other activities are strictly controlled by the 1980 Act. The following list of offences is not exhaustive. All prosecutions are before the magistrates' court and the level of fine is shown:

1. Cause damage to a highway, perhaps by digging it up (s.131 – level 3).
2. Make unauthorised marks on the highway (s.131 – level 3).
3. Plough up a public footpath (s.134 – level 3).
4. Cause a wilful obstruction to a highway – note that no actual intention to obstruct is required as long as the act which leads to the obstruction is intended (s.137 – level 3).
5. Place a rope across a highway (s.162 – level 3) or allow water to fall or flow onto a highway (s.163 – level 1).
6. Pull down, remove or obliterate traffic signs (s.131 – level 3).

It is also an offence:

1. To place a skip on a highway without the consent of the highway authority (s.139). The highway authority may impose conditions

when giving consent as to the positioning of the skip, its size and any other safety precautions which it feels are required (level 3).

2. To erect scaffolding over the highway without obtaining the highway authority's consent (s.169). Again, the authority may impose conditions on the grant of consent to ensure safety for road users (level 5).

3. To mix mortar on a highway in such a way that any deposit is left or any residue enters the highway drains (s.170 – level 4).

4. To carry out works which might affect the safety of those using the highway without taking proper precautions, such as the erection of barriers, warning lighting, traffic signs, etc. (s. 174 – level 3).

Lastly, if an accident occurs on the highway when building operations are taking place, the builder can be prosecuted under s.168 unless he can prove that he took all reasonable precautions to protect the public (level 5).

Adjoining land

Where the highway authority believes that land adjoining a highway is dangerous, it may require the owner or occupier to obviate the danger (ss.165–166). Owners or occupiers are also liable to members of the public who are injured by reason of the disrepair or danger presented by adjoining buildings. This includes the presence of glass, barbed wire and spikes, as well as trees which hang over the highway. The highway authority may take action to remove the danger and recover any costs from the owner (s.164).

CONCLUSION

This chapter highlights many of the additional constraints which are placed on the builder and the other members of the development team. Unfortunately, it cannot be a comprehensive list, but it does try to identify those areas of most significance. It makes clear that statutory control reaches into vast areas, from safety precautions for employees whilst they are at work, to precautions to protect trespassers.

CHAPTER 8

COMPULSORY PURCHASE AND COMPENSATION

COMPULSORY PURCHASE

Historical introduction

Compulsory purchase of interests in land authorised by Parliament has existed for more than three hundred years, being employed in the early days to facilitate the provision and extension of canals, the enclosure of land and, later, the development of the railway network and more general requirements for road-building and redevelopment.

There was no general code of compulsory purchase and each new proposal required a private Act of Parliament – a very expensive, time-consuming and uncertain process. Such an Act, introduced in 1801, not only empowered the promoters to take land but set out the procedural basis for acquisition and compensation.

The first Act of general application was the Lands Clauses Consolidation Act 1845 which was to be incorporated into every subsequent Act unless specifically excluded. Over the years, various amending legislation has been passed but the 1845 Act remained the bedrock of compulsory purchase until the passing of the Compulsory Purchase Act 1965. As with the 1845 Act, the provisions of the 1965 Act provided the procedural rules for acquisition and the assessment of compensation which were incorporated into each special public or private Act unless specifically excluded. Now, acquisitions are usually made under public Acts, although it is still possible for a promoter to obtain a private Act with a specific objective incorporating the appropriate part of the compensation procedure. (An example of a recent private Act is the Channel Tunnel Act 1987.)

AUTHORISATION FOR COMPULSORY PURCHASE

Earlier compulsory powers are now consolidated in the Acquisition of Land Act 1981 which applies to the majority of Acts authorising acquisition by public authorities and government departments. There are slight differences of detail in procedure between those prescribed for local and public authorities and those set down for government departments.

Constant codes of compensation

Whatever the authority for acquisition, the procedure and compensation codes are, in the main, constant (although there is an important exception in the case of certain land to which the Third Schedule of the Town and Country Planning Act 1990 applies). Compensation now has its provisions in four separate acts: the Land Compensation Acts 1961 and 1973, the Acquisition of Land Act 1981, and the Planning and Compensation Act 1991.

The final and enduring piece of the jigsaw has been the creation of the Lands Tribunal (replacing the role of Official Referees in this regard) by the Lands Tribunal Act 1949. The tribunal is a specialist court dealing with all aspects of compulsory purchase but, inevitably, the level of compensation (often requiring a consideration of the legal principles determining the basis of the assessment) is the most common cause for reference. The tribunal has a legal chairman but its members tend to be distinguished surveyors of long experience, reflecting the need to interpret the technical valuation arguments often forming the basis of a case. The status of the tribunal is such that there is no appeal against its decisions except on a point of law which then goes either to the Court of Appeal or in certain limited categories of case, direct to the House of Lords.

GENERAL POWER FOR PUBLIC BODIES

In the case of local authorities and other public bodies there exists a general power of compulsory purchase for specific purposes.

Prescribed form   A draft compulsory purchase order must be in the prescribed form (Compulsory Purchase of Land Regulations 1982), served on the interested parties and publicised in one or more local newspapers, inviting objections, describing the purpose for which the land is to be acquired, where a copy of the order and map can be inspected, and specifying the time within which objections must be made to the appropriate minister as confirming authority. At least twenty-one days must be given for objections to be made.

'Interested parties' include every owner, lessee and occupier (except tenants for a period of a month or less). An owner is defined as a person who is entitled to dispose of the fee simple including a tenant with an unexpired term exceeding three years (but not including a mortgagee not in possession). 'Land' includes messages, hereditaments and any other interest defined as land in the Act authorising compulsory purchase.

Creation of new rights over land

The beneficiaries of existing easements over any land affected are not owners within the definition and not included in those groups of people entitled to be served with notice; however, where the acquiring authority wishes to create new rights over land they must be specified in the order and the owner of the servient tenement notified.

Where the owner of land affected cannot be traced, the notice may be delivered to the premises or, if unoccupied, fixed to a conspicuous object on the land.

Written statement of reasons recommended

It is recommended that a written statement of reasons accompanies the formal notice. Where an objection is made and not subsequently withdrawn, a statement of reasons must be sent to individual objectors and to the minister at least twenty-eight days before the date of any public local inquiry. The minister must be informed where the order includes a listed building or land within a conservation area. Where an objection is made to an order by an affected owner or occupier and the notice is not withdrawn, the minister shall hold a public local inquiry or a hearing which requires no public notice that it is to take place.

Concurrent hearings

A highway scheme to which objections have been received and not withdrawn must also be subject to an inquiry under the Highways Act 1980 but both this and the public local inquiry may be heard concurrently. In this case the inspector is appointed by the Lord Chancellor.

Objections other than by owners or occupiers

Persons other than owners or occupiers may object to the order but the minister is not required to hold an inquiry into their objections.

Costs of statutory objector

A statutory objector who is successful is entitled to costs unless exceptional reasons exist for not awarding costs. He is 'successful' where the order is not confirmed or his land is wholly or partly excluded from the order.

Confirmation of order

The inspector reports his findings of fact and makes his recommendations to the minister who may then confirm the order, with or without modification. It was not always the case, but the minister is now required to give reasons for his decision. The confirmation must be publicised in one or more local newspapers and the parties originally entitled to notice informed of the outcome. The acquiring authority must then exercise its powers within three years.

Challenge once confirmed

Once confirmation has taken place, the order can be challenged only by bringing an action in the courts for a declaration or an application for an order of certiorari.

Special Parliamentary Procedure

A compulsory purchase order in respect of National Trust land, held by the Trust inalienably where an objection has been made and not withdrawn, land forming part of a common or open space or being the site of an ancient monument or other object of archaeological interest is subject to special parliamentary procedure. There are exceptions in the case of common land where land is being given in exchange or the amount of land involved is very small (less than 250 square yards).

Order laid before Parliament

The order is laid before Parliament and petitions against it may be presented within twenty-one days when the order comes into operation unless a resolution to annul the order is made by either House.

Challenging the validity of an order

Any aggrieved person (i.e. any person with an interest in the land covered by the order) may challenge the validity of a compulsory purchase order in the High Court on certain grounds concerned with powers or procedure, provided he does so within six weeks of the date of publication of confirmation of the order. An order may be challenged on the ground that it is beyond the power conferred by the 1981 Act or the enabling Act or that the rules have not been complied with, resulting in substantial prejudice to the interests of the person making the application. A minister's decision to make an order or not to confirm an order may be subject to judicial review.

Notice to treat

Notices to treat must be served within three years of confirmation of the compulsory purchase order on all those having an interest in the land specifying the property to which it relates and requiring details of the rights owned and the amount claimed for purchase and any damage that may result from the execution of the works. The notice must be served personally on the person or persons who have an interest in the land and power to sell and convey or release the land or, where they are not known or cannot be traced, affixed to the land. The notice will lose its validity after three years unless:

1. Compensation has been agreed, or
2. The acquiring authority has taken physical possession or served a general vesting declaration, or
3. The matter of compensation has been referred to the Lands Tribunal.

Deemed service

A notice to treat is deemed to have been served in the case of a blight or purchase notice and cannot be withdrawn by the acquiring authority. The claimant's claim in answer to the notice to treat must be submitted within the time limit specified, normally twenty-one days. The response should state the nature of his interest and details of the compensation claimed, including the method of calculation of the amount of each head of claim. Lack of information of this nature may entitle an acquiring authority to withdraw the notice to treat.

Non-submission of claim

In the event of non-submission of a claim or lack of agreement on compensation payable, there is provision for the question of compensation to be referred to the Lands Tribunal. Either party may make such a reference. The Lands Tribunal must ignore any building work or creation of interests which was not reasonably necessary and was undertaken with a view to influencing compensation.

Power to take possession

Service of a notice to treat gives the acquiring authority the right to serve fourteen days' notice of entry and to take possession before compensation has been agreed and paid. In such cases the eventual compensation will carry interest at the prevailing rate from the date of taking possession.

Inferior interests

Inferior interests may be acquired by negotiation after notice to treat or the authority may choose to use landlord and tenant procedures to gain possession, in which case the tenant may not be entitled to compensation. Where the tenant is so entitled, it will be as a result of the contractual landlord and tenant relationship and not arising directly from the compulsory purchase procedures (e.g. compensation for loss of tenancy and tenant's improvements under the Landlord and Tenant Acts 1927 and 1954).

Obtaining possession

Possession may be obtained, if necessary, by instructions to the sheriff and at the expense of the person in occupation. Any entry without authority will involve payment of damages to the occupier.

General vesting declaration

Where the acquiring authority wishes to speed up the procedure it may use the general vesting declaration procedure by serving notice of intent on any owner, lessee or occupier (except tenants for a month or less) at the same time or after making or confirmation of the compulsory purchase order. It cannot be used in cases where a notice to treat has already been served. The declaration can take effect at the expiration of two months or earlier if all occupiers agree in writing, when title to the interests in the land will vest with the authority, conferring on it the right to enter and take possession. The vesting date must be not less than twenty-eight days after the declaration.

Severance

Once these procedures have been completed the authority cannot withdraw, subject to the proviso that, in a case where a notice of severance is served within twenty-eight days of notification of the execution of the declaration, the authority has three months in which to notify the owner that they are not proceeding with the acquisition or that the whole of his land is now included in the general vesting declaration. Alternatively, the authority may refer the notice of objection to severance to the Lands Tribunal. Should the authority fail to take any of the steps described within the time limits, they will be regarded as having withdrawn from any acquisition of the land concerned. Finally, should both parties agree, the acquisition may be discontinued.

Owners unable or unwilling to convey

Owners who are unable or unwilling to convey the property, and in cases where the owner is absent or cannot be traced, may be dealt with by payment of the compensation into court on the basis of a valuation provided by the Lands Tribunal, when the title will be conveyed by deed poll. If the owner subsequently proves his title, he may receive the compensation paid into court and may refer the amount of compensation to the Lands Tribunal. Monies paid into court and not claimed within twelve years can be reclaimed by the authority.

Discovery of other interests

Where an interest is not acquired because of ignorance of its existence, on discovery the authority may remain in possession subject to paying the capital value of the interest and any mesne profits within six months of discovery.

Permission for more valuable use

The Planning and Compensation Act 1991 makes provision for additional compensation where planning permission is obtained for a more valuable use within ten years of acquisition. The compensation is to be reassessed assuming that the further permission was available at the time of the original acquisition date. The additional compensation assessed in this way, together with interest thereon, is to be paid to the claimant.

Wilful entry

Where the acquiring authority or its contractors wilfully enter the land without following one of the procedures outlined above, there is a fixed penalty in addition to which the owner may resort to his common law rights. Where the acquiring authority enters on land through mistake or oversight, the owner will not be able to regain possession: the authority may regularise the position by purchasing that interest, paying interest from the date of entry and recompensing lost profits.

PURCHASE AND BLIGHT NOTICES

In certain circumstances the owner can take the initiative and require an authority to purchase his land. A purchase notice is the appropriate method where planning permission is at issue, whereas a blight notice will be appropriate where a particular property is affected by certain specified events rendering the property unsaleable. In either case, the authority may be required to purchase in advance of their requirements and formal procedures so as to mitigate hardship.

Purchase notices

A purchase notice, whereby an owner can require a local authority to purchase his land, may be served under powers derived from planning or housing legislation.

Under planning legislation

An owner may serve a purchase notice where:

1. Planning permission has been refused or granted subject to conditions, and

   (a) the land has become incapable of reasonable beneficial use either in its existing state or because of the conditions attaching to a planning permission, and
   (b) the land is incapable of reasonable beneficial use for any existing permission or one which the local authority or Secretary of State has undertaken to grant.

2. Planning permission has been revoked or modified; where a discontinuance order is served requiring discontinuance of use, alteration or removal of buildings or works; where listed building consent is refused or granted provisionally, and in certain cases where provided by a tree preservation order to advertisement control regulations.

   In each case the test is whether the land has become incapable of reasonable beneficial use.

Time limits

The purchase notice must be served within twelve months of the decision on the district (or London Borough) council, the council to serve within three months a counter-notice stating either that the council or another specified authority is willing to purchase the land, or that neither authority is willing to purchase the land and that a copy of the notice has been sent to the Secretary of State.

Representations

The Secretary of State invites representations from all parties, holding a hearing or public local inquiry if required to do so. As a result he may confirm the purchase notice (substituting another authority for the council if appropriate), refuse to confirm the notice and grant planning permission or vary any of the conditions imposed or direct that planning permission be granted for development other than that applied for originally.

Effect of earlier planning permission

The Secretary of State is under no duty to confirm a purchase notice where the land should, in accordance with a previous planning permission, remain undeveloped or preserved or laid out as amenity land for the larger area for which planning permission was granted.

Confirmation

Except where there is an appeal against the planning decision before the Secretary of State, the purchase notice will be deemed to be confirmed if the Secretary of State has not made a decision within nine months of the service of purchase notice or six months of the transmission to him of a copy, whichever is the earlier.

Acceptance by council

Acceptance of a purchase notice by the council or other authority or confirmation by the Secretary of State acts as a deemed notice to treat. The matter then proceeds under the provisions for compulsory purchase.

Under housing legislation

An owner may require a housing authority to acquire his premises by service of a purchase notice in two cases:

1. Where a building is so obstructive to other buildings as to make them dangerous or injurious to health, the housing authority may make an obstructive building order requiring it to be demolished. The owner may offer his interest to the local authority which is then responsible for demolition as soon as possible after possession is obtained.

2. Where a housing authority serves a notice requiring improvement of a dwelling in a general improvement area or housing action area or a house outside such areas where occupied by a tenant, the owner may serve a notice within six months requiring the authority to purchase his interest. The authority is deemed to have served a notice to treat and the acquisition proceeds as if it were a compulsory purchase.

Blight notices

**Deemed notice
to treat**

Where local authority planning proposals or decisions result in circumstances in which a property becomes unsaleable it may be possible for the owner to require an authority to acquire the 'blighted' property in response to a deemed notice to treat taking effect two months after the blight notice was served, except where the blight notice was challenged and in which case the date is fixed by the Lands Tribunal. To be successful, the landowner must show that he has made reasonable endeavours to sell and has been unable to do so except at a price substantially below the market value.

This requirement is now waived where a compulsory purchase order exists or where the land is authorised to be acquired by a special Act.

*Withdrawal of blight
notice*

The blight notice may be withdrawn at any time prior to determination of compensation by the Lands Tribunal. Withdrawal has the effect of nullifying the deemed notice to treat.

Fifteen categories of blighted land qualify for service of a blight notice, including:

1. Land included in a structure plan, local plan or unitary plan for the purposes or functions of local authorities.

2. Land indicated on a development plan or land adjacent to the line of a highway and required for a highway or a highway improvement.

3. Land shown on a plan approved by a local highway authority as land required for a new highway or for highway improvements.

4. Land shown on a plan published by the Secretary of State as land required for a trunk road or motorway.

5. Land within a compulsory purchase order authorising the acquisition of rights over the land, but only where a notice to treat has not yet been served.

6. Land in a general improvement area.

7. Land authorised to be acquired by a private Act.

8. Land within an area described as or designated as a new town.

9. Land within an area affected by a slum clearance resolution.

10. Land within a new street order.

11. Land indicated in a plan, not being a development plan approved by a local planning authority as required for the purposes of a public authority.

Persons entitled

The classes of person entitled to serve a blight notice are restricted to:

1. Owner occupiers of any hereditament (including business premises) with a net annual value (NAV) for rating purposes not exceeding £18,000.

2. Owner occupiers of a private dwelling.

3. Owner occupiers of agricultural units.

In each case, the owner occupiers must have been in occupation of the whole or a substantial part of the hereditament for six months immediately preceding the service of a blight notice or a period of six months ending not more than twelve months before the blight notice, since when the property has been unoccupied.

An owner occupier is defined as the freehold owner or a leaseholder with at least three years unexpired; the right to serve a blight notice extends to a mortgagee where he is entitled to exercise his powers of sale, can give vacant possession and has been unable to sell the interest except at a reduced price. Similarly the personal representative of a deceased owner occupier is entitled to serve a blight notice.

Grounds of objection

The authority may serve a counter-notice objecting to the blight notice within a period of two months. The grounds of objection include:

1. That the land is not within the categories of planning blight.
2. That the authority has no intention to acquire any of the land (with, in some cases, a specific number of years quoted).
3. That the person who served the blight notice had no interest in the land on the date it was served.
4. That the claimant does not otherwise qualify (with reasons).

COMPENSATION PROVISIONS

Purchase money

The basis of compensation is market value, although for this purpose the 'market' is defined.

Statutory assumptions are made regarding the planning position although it may be necessary to obtain a formal determination from the local planning authority in the shape of a certificate of alternative permitted development. These assumptions are likely to affect the level of compensation payable and apply in certain specific situations such as comprehensive development areas, buildings of architectural and or historic interest, slum clearance areas and agricultural holdings.

Additional amounts such as home and farm loss

payments are provided for but are not based on valuation principles and are subject to special rules.

Injurious affection

Compensation for injurious affection is applicable only where an owner does not have all or, in some cases, any of his land acquired by compulsory purchase. In such a case the owner has a claim not only for the value of the land acquired but also for any damage to the retained part of the holding arising from its loss. In some few categories, an owner who has no land taken is entitled to compensation also. The rights to such payments have been extended by recent legislation, particularly in the case of depreciation in value caused by the use of public works such as highways. This aspect is dealt with later.

Severance

Provisions for the payment of compensation for severance operate in similar conditions to injurious affection and are aimed at mitigating the effect of the acquisition by providing accommodation works such as fencing of the new boundary or the provision of a cattle creep under a motorway where the roadworks divide the farmland. Although such works are often expensive, the effect is to reduce the inconvenience and therefore possibly to reduce the level of the claim for market value.

Disturbance

In the case of compulsory purchase, the owner may expect to obtain not only the market value of the land but also compensation recognising his right to be placed, so far as money can do it, in the same position as if the land had not been taken from him.

The code accepts that other matters, inappropriate in a normal market transaction, may be compensatable where the acquisition is the result of compulsory purchase powers.

In order to establish a claim for disturbance compensation, the claimant must be an occupier having received a notice to treat (i.e. a freeholder or lessee with an unexpired term exceeding one year).

Acquisition of part only of owner's land

A claimant is entitled to claim disturbance where part

only of his land is acquired, and also where a blight or purchase notice is accepted even though a notice to treat has not been served by the acquiring authority.

Changes in legislation: investment property

Recent changes in legislation have extended the right to an investment owner (i.e. not an occupier) who reinvests in property to claim the incidental costs of purchasing a replacement property within one year of the date of entry.

Compensation under each of the above four subheads (purchase money, injurious affection, severance, and disturbance) is described in more detail below.

The assessment of compensation

Statutory provisions exist to ensure that, as far as possible, the claimant is treated fairly in accordance with the principle of market value, whilst recognising that there should be special provisions to acknowledge, particularly in the area of types of property without a market value and incidental costs and expenses, that the claimant is being required to move.

Compensation rules

There are six rules which are of great importance in the province of compulsory purchase.

Rule 1:
No special allowance

No allowance shall be made on account of the acquisition being compulsory.

This provision is necessary because, in the absence of specific provisions in the early general legislation, the courts had countenanced the basis of value as being value to owner. The practical effect was for valuers to make an addition – ten per cent became customary – to the market value to reflect the reluctance of the vendor, who was in effect forced to sell. In some instances, for example home loss payments, an addition to market value is now sanctioned by statute.

Rule 2:
Willing seller

The value of the land shall, subject as hereinafter provided, be taken to be the amount which the land if sold in the open market by a willing seller might be expected to realise.

This rule reinforces rule 1 in emphasising that the value of the land must be assessed in general at the value which the owner could expect if he wished to make a sale and placed the land on the market. The value will reflect hope value, marriage value and other possible influences which may have the effect of inflating the value, but subject to the limitations of rule 3.

Rule 3:
Special suitability
of land

The special suitability or adaptability of the land for any purpose shall not be taken into account if that purpose is a purpose to which it could be applied only in pursuance of statutory powers, or for which there is no market apart from [the special needs of a particular purchaser or] the requirements of any authority possessing compulsory purchase powers.

Following this rule it has been held that the fact that stone from a quarry had a special value to the acquiring authority could not be reflected in the compensation because that increase was entirely due to the scheme for which the land was acquired – in this case to provide a source of stone required in the construction of a nearby naval base (*Pointe Gourde Quarrying and Transport Co. Ltd* v. *Sub-Intendent of Crown Lands* (1947)) The additional value attaching to an interest because of, for example, the marriage value opportunity is a normal market consideration and should be taken into account in the valuation. The rule as amended (excluding the words in the square brackets) preserves the protection afforded to the acquiring authority not to pay compensation for an element of value which could be realised only by a public body or by the exercise of statutory powers. At the same time, it recognises that in the ordinary market, land sometimes has a special value to an adjoining owner, the special needs of a particular purchaser.

Rule 4:
Unlawful use of land

Where the value of the land is increased by reason of the use thereof or of any premises thereon in a manner which could be constrained by any court, or is contrary to law, or is detrimental to the health of the occupants of the premises or to the public health, the amount of that increase shall not be taken into account.

The most likely contravention would be where the land was being used without planning permission, or where the permission did not wholly cover the current use. Any prospective purchaser would tend to consider the likelihood of action by the local planning authority and of the prospect of its success, in deciding whether to include all or any part of the value attributable to such unauthorised use in the offer made for the land. The 1991 Act changes the period within which enforcement action against breaches of planning control can be taken to ten years. After that time, an unlawful change of use will become lawful. The four year period is retained for building operations and changes of use to a single dwelling.

Rule 5:
Equivalent reinstatement

Where land is, and but for the compulsory acquisition would continue to be, devoted to a purpose of such a nature that there is no general demand or market for land for that purpose, the compensation may, if the Lands Tribunal is satisfied that reinstatement in some other place is bona fide intended, be assessed on the basis of the reasonable cost of reinstatement.

This rule is an extremely valuable one to the claimant in providing an alternative basis of claim in certain cases. It ignores value and enables the claimant to base his claim on the reasonable cost of reinstatement, the land cost and associated fees and expenses. The basis is valuable in the circumstances where it is available because the market value, even if it could be estimated, would be likely to be far less than the cost. The rule has been applied to the reinstatement of churches, hospitals, schools, theatres and working men's clubs.

It will be noted that the Tribunal has a discretion as to whether or not the basis should be used.

Payment for additional facilities   The claim may extend to the provision of enhanced facilities to comply with building regulations or additional planning requirements. For example, should the authority require the provision of car parking spaces where none had previously been provided, the additional claim would embrace both the expense of laying out and constructing the car park and the cost of the additional land necessary to meet the requirements. Increased costs due to unnecessary delay are unlikely to be granted, and the valuer or Tribunal will have regard to the cost of any essential repairs necessary to the existing building by deducting an appropriate amount from the reinstatement cost determined by him or it.

Rule 6:
Disturbance, etc.

The provisions of rule 2 shall not affect the assessment of compensation for disturbance or any other matter not directly based on the value of the land.

The rule is no more than clarification that claims for disturbance can be assessed and pursued in the normal way.

Annual tenants,
tenants at will

For the first time, a tenant with a minor interest is given a right to compensation for 'damage done to him', enabling the effect of termination on other holdings occupied by him as, whether as a freeholder or tenant, to be considered.

BETTERMENT

Principle of set-off

The intention of an authority with powers to purchase compulsorily or the actual acquisition of land may result in an increase in the value of other land. There have been numerous attempts to legislate for the recoupment of such increases in value.

There is no authority to claim for betterment from landowners benefiting from the scheme in some way unless part of the land in the same ownership has been acquired. In such a case, betterment of contiguous or adjacent land retained by the person entitled to the relevant interest in the same capacity may be claimed as a set-off against compensation otherwise payable for the land taken.

DATE OF VALUATION

General understanding

For many years it was generally understood that the date of valuation was fixed by the date of service of a notice to treat by the acquiring body. Such a rule would tend to lead to under-compensation in inflationary times and the issue was tested in *Birmingham Corporation* v. *West Midlands Baptist (Trust) Association*, decided by the House of Lords in 1969 (a rule 5 case) where the basis of compensation was that of equivalent reinstatement. The Lords held that the proper date to assess the cost was the date on which reinstatement could reasonably commence.

In the more usual case of an assessment of value on the basis of market value (rule 2), the appropriate date for assessing the value of the estate or interest to be acquired is the date when compensation is agreed or assessed (unless possession has already been taken, in which case the date on which possession was taken is the appropriate date).

The circumstances existing on the date of valuation have to be taken into account. For example, if the tenant has vacated the premises at the date of valuation, no account will be taken of the lease terms under which he occupied when valuing the interest of the landlord. The change in circumstances could, in some instances, have a significant effect on value. There is an exception where the acquiring authority has rehoused a tenant of residential accommodation in pursuance of its statutory obligation, when the acquiring authority is deemed to have taken possession on the date on which the tenant is rehoused. As a result, the valuation will be subject to the existing tenancy, preventing the owner from gaining a financial benefit from being able to offer the property with vacant possession.

When compensation is assessed by the Lands Tribunal, the date of valuation is the date of the award: the date remains the same even if there is an appeal to the Court of Appeal following which the case is remitted to the Tribunal.

Where the general vesting declaration procedure is used, the date of valuation is the date of vesting when title passes to the acquiring authority together with the right of entry.

COMPENSATION WHERE NO LAND IS TAKEN

Limited rights to compensation

An owner whose land is affected by actions of the acquiring authority but none of whose land is acquired has only limited rights to compensation. Such an owner may qualify for compensation for injurious affection caused by the construction or execution of public works and/or depreciation caused by the subsequent use of the works.

Damage caused by execution of works

Where damage is caused by execution of the works, statutory compensation is payable but the claimant must first satisfy each of the following rules (the McCarthy rules) laid down in *Metropolitan Board of Works* v. *McCarthy* (1874):

1. The action causing injury to or depreciation of the claimant's land is authorised by statute.
2. That injury would be actionable at law but for the existence of statutory authority.
3. That damage arises from a physical interference with some public or private right in land which the owner of that interest is entitled to enjoy.
4. The damage must arise from execution of the works and not by their subsequent use.

Assessment of compensation

Compensation is assessed on the basis of the diminution in value of the claimant's land on the date when the works are completed. The claim should include both present and future depreciation in value since it is not possible to make a further claim.

Liability is restricted to cases where there is express or implied immunity. Where it is claimed that there is no such immunity (resulting in failure of the claim for compensation), the claimant may later proceed in nuisance in respect of which the authority cannot claim immunity.

Depreciation caused by use of works

Where depreciation is caused by the use (as contrasted to the execution) of public works there is provision for compensation whether or not land is taken.

Physical factors caused by use of public works

Where the value of an interest is depreciated by physical factors caused by the use of public works, the interest qualifies for compensation.

The public works are defined as any highway, any aerodrome and any works on land (not being a highway or aerodrome) provided or used in the exercise of statutory powers. The physical factors are defined as noise, vibration, smell, fumes, smoke, artificial lighting and the discharge onto the land in respect of which the claim is made of any solid or liquid substance.

Assessment of compensation

Compensation is assessed on the basis of a valuation date twelve months after use of the works commenced (the relevant date). The depreciation in value should be assessed giving credit for any grant-aided work undertaken to mitigate the effect of the public works. The effect on any building or extension completed after the relevant date is excluded from consideration, as is a change of use.

Occupiers of mobile homes, etc.

Occupiers of mobile homes, caravans, etc. affected by noise from the construction or use of public works may benefit from a discretionary power available to acquiring authorities to make a payment.

DISTURBANCE

Rule 6 providing for the assessment of compensation for disturbance envisages payment for loss occasioned by disturbance to the owner and which is not related to or reliant on any determination of market value.

The general principle of disturbance is that loss sustained by the dispossessed owner may be properly compensatable provided that, 'it is not too remote and that it is the natural and reasonable consequence of the dispossession', [*Harvey* v. *Crawley Development Corporation* (1957)]. Disturbance is payable to any occupier, freeholder or lessee with an unexpired term exceeding one year, where the land is acquired compulsorily.

Expenditure before notice to treat

In a series of cases it has become clear that compensation for disturbance may include relevant expenditure incurred or losses accrued before service of notice to treat if the disturbance is the natural and reasonable consequence.

Duty to mitigate loss

The claimant has a duty to mitigate his loss and in general will be required to set benefits against his claim. Where a claimant gains value for money from expenditure on any replacement property, a disturbance claim will not succeed (although, as noted later, costs of adaptation may well qualify).

Total loss of goodwill

In certain limited cases, the total loss of goodwill may be claimed. The provision applies where the claimant is over sixty years old, occupied premises having a rateable value not exceeding £18,000, and has not and will not dispose of the goodwill of the whole of the trade or business.

In all cases a claimant must take all reasonable steps to mitigate his loss. If, in so doing, he receives value for money, such expenditure will not be recoverable in a claim for compensation.

Goodwill generally

Apart from the special provisions noted above, a diminution or complete loss of goodwill is potentially compensatable, subject to the duty to mitigate loss.

Costs of reinvestment

Hitherto, only occupiers could claim disturbance compensation. This limitation has now been lifted to enable owners of investment property to claim incidental costs of purchase when a replacement property is purchased within one year of the date of entry.

Taxation of disturbance compensation

Disturbance compensation will be taxable where any part of it represents taxable capital or income. It follows that disturbance compensation should be payable gross of tax and dealt with in the accounts of the business in the normal way.

Development value

Where the owner establishes development value as the basis of compensation for his holding, it is not possible also to claim disturbance to the activity carried on which would disappear on redevelopment.

Fees

The claimant is entitled to claim professional fees, covering legal expenses and surveyors fees, based on a scale agreed between the Inland Revenue and the Royal Institution of Chartered Surveyors (Ryde's Scale).

Use of public works

Statutory recognition was given in 1973 to the concept that use of public works could result in depreciation which should, in certain circumstances, be compensatable.

Admissibility

A claim for compensation is admissible where it can be shown that depreciation in the value of an interest in land is due to physical factors – noise, vibration, smell, fumes, smoke, artificial lighting or the discharge into land of any solid or liquid substance – caused by the use of the works where the authority is immune to an action in nuisance by virtue of its statutory powers (except in the case of a highway where there is a claim regardless of whether or not the authority is immune from action for nuisance).

Physical factors

The physical factor(s) cited must be on or in the public works except in the case of an aerodrome where the effects of aircraft arriving and departing are to be treated as caused by the use of the aerodrome even when outside its boundaries.

Qualifying interest

The claimant must have held a qualifying interest in a dwelling or land at the relevant date. A qualifying interest is defined as an owner's interest being either a fee simple or a tenancy with three years or more to run, in the latter case the owner occupying the dwelling as his residence at the relevant date.

Status of owner

Where the interest is in land other than a dwelling, the claimant must not only have an owner's interest but also be an owner occupier, being a person who occupies the whole or a substantial part of the land and with a rateable value or net annual value, where not a dwelling or an agricultural unit, not exceeding £18,000.

Costs

Legal costs together with stamp duty on the purchase of another (comparable) property may be claimed and surveyors fees in reporting on that property. Such claims were restricted to owner occupiers, but in certain circumstances the incidental costs of replacing investment property may now be claimed.

Costs of the conveyance of land acquired are payable by the acquiring authority. Expenditure prior to notice to treat is not covered by this provision, though it may be possible to claim such expenses as part of the general disturbance claim. Where the purchase does not proceed, the owner will have no right to claim for reimbursement of costs unless the negotiations took place on the basis that reasonable fees would be paid regardless of the outcome of the negotiations. There is provision for taxation of costs.

Fees

Professional fees for the negotiation of the claim and the legal work entailed are not part of the claim but are paid by the acquiring authority on the basis of published extra-statutory scales in respect of both solicitors' and surveyors' fees (see Appendix 2).

Interest

Interest is payable on the unpaid purchase monies from the date of entry (whether under the powers of entry or on entry by consent) at a rate prescribed by statutory order from time to time.

Interest where reference to tribunal

Where the matter is referred to the Lands Tribunal, it may award interest on the amount of compensation determined from the date of the award. Interest is not at the statutory rate (above) but, by virtue of a provision in the Arbitration Act 1950, at that rate which could be awarded by a court on a judgement debt.

Disturbance payments

Eligibility

A person with an interest in land which is acquired compulsorily is entitled to compensation for disturbance over and above the value of the interest acquired, as described earlier.

Where an occupier in lawful possession has no compensatable interest in land, he may nevertheless be eligible for a disturbance payment where he is displaced in one of the following circumstances:

1. By compulsory purchase.
2. By the making or passing of a housing order or resolution.
3. By redevelopment of land already acquired by an authority possessing compulsory powers.

In particular, a disturbance payment is not available where an owner occupier's supplement is payable.

Amount of payment

The amount of the payment is to be equal to the reasonable expenses of removal together with, in the case of a trade or business, any loss resulting from disturbance. The latter provision requires regard to be had to the likely security of tenure and the availability of suitable alternative premises (except in the case of traders aged sixty or over who opt for compensation for total extinguishment). Payments are not taxable.

Business tenant choice

A business tenant may have a compensatable interest under s.37 of the Landlord and Tenant Act 1954 but, if that is the case, he is entitled to choose between that and a disturbance payment.

Further payment

A further payment may be claimed where a dwelling has been modified structurally to meet the special needs of a disabled person, the amount to be assessed so as to provide reasonably similar alterations to the new premises.

Discretionary payments

There is provision in certain limited classes of case to make discretionary payments for disturbance.

Disputed payments

Any dispute as to the amount of a disturbance payment is referred to and determined by the Lands Tribunal.

Home loss payments

Any person who is displaced from a dwelling is entitled to a home loss payment, subject to the following qualifications. The person displaced must have occupied the dwelling as his main residence for a minimum of five years. The claim must be made within six months of displacement. Where the applicant has lived in the property for five years but not for the whole of that time in a qualifying capacity, the period can be achieved by including the period of occupancy of his predecessors.

Provisions have been introduced to enable the spouse of an owner who no longer occupies the matrimonial home to qualify for a home loss payment. Compensation must then be paid not later than three months after the date of the claim.

No payment is available where the dwelling is acquired by agreement.

Availability of loan

Where a person is entitled to a home loss payment, the acquiring authority may grant a loan to enable that person to acquire or construct another dwelling in substitution for the house which has been acquired. To be eligible, he must either have been the freeholder or have held a lease with not less than three years unexpired at the date of acquisition. The loan is repayable and will be secured by a charge on the new dwelling. In addition, the acquiring authority may pay any expenses incurred by the displaced person in acquiring a substitute dwelling.

Occupier of agricultural unit

The occupier of an agricultural unit displaced from his dwelling is also entitled to a home loss payment where the conditions are satisfied.

Farm loss payments

Farm loss payments are provided to compensate temporary losses incurred in moving as a result of compulsory purchase from one unit to another.

To qualify, the claimant must be in occupation as

freeholder or as a tenant (including an annual tenant). He must be displaced from the whole or a sufficient part (defined as not less than 0.5 hectares) of the land and begin farming again elsewhere not more than three years after the date of displacement. Where the annual tenant is served with a notice to quit, he may elect to claim compensation as though notice of entry had been served. This provision has been extended to apply to tenants of Crown Lands.

Move in advance

The claimant may move from the holding in advance of displacement and at any time after the making of the compulsory purchase order, even where the acquiring authority has not required him to do so. The 1991 Act provides for payment even where the farm is compulsorily acquired following service of a blight notice by the claimant.

Amount of claim

The claim is equal to the average annual profit derived from the use of the land over a period of the last three years, with provision where the land has been occupied for a shorter period, that period. In computing profits, a notional rent is deducted (in place of any rent actually paid) and there are provisions to exclude profits arising from any activity where compensation representing temporary or permanent loss of profits has been agreed. Where the value of the farm compulsorily acquired exceeds that of the new farm, the amount of the farm loss payment will be reduced proportionately. Also, there are limitations where the land has development value.

Time limit for claims

Claims must be made within twelve months of the claimant starting to farm the new unit.

Home loss payments

The occupier of an agricultural unit displaced from his dwelling is entitled to a home loss payment in accordance with the general principles of such payments.

Costs and interest

Reasonable valuation and legal costs may be included and interest runs on unpaid payment from the date the claimant starts to farm.

Discretionary payments
when acquisition is
by agreement

There is provision for discretionary farm loss payments where land acquired by agreement by an authority possessing compulsory powers would have qualified for a payment had the acquisition been compulsory.

THE LANDS TRIBUNAL

Jurisdiction

Where there is a dispute as to the amount of compensation to be paid on an acquisition by compulsory purchase the matter may be referred to the Lands Tribunal. The tribunal also has jurisdiction in appeals from decisions of local valuation courts and determinations by government departments; disputes in relation to compensation on compulsory purchase or capital taxes, applications for the modification or discharge of restrictive covenants, and settlements of compensation payable where an owner is absent or unknown. The tribunal may also act as an arbitrator under a reference by consent.

Reference to the Lands Tribunal

The acquiring authority can refer to the Lands Tribunal any case where the person served with a notice to treat does not within twenty-one days of service state particulars of the claim or treat with the acquiring authority. The tribunal may also deal with the apportionment of rent or rent-charge under a lease of land where only a part is being acquired. It will also determine any dispute as to the question of a blight notice. The claimant may initiate proceedings by giving notice of reference to the registrar.

General procedure

Any reference is registered and a copy sent to the other party or parties. The tribunal sits in public and receives evidence given orally. A party may appear in person, by counsel, solicitor (who has a right of audience) or, with leave of the tribunal, by any other person.

The tribunal will normally consist of one member, or two where the case is of some complexity. The number of expert witnesses is limited to one on each side subject to the ability of the Tribunal to waive the limitation where it thinks fit and to allowing a further witness on either side in relation to a claim for business disturbance or minerals.

Sealed offers and costs

In cases of disputed compensation on compulsory purchase, the acquiring authority is likely to make an unconditional offer in writing of the sum which it is prepared to pay as compensation; a sealed copy is provided to the tribunal marked 'sealed offer'. Once the tribunal has made its award, the sealed offer will be opened. The amount of the offer in relation to the award will determine liability for costs. Where the tribunal awards an amount in excess of the sealed offer, the acquiring authority will be liable for costs. Where the amount awarded is equal to or less than the sealed offer the claimant will be liable for all costs incurred after the offer was made. The tribunal may direct that any sum awarded carries interest from the date of the award. Where appropriate, the expert witnesses' valuation and other details must be submitted in advance and copies will be sent to the other party. Evidence is given under oath. The tribunal will act as an arbitrator and base itself on the evidence presented, using its expert knowledge only in interpretation, not in determination.

Case stated

Either party may ask the tribunal to state a case on a point of law within six weeks of the award. The hearing will be by the Court of Appeal or, in certain limited categories of cases, may be referred direct to the House of Lords.

Preliminary hearing on point of law

The tribunal may hold a preliminary hearing on any point of law. The decision must be given in writing together with a statement of the tribunal's reasons. Where dependent upon a decision on a point of law, the tribunal should give an alternative award had the question of law been decided differently.

CHAPTER 9   # GRANT AID FOR DEVELOPMENT PROJECTS

GRANT AID IN THE 1990s

For certain types of development project the availability of grant aid is a significant or even critical factor in the decision to go ahead. In the inner cities in particular, many schemes under construction, companies in expansion, or dwellings in occupation, owe their existence to direct or indirect grant support. This does not mean that the grant was the only source of funding, but it can be, and often is, a substantial percentage. When government, public agencies or private trusts wish to encourage development, economy diversification, conservation, or some other activity which may be, at best, marginally profitable, grants or favourable loans, even in our market-led society, are possible where the scheme is carefully devised to qualify. A full list of grant-making bodies would be lengthy indeed. This chapter shows the main sources of funds, selected on the basis of their scale and relevance to the general field of land, buildings and environment. The larger grant-making organisations, and the larger grants, tend to involve property and building-related projects.

The first substantial development-related grant aid came about in the post-war period as governments attempted to influence developers and industrialists in their decisions where to build. The modern equivalent of these grants remains in the Department of Trade and Industry's Regional Selective Assistance supported by other government and European Community programmes which have emerged in the past two decades. The maximum utilisation of different sources of assistance is a skill in itself but it would not be out of the question for a mixed commercial and industrial project in an inner city to attract support from three or four grant programmes if it happens to occupy the right site.

PRINCIPLES OF GRANT AID

Grants are offered for a variety of reasons, some quite obvious and others much less so. A grant may be received for undertaking an action which one was committed to in the first place: in which case it is a luxury. More frequently it is something which is necessary to make a project viable and is calculated to be no greater than the minimum to achieve this objective. In some cases, it may be offered as an inducement to undertake a scheme which would not otherwise have been considered. Many grant-awarding powers allow the giving of loans or a mix of loan and grant. Loans may be very favourable with deferred payments and low or nil interest.

APPLYING FOR GRANT AID

A few general rules apply to most forms of grant aid which, if followed, make the chances of a successful outcome more likely.

1. Most grants are discretionary, or at least some element in the process of grant-making, perhaps timing or the amount of help, is a matter for the grant body's judgement. The case should be presented carefully and politely.
2. Usually the grant application should be made in advance. In certain cases the start of work will disqualify the scheme from assistance. It is important to allow sufficient time for the application to be processed. This may be months in some cases.
3. It is sometimes necessary to have already secured other approvals necessary for the scheme to go ahead. Planning permission, for instance, may be required or at least some informal support for the development indicated by the local authority.
4. The scheme may need to be worked up to quite a level of detail. This often means a full exercise in costing and valuation. The grant-making body will often wish to see the margin by which the scheme falls short of being self-financing and may have its own ways of checking submitted costs, estimates and accounts. The grant-making body may have rules requiring a building project to be supported on the basis of the lowest of competitive tenders.
5. A statement may have to be submitted identifying the financial health of the company or other organisation making the application. The grant-making body may be concerned not just with the balance sheet but with the character and scaie of the applicant company. For example, is it part of larger, wealthy group? What are its articles of association? And how is it

controlled? Means testing of individuals is quite common for housing and related grants.

6. The public benefit of the project will usually have to be made quite clear. How many jobs is it creating? Or how important is the building or site to the community? The application may have to be supported by information to demonstrate its value in this respect. Photographs, statements of support from others, and so on, may be essential. Some grant-making bodies may not know the site in question and come to their decision on the basis of written submissions alone.

7. In some cases the rules of one grant-making body may prohibit a payment where other grant help has been given. This is common with some types of government assistance where the department involved may wish to ensure it is not helping a project which is already receiving support from another public source.

THE OFFER OF SUPPORT

The addage 'there is many a slip between cup and lip' is worth remembering with grant aid. Grant offers are seldom made without conditions and cheques are not usually released until the work is completed or at least at a certain stage. Conditions can be wide-ranging, covering work quality, recording of progress, independent audit, and so on. Indeed, almost anything may be required (for example, listed building grants might include a requirement to permit public access to the property, even if it is your own family house). In most cases the grant will be subject to a time limit on its uptake. This is clearly important from the grant body's accounting point of view. It will not wish to give an open-ended commitment. In some cases the grant must be accepted within a matter of weeks and the work completed within the financial year. If the conditions are not acceptable then do not go ahead with the work. The selling-on of the completed project might be forbidden under the grant, at least for a certain number of years. It is dangerous to assume that once the cheque is in your hands the money is safe since many grants are subject to 'clawback' provisions which, if properly drafted, are entirely enforceable.

PROFESSIONAL HELP WITH GRANT AID

In cases where the project is large or complex, or the potential for grants from more than one source exists, the appointment of specialist advisers may be necessary. The professional discipline of these consultants will vary depending upon the case but their job will be to maximise the grants/loans available avoiding adverse terms and conditions. An example of how they might help may be useful. The project might be, say, to repair, refurbish and extend a block of properties, some of which are listed, in an urban area. The consultant's job is to assign elements of the work to particular categories of grant. Thus repairs to the listed building are targeted to a conservation source, general refurbishment to another, and some element of the revenue costs to a third. If you or your organisation does not qualify for grant aid it may be necessary to set up a company, partnership or trust that does. Other parties may need to be drawn in to help make the scheme qualify. Some parts of the project may have to be set up as stand-alone elements. An additional trick is to make sure none of these bodies impose conditions which conflict with another. It may be comforting to know that in most cases the cost of employing consultants can usually be included in the overall project sum for which grant aid is being sought.

SOURCES OF GRANT AID

Architectural Heritage Fund
27 John Adam Street
London   WC2N 6HX
071-925 0199

Low-interest loans
Short-term, low-interest loans are granted by the Fund for conversion or rehabilitation of historic buildings, structures and gardens to registered revolving building preservation trusts and other charitable organisations. Usually limited to not more than fifty per cent of costs, with an upper limit of £175,000 and a repayment period of two years. The usual intention is to provide working capital to charities operating a rolling programme of acquisition, repair and sale. The annual rate of interest is five per cent.

Feasibility studies grants
The Fund may give a feasibility studies grant where projects involve buildings likely to qualify for an Architectural Heritage Fund loan but which cannot proceed without a feasibility study to examine complex structural, end use, or financial problems.

Feasibility studies grants are intended for problem buildings involving more than basic repair and rehabilitation, and are payable to revolving trusts only. Grants are normally up to fifty per cent of cost (but an Architectural Heritage Fund contribution will not exceed £5000), and are paid on completion of the feasibility study.

Arts Council of Great Britain
14 Great Peter Street
London   SW1P 3NQ
071-333 0100

An annual budget (£50,000 in 1990) assists feasibility studies for building projects involving museums and art galleries.

Department of the Environment
Inner Cities Division
Marsham Street
London   SW1P 3EB
071-276 3000

Except for urban programme grants, the most useful first point of contact will be the appropriate regional office (see Appendix 3).

The Secretary of State for the Environment has designated fifty-seven areas of England which are eligible for Urban Programme funding under the Inner Urban Areas Act 1988. Designation allows certain types of Department of the Environment (DoE), local authority and EC monies to be spent in these areas including City Grants and Urban Programme Grants referred to below. The designated areas are split between partnership status and programme status with the former receiving more generous provision. The full lists are:

> *Partnership:* Birmingham, Islington, Manchester, Gateshead, Lambeth, Newcastle, Hackney, Liverpool, Salford.
>
> *Programme:* Barnsley, Blackburn, Bolton, Bradford, Brent, Bristol, Burnley, Coventry, Derby, Doncaster, Dudley, Greenwich, Halton, Hammersmith and Fulham, Haringey, Hartlepool, Hull, Kensington and Chelsea, Kirklees, Knowsley, Lanbaurgh, Leeds, Leicester, Lewisham, Middlesbrough, Newham, North Tyneside, Nottingham, Oldham, Plymouth, Preston, Rochdale, Rotherham, St Helens, Sandwell, Sefton, Sheffield, South Tyneside,

Southwark, Stockton-on-Tees, Sunderland, Tower Hamlets, Walsall, Wandsworth, Wigan, Wirral, Wolverhampton, The Wrekin.

City Grant

A City Grant is a grant or loan towards any employment generating or private housing project in one of the fifty-seven areas listed above. The grant guarantees scheme feasibility including reasonable developer profit, and projects may involve new buildings and/or building refurbishment. In order to qualify, completed work must have an end value exceeding £500,000. Individual grants can be large (frequently measured in millions of pounds). The DoE can be flexible depending on the nature of the scheme and the particular area but usually seeks a private sector weighting of better than 3:1. This grant was introduced in 1988 replacing Urban Development Grant, Urban Regeneration Grant, and Private Sector Derelict Land Grant.

Urban Programme Grants

Urban Programme Grants are made for schemes which provide economic, social, environmental benefits in one of the fifty-seven designated inner areas. Typical projects might include conversion of a building to provide workshops, offices, sports or community facilities. Projects must be submitted to the DoE through the local authority, which must indicate support. Money then comes from the local authority which receives seventy-five per cent of its outlay from the DoE. Enquiries should be to the district council, although in some cases the applicant may be encouraged to discuss his case with the county council.

Derelict Land Grants

A Derelict Land Grant may be paid to local authorities for restoration of land which is incapable of reasonably beneficial use to bring it to a condition where it has improved value, utility or appearance. Schemes which involve a 'hard' end use, that is one which involves some form of building or other development, are particularly sought. Rates vary from fifty to one hundred per cent depending on the area of the country.

City Challenge

The City Challenge is a packaging arrangement for City Grants, Urban Programme Funds, Derelict Land Grant, and Housing Corporation funds introduced in 1991. The fifty-seven cities, boroughs and towns designated under the Inner Urban Areas Act 1988 are invited to bid for blocks of money top-sliced from these sources and guaranteed to the authority's area over a five year period. City Challenge has winners and losers. The successful areas in 1991 and 1992 have been promised £37.5 million over the five years to spend on one particular part of their area (in most cases between 150 and 400 hectares). Successful bids for City Challenge have to show vision, value for money (in grant terms), and promise successful delivery of projects within the five year period. During publication of this book the Secretary of State has indicated he will not invite City Challenge submissions in 1993.

Department of Trade and Industry
Kingsgate House
66–74 Victoria Street
London   SW1E 6SW
071-215 0574

Regional Selective Assistance

Regional Selective Assistance is designed to encourage the creation of or safeguard employment in the manufacturing and service sectors in Assisted Areas under Section 7 of the Industrial Development Act 1982. Grants are discretionary and need must be demonstrated. The amount is based on the fixed capital cost of the project and the number of jobs to be created/safeguarded: assessors expect to see the major part of the project funded from private sources. The grant is paid in stages related to private investment or the actual creation of jobs. The DTI will usually direct applicants to the regional DTI office for detailed guidance.

Regional Enterprise Grants

The Regional Enterprise Grant is for investment projects involving firms with fewer than twenty-five employees in the Assisted Areas. A maximum fifteen per cent of eligible costs is payable, with a ceiling of £15,000. The grants are designed to encourage projects which involve investments in fixed assets or the development of new products and processes but this can include building/property-related work in some circumstances. There is no requirement to produce any new jobs. The DTI will usually direct applications to the regional DTI office for detailed guidance.

English Heritage
(Historic Buildings and Monuments Commission for England)
Fortress House
23 Savile Row
London   W1X 2HE

Building in Conservation Areas Grants (s.77 Planning (Listed Buildings and Conservation Areas) Act 1990)

The Buildings in Conservation Areas Grant is a discretionary award for structural repairs (walls, roofs, dry rot, etc.) and restoration of important features of listed and unlisted buildings in conservation areas. The grant usually forms part of a programme of work which the Historic Buildings and Monuments Commission (HBMC) has invited or which the local planning authority has encouraged as a joint venture involving a number of properties. The grant can sometimes be used initially for just one important local building as a way of encouraging other repair work nearby. Environmental works, particularly in the vicinity of buildings being repaired, are also subjects for grant-aid. The total value of work must exceed a minimum figure, and the grant is usually twenty-five per cent of project costs. There must be a minimum of £4000 of eligible works.

Outstanding Buildings Grants (s.3A Historic Buildings and Ancient Monuments Act 1953)

Outstanding Buildings Grants are for exceptional secular buildings and places of worship in use which are in need of comprehensive major repairs. The description can be extended to cover special furniture items, outbuildings, garden structures, and so on. Applicants can include individuals, trusts and local authorities, but not government departments or public agencies with more than fifty per cent funding from the exchequer. The grant is usually set at forty per cent of eligible costs, although churches may receive up to fifty per cent, and minimum eligible works must exceed £10,000 (reduced to £5000 for churches). Buildings must be determined 'outstanding' by English Heritage, and only some two to three per cent from the statutory list would be likely to qualify. Grade I status is not a guarantee, and some grade Grade II* and even Grade II buildings do qualify on detailed inspection.

Town Scheme Grants (ss.79–80 Planning (Listed Buildings and Conservation Areas) Act 1990)

A Town Scheme is an arrangement whereby the HBMC and the local authority conclude a repair grant scheme setting aside matching sums of money for grant aid within a conservation area. Listed properties and unlisted properties with townscape importance qualify. Structural and external items are the main targets. The total support to the applicant is normally forty per cent of eligible works (that is, twenty per cent from the council and twenty per cent from the HBMC). The majority of Town Schemes are now administered by local planning authorities under delegation agreements from the HBMC.

Acquisition Grants (s.5B National Heritage Act 1983)

Acquisition Grants are available to local authorities who use the compulsory purchase provisions to acquire a building which is at risk. The HBMC must be satisfied that the building has real value, that the local planning authority's action is necessary, and that an adequate provision is being made for repair and use. Some repayment may be necessary if the building is sold at a profit.

Buildings at Risk Grants (s.3A Historic Buildings and Ancient Monuments Act 1953, or s.77 Planning (Listed Buildings and Conservation Areas) Act 1990)

Buildings at risk are dealt with as special s.77 or s.3A cases. Grants are intended to ensure a listed building in poor condition survives until a new use can be found. The grant is usually payable at twenty-five per cent of eligible costs, although councils taking Repairs Notice action and unable to recover costs from the owners may attract up to fifty per cent support. Preservation Trust and amenity societies are encouraged to apply.

London grants

London grants are available (usually up to twenty-five per cent of eligible costs) for listed buildings in pursuance of English Heritage's special responsibility for the former GLC area. Recent changes have lead to such grants being available only for buildings which are seen to be at risk.

Grant to National Trust (s.5B, Historical Buildings and Ancient Monuments Act 1953)

Discretionary grants are made to the National Trust to defray, in whole or in part, the Trust's costs in acquiring buildings and gardens of historic interest and any adjacent associated lands.

Scheduled Ancient Monuments Grants (s.24 Ancient Monuments and Archaeological Areas Act 1979)

Schedule Ancient Monuments Grants are given for repair and conservation and, exceptionally, for acquisition. The amount is normally forty per cent of eligible costs.

Gardens grants

Garden grants have been given for tree clearance and replanting in gardens of historic interest damaged during the two major storms in 1987 and 1990. This has been the only grant aid directly available to gardens. In many cases, garden buildings, bridges, and other built features within gardens may attract grant aid in their own right under regimes referred to above. HBMC has set out a plan to make general garden repair and restoration grants available from 1 April 1993.

Cathedrals grants

The new grants scheme (initially of three years duration) started in 1991 is designed to ensure that urgent repairs to cathedrals are carried out promptly and to an appropriate standard in tandem with the new Care of Cathedrals Measure.

Scheduled Ancient Monuments Management Grants (s.17 Ancient Monuments and Archaeological Areas Act 1979)

Small management payments are made to owners of certain scheduled ancient monuments for sympathetic management.

English Tourist Board
Thames Tower
Black's Road
Hammersmith
London   W6 9EL
081-846 9000

Tourism Development Grants

Tourism Development Grants are made towards conversions, refurbishments and new buildings in connection with visitor accommodation, particularly using redundant farm buildings. The system has assisted for example in the creation of hotels in historic towns. Tourism Related Grants both of up to £200,000 (and occasionally more) were available until suspension in 1989 when it was considered there was adequate private investment to make tourism projects successful. The legal provision for grant payment remains (s.4 Development of Tourism Act 1969), though, and with the tourism industry in the doldrums the possibility of reintroduction for capital projects cannot be discounted.

Tourism Development Grants remain available in Wales and are covered later under 'Welsh Tourist Board'.

European Commission
London Office
8 Storeys Gate
London   SW1P 3AT
071-973 1992

Cultural Activities Grants

Grants for cultural property have been available from the EC since 1984. For the first few years of operation of the grant programme any projects involving properties of 'European renown' could qualify. Since 1988 grants have been encouraged which comply with a theme for the particular year. The theme for 1992 was that of conservation projects in towns and villages where the setting of monuments and buildings would be improved. The theme for 1993 is the conservation and restoration of historic gardens. ECU 3 million is available, and individual projects are restricted to a maximum grant of ECU 150,000. English Heritage can supply information and offer advice.

European Regional Development Fund (ERDF)

The ERDF was set up in 1975 and aimed mainly at large, public-sector capital schemes. The grant level is usually fifty per cent of eligible costs. The objective of this grant programme is to help eliminate the disparities in levels of development and wealth between different regions. Grants can be available for basic infrastructure, industrial estate provision, workshop units, conversion of factories, and so on. Schemes such as conference facilities, sports facilities and museums, could qualify but only where it is clear they would have a significant impact on tourism and not be simply local facilities. The Fund is restricted to areas defined as disadvantaged but this includes much of midland and northern Britain. The relevant Regional Office of the Department of the Environment provides guidance.

European Agricultural Guidance and Guarantee Fund (EAGGF)

All parts of the UK can qualify for assistance towards alterations to farm buildings and structures which bring about diversification into tourism, craft trades, manufacture and sales. The Ministry of Agriculture, Fisheries and Food can provide detailed guidance.

European Coal and Steel Community Loans (ECSC loans)

ECSC loans are available to almost any private industries towards schemes which will improve economic and social conditions in the declining coal- and steel-producing regions of the EC. Loans can cover up to fifty per cent of the capital cost of a project and are fixed at a very low rate of interest. In addition, capital repayment can be deferred up to five years. The Department of Trade and Industry regional office provides guidance.

Foundation for Sport and the Arts
P.O. Box 666
Liverpool   L69 7JN
051-524 0235

The Foundation was set up in 1991 by the major pools organisations. Its budget for the first year of operation (1991–92) was £64 million and is likely to increase. All parts of the country qualify for assistance and the aims of the trust permit grant aid to a wide variety of sport, games and arts projects. Although a significant proportion of the trust's support may go to supporting the activities of sporting and performing clubs and individuals, the fund seems large enough to provide help with the provision of entire new buildings and facilities and the improvement of existing ones. Early objectives include improving access to sport for the disabled and for the young, and for the provision of reliable, safe equipment.

Interbuild Fund
11 Manchester Square
London   W1M 5AB
071-486 1951

The Interbuild Fund is controlled by trustees charged with using their funds for the benefit of the UK construction industry. Grants are made for research, economic forecasting, and the publication of reports. The results of the work must be available for the construction industry as a whole. Grants are limited to £10,000; any group associated with the construction industry may apply.

J. Paul Getty Trust Grant Program
401 Wiltshire Boulevard
Suite 1000
Santa Monica
California   90401-1455
Tel. 213/393-4244

The Trust is a foundation devoted to the visual arts and related humanities throughout the world. Grants are available across a wide field, including monies for project feasibility studies as well as for implementation. Non-profit organisations are eligible, and schemes linked to training are often favoured. Grants usually require a matching sum from another source.

Local authorities

Housing grants

Major changes to the housing improvement grant system were made on 1 April 1990, bringing to an end the 1974 system. Ten categories of grant were introduced. The new arrangements have been criticised and the government intends to publicise a range of possible changes during 1992 (but still not produced at the time of writing in October 1992). In the meantime there are two main categories. The first is Renovation Grants (replacing the former Improvement, Intermediate and Repairs Grants). Renovation Grants are means-tested and cover works to bring a property to a standard of fitness. A further discretionary award can be used to improve the property to full standard. Neither has any eligible expense limits. The second is Group Repair Grants which replace the old enveloping arrangements for dealing with external repair to whole blocks of houses. The scope of work is similar. The maximum average cost is £10,000 per property. Assistance is means-tested but there is a maximum contribution of twenty-five per cent in renewal areas and fifty per cent elsewhere. Owner occupiers and private landlords are eligible, and enquiries should be made to the housing department of the district council.

Historic Buildings Grants and Loans (s.57 Planning (Listed Buildings and Conservation Areas) Act 1990)

The local authorities have wide-ranging discretionary powers to offer grants or loans from their own resources. Grants and loans may be for repair and maintenance of listed and unlisted buildings, buildings in conservation areas and unlisted buildings of historic interest elsewhere. They can also be used to maintain or restore historic gardens. The level of grant, conditions and limits all vary from district to district. There is no obligation on councils to have such a programme, but both county and district councils are able to offer grants if they wish. Contact the conservation officer at either council for advice.

Town Scheme Grants

Town Scheme Grants are available for listed and unlisted properties in conservation areas. Contact the county or district council conservation officer to see if a town scheme is in operation. A full account of Town Scheme operations is given in the section on English Heritage earlier in the chapter.

Urban Programme Grants

See 'Department of the Environment' earlier in this chapter.

Ministry of Agriculture, Fisheries and Food
Whitehall Place
London   EC4Y 0BN
071-270 3000

The Ministry administers a large number of grant programmes, most of which are related to agricultural production, woodland and hedgerow management, nature conservation and landscape enhancement. There are several programmes, however, which relate to buildings and development, two of which are described below.

Traditional Farm-Buildings Grants

On many farms, traditional buildings continue to serve an agricultural use but the cost of repair or renovation can come to outweigh their agricultural value with the result that they fall into disrepair and may be lost. Thirty-five per cent grant aid can be given (up to a fixed investment ceiling) towards keeping existing farm buildings in farming use. The grant can also be used to help with reinstatement of walls built in traditional materials. Applicants in Wales should apply to the Welsh Office.

Farm Diversification Grants

Setting up a new farm-based enterprise can require heavy capital investment. Thorough and expensive preparation, market analysis and other research may also be necessary. Diversification grants are intended to give twenty-five per cent support up to a limit of £35,000 for capital investments to encourage diversity of activities which keep farms from running into financial difficulties. Farm shops, tourist accommodation, craft manufacture, machinery repairs and similar projects consistent with the farm environment can be considered. Applicants in Wales should apply to the Welsh Office.

National Heritage Memorial Fund
10 St James Street
London   SW1A 1EF
071-930 0893

Powers exist for the trustees of the fund to acquire buildings, land, furniture, art, etc. of outstanding aesthetic, architectural or scientific importance. Help may also take the form of a grant to non-profit-making organisations for acquisition, repair or maintenance of historic buildings. The Fund sees itself as a last line of support for special cases where all other efforts have failed.

The Pilgrim Trust
Fielden House
Little College Street
London   SW1P 3SH
071-222 4723

The Pilgrim Trust was established in 1930 by the American philanthropist Edward Harkens with an endowment of £2 million. It now has an income of around

£1.5 million per year and assists schemes under the headings Preservation, Arts and Learning, and Social Welfare.

Royal Institute of British Architects
66 Portland Place
London   W1N 4AD
071-580 5533

Community Projects Fund

The Community Projects Fund provides small grants to voluntary and community groups, through the Community Architecture Resource Centre, to help with feasibility reports for building and environmental improvement projects. Grants are usually up to £1000 but can be to £3000 in certain cases. The Fund was supported by the DoE for nine years but lost this help in April 1992. It continues with private-sector and trust sponsorship.

Rural Development Commission
141 Castle Street
Salisbury
Wiltshire SP1 3TP
0722 336255

Funded Partnership Schemes

Available within Rural Development Areas, Funded Partnership Schemes give grants of up to fifty per cent to councils, non-profit-distributing trusts and charities engaged in conversion of buildings for commercial, industrial or workshop uses. These are usually schemes for local employment which the private sector would find unattractive.

Redundant Buildings Grants

Redundant Buildings Grants are available within the Rural Development Areas at a rate of twenty-five per cent of eligible costs (occasionally more) for conversion of farm and countryside buildings (barns, chapels, schools, etc.) to new commercial uses. Grants are usually between £1000 and £50,000, with a maximum of £75,000.

Village Halls Grants and Loans

Village Halls Grants and Loans are available to local communities for renovation, alteration and construction of village halls within Rural Development Areas. Local authorities must match the offer of grant or loan.

Sports Council
16 Upper Woburn Place
London   WC1H 0QP
071-388 1277

Under a Royal Charter the Sports Council may grant aid to provide or improve sports opportunities by building new facilities or adapting existing ones. Social accommodation to support sports facilities may also be assisted. There must be evidence of need to the extent that the project would not go ahead unless it is grant-aided. There must be good public access. Grants are individually assessed, and although there is no upper limit, funds are limited. The Sports Council will direct enquiries to its appropriate regional office for detailed discussion.

Welsh Tourist Office
Brunel House
2 Fitzalan Road
Cardiff   CF2 1UY
0222 499909

Tourism Development Grants

Tourism Development Grants in Wales are similar to those that were offered by the English Tourist Board in England (see under 'English Tourist Board' earlier in this chapter).

PENALTIES IN THE MAGISTRATES' COURT

The maximum fines applicable in the magistrates' court are either specified within the body of the legislation and any amending legislation or stated as being in accordance with the standard scale which was established by the Criminal Justice Act 1982, ss.37 and 75.

This scale has subsequently been increased, most recently by s.17 of the Criminal Justice Act 1991. The current standard scale is as follows:

Level 1	£200
Level 2	£500
Level 3	£1000
Level 4	£2500
Level 5	£5000

Some legislation states that the penalty applicable is the 'statutory maximum' in the magistrates' court. This is a fine of £5000 and/or six months' imprisonment. Where two or more offences are tried together in the magistrates' court, the maximum is a total of £5000 in fines and/or one year's imprisonment.

As from the 1 October 1992, sentencing on the basis of 'unit fines' becomes mandatory in the magistrates' court. The aim is to create greater fairness by linking the fine to the offender's disposable income. With this method, the seriousness of the offence is assessed in units on a scale from 1 to 50 and this is multiplied by the offender's disposable weekly income, thus providing a means-tested punishment system. The link with the levels listed above is preserved by calculating a maximum disposable weekly income of one-fiftieth the cash ceiling of the level. For example, the maximum weekly disposable income for a level 1 fine would be £4; and £100 for level 5. A level 5 offence assessed at 40 in seriousness would equate to a £4000 fine for a person with £100 weekly disposable income and £1200 for a person with only £30.

RYDE'S SCALE
(1991 REVISION)

Ryde's Scale is long established as the basis of the reimbursement of valuer's fees in the preparation and negotiation of a claim for compensation consequent upon the exercise of compulsory powers or on a purchase by agreement where there exists the ability to invoke compulsory powers. The prescribed fees are intended to cover all work necessary by the valuer in formulating, negotiating and concluding a claim, including the specification of any accommodation works necessary (the fee does not extend to the supervision of their satisfactory completion).

The scale has been agreed with the principal professional institutions but does not bind either side in the transaction. It is recognised that there will be cases where the application of the scale fee would be inappropriate and where the fee should be the subject of negotiation to take account of the particular circumstances.

The scale applies only to concluded negotiations. Where negotiations take place in advance of the existence of compulsory purchase powers, it is usual for the valuer or solicitor for the claimant to obtain an undertaking from the acquiring authority that it will reimburse fees for abortive work in the event that the acquisition does not proceed.

There is a basic scale with additions where leasehold interests are involved and for claims for compensation for disturbance and/or severance and injurious affection. There is a separate scale for agricultural land, such land being defined by s.96(1) of the Agricultural Holdings Act 1986 (in England and Wales). Where the compensation payable has been reduced to reflect betterment, the fee should be calculated on the gross amount of compensation negotiated.

The supervision of accommodation works is not included in either the basic scale or the agricultural scale but an additional fee may be negotiated where such work is undertaken. The scale is inclusive of office expenses but travelling and other out-of-pocket expenses may be claimed. VAT payable forms an additional claim but only where the claimant is not registered for tax. Where the claimant is registered for VAT, whether fully taxable or partially exempt, he will be able to reclaim any VAT paid.

No fee is payable where the payment is prescribed by law and not subject to negotiation (for example, well maintained and home loss payments). Reasonable legal and valuation expenses may be claimed for preparing and negotiating farm loss payments.

The scale does not extend to payments for attendance in court or before the Lands Tribunal.

The basic scale

On the first	£10,000	£262.50 minimum fee
On the next	£40,000	£262,50 plus 1% on the amount over £10,000
On the next	£250,000	£2162.50 plus 0.75% on the amount over £50,000
On the remainder		£2537.50 plus 0.5% on the amount over £250,000

Fractions of £100 compensation are rounded up to the next £100.

Additions to the basic scale

1. *For leasehold interests*
Where the rent payable by the claimant at the valuation date (exclusive of payment for rates, utilities, services or incidental charges) exceeds one-tenth of the rack rental value, the fee payable under the basic scale is increased according to the annual rent payable:

On the first	£300	of annual rent 7.5%	(no minimum fee)
On the next	£700	£22.50 plus 4.5%	of the rent over £300
On the next	£1,500	£54.00 plus 3.0%	of the annual rent over £1,000
On the next	£2,500	£99.00 plus 2.0%	of the annual rent over £2,500
On the next	£5,000	£149.00 plus 1.0%	of the annual rent over £5,000
On the next	£15,000	£199.00 plus 0.5%	of the annual rent over £10,000
On the remainder		£274.00 plus 0.25%	of the annual rent over £25,000

2. *For disturbance and/or severance and injurious affection*
Where the compensation under this head is for a sum of not less than £100, or five per cent of the total compensation, whichever is the higher, the basic fee is to be increased:

1. Where the property was occupied wholly as a private dwelling: *by* 10%
2. Where the property was occupied wholly for purposes other than a private dwelling *and* the disturbance content is less than 25% of the total compensation: *by* 30%

Where the property is partly occupied for the purposes of a private dwelling and partly for other purposes, the addition should be fixed between 10% and 30% according to what is reasonable in the circumstances of the case.

In circumstances where the disturbance element of the claim is greater than 25% of the total compensation, the fee is increased as follows:

Where the disturbance content of the claim

Exceeds 25% but is less than 50%,	the basic scale fee is increased by 45%
Exceeds 50% but is less than 75%,	the basic scale fee is increased by 60%
Exceeds 75%,	the basic scale fee is increased by 75%

The scale for agricultural land

The fee for negotiating compensation where the land is used for agricultural purposes and for compensation for pipeline and sewerage work, works under the Land Drainage Act 1976 and survey damage claims is set out in a separate scale:

On the first   £200   £276.25 minimum fee

The fee rises steeply up to £700, then increases at rates between 2.75% and 4.25%

At	£5,000	the fee is £552.50	
On the next	£45,000	£552.50	plus 2.4% on the amount over £5,000
On the next	£250,000	£1,632.50	plus 1.8% on the amount over £50,000
On the remainder		£6,132.50	plus 1.2% on the amount over £300,000

Fractions of £100 compensation are rounded up to the next £100.

RELEVANT ORGANISATIONS

The following bodies, listed alphabetically, are among the ones most relevant to the purpose of this book. Unless stated, the address given is the administrative head office.

Ancient Monuments Society
St Andrews-by-the-Wardrobe
Queen Victoria Street
London   EC4V 5DE
071-236 3934

The AMS exists to save historic buildings of all ages and types. Its main function is to advise planning authorities, which are required to inform the Society of all applications involving any degree of demolition of a listed building. Membership is open to interested individuals. Advice on the protection of threatened buildings is given.

Architectural Heritage Fund
27 John Adam Street
London   WC2N 6HX
071-925 0199

The AHF was established with government and private-sector support to provide low-interest loans to those building preservation trusts throughout the UK which engage in purchase, repair and resale of historic buildings. It also offers advice on forming and running a preservation trust and managing a preservation project.

Association of Conservation Officers
The Secretary
54 Pulens Lane
Sheet
Petersfield   GU31 4DD
0730 66653

The ACO acts as an active forum and support organisation for those working through local authorities for the conservation of the built environment and has around seven hundred and fifty members. The Association's primary objective is to promote the preservation and enhancement of the built environment. The Association can assist with speakers.

Association of Preservation Trusts
c/o Architectural Heritage Fund
Environmental Institute
Greaves School
Bolton Road
Swinton
Manchester   M27 2UX
061-794 8035

The APT was formed in 1988 in order to increase the size and effectiveness of the building preservation trust movement. The Association has close links with the Architectural Heritage Fund.

British Property Federation
35 Catherine Place
London   SW1
071-828 0111

The Federation exists to promote the interests of property owners. Membership includes both individuals and organisations.

British Standards Institution
2 Park Street
London   W1A 2BS
071-629 9000

The BSI was formed in 1901 to establish and maintain standards for units of measurement and technical terminology. British standards exist for a wide range of materials, techniques and services in the construction and property industries.

British Waterways Board
Melbury House
Melbury Terrace
London   NW1 6JX
071-723 8486

The BWB was established under the Transport Act 1962 and is responsible for two thousand miles of canal and river navigations in England, Wales and Scotland. It has powers to develop its resources for recreational purposes. Its waters are designated cruising waterways, commercial waterways, and remainder waterways. British Waterways, although limited in its own funds, is active in seeking to achieve suitable development related to its land and waterways.

Building Cost Information Service Ltd
and
Building Maintenance Information Ltd
85–87 Clarence Street
Kingston-upon-Thames
Surrey   KT1 1RB
081-546 7554/5

The BCIS and BMI were set up by the Royal Institution of Chartered Surveyors in 1971. Both are subscription services. The BMI promotes the exchange of occupancy cost data, and provides information for planning, estimating, budgeting, forecasting and performance review. The BCIS operates similarly in relation to building cost data for new work and refurbishment.

Building Employers Confederation
82 New Cavendish Street
London   W1
071-580 5588

The Confederation is a trade association of building contractors which also acts to assist many smaller allied associations. It advises government on building matters, and negotiates wages and working conditions in the industry. It has local and regional offices throughout England and Wales.

Building Research Establishment
Bucknalls Lane
Garston
Watford
Hertfordshire   WD2 7JR
0923 664040

The BRE, founded in 1921, is the main organisation in the UK carrying out research into building, construction and the prevention of fire. It offers an extensive range of publications, an enquiry service and an online bibliographic service.

CADW (Welsh Historic Monuments)
Ninth Floor
Brunel House
2 Fitzalan Road
Cardiff   CF2 1VY
022 465511

CADW is the division of the Welsh Office which advises the Secretary of State for Wales on matters relating to the built heritage of the principality. CADW is the approximate equivalent in Wales of the Historic Buildings and Monuments Commission for England (English Heritage), providing grants for building restoration and repair.

Chartered Institute of Building
Englemere
Kings Ride
Ascot
Berkshire   SL5 8BJ
0344 23467

The CIOB is a professional institution with objectives to promote the science and practice of building, educate in these areas, publish research, and establish and maintain standards.

Chartered Institution of Building Services Engineers
Delta House
222 Balham High Road
London   SW12 9BS
081-675 5211

The CIBSE is the professional organisation for electrical, mechanical and environmental engineers in the building industry. It was formed in 1977 following amalgamation of various specialist engineering bodies. The Institution has several divisions, including lighting, information technology, public health, electrical services, and air conditioning. The CIBSE organises conferences and lectures.

Civic Trust
17 Carlton House Terrace
London   SW1Y 5AW
071-930 0914

The Civic Trust is an independent agency concerned with the improvement and regeneration of the built environment, particularly in areas of architectural or historic interest. It has established a nationwide network of one thousand amenity societies.

Commission for New Towns
Glen House
Stag Place
London   SW1E 5AJ
071-828 7722

The CNT was set up in 1959 to manage the assets of completed new towns, taking over the residual interests of development corporations as they wind up. It takes over property with a view to eventual disposal, but it must have regard to the convenience and welfare of residents in its decisions. The CNT carries responsibility for completing the development programmes of some new towns taken into charge.

Commons, Open Spaces and Footpaths Preservation Society
25a Bell Street
Henley-on-Thames
Oxfordshire   RG9 1BA
0491 573535

The Society advises local authorities, commons committees and voluntary bodies on the protection of commons, village greens, public rights of way and other open spaces as well as campaigning for their preservation.

The Construction History Society
c/o Chartered Institute of Building
Englemere
Kings Ride
Ascot
Berkshire   SL5 8BJ
0344 23355

The Society exists for the study of historic methods of construction, contracts, tools and materials. It arranges meetings and visits throughout the UK and publishes occasional papers.

The Construction Industry Council
26 Store Street
London WC1E 7BT
071-637 8692

The Council represents the majority of professional institutes in the building industry. It promotes increased efficiency, quality and improved service to clients, and attempts to provide a single voice for the construction industry.

Construction Industry Research and Information Association
6 Storeys Gate
London SW1P 3AU
071-222 8891

CIRIA is a non-profit-making, co-operative research association. It has no central laboratories of its own, but arranges for and finances the research that its members need. Membership is open to firms and organisations engaged in or concerned with civil engineering and building in the widest sense. Reports and notes produced are available to non-members at a charge.

Council for British Archaeology
112 Kennington Road
London SE11 6RE
071-582 0494

The CBA provides liaison at a national level between archaeological institutions (societies, museums, units, universities) and the government bodies concerned with the preservation of monuments and historic buildings. It serves as the national information centre on all aspects of British archaeology. Funding comes mainly from British Academy grants.

Council for the Care of Churches
83 London Wall
London   EC2M 5NA
071-638 0971

Established in 1921, the CCC is a permanent commission of the General Synod of the Church of England with a wide range of responsibilities for the care of churches. It provides information and views on architectural and historical qualities in churches and allocates grant aid.

Council for the Protection of Rural England
Warwick House
25 Buckingham Palace Road
London   SW1W 0PP
071-976 6433

A voluntary body concerned with the protection of rural landscape, the CPRE campaigns inside and outside Parliament in the cause of conservation. Forty-four local branches seek to influence the planning and development control decisions of local authorities. Concerns relate to the loss of landscape quality through farming and other management actions, as well as loss of land to development.

Council for the Protection of Rural Wales
Ty Twyn
31 High Street
Welshpool
Powys   SY21 7JP
0938 552525

A voluntary body concerned with the protection of the Welsh rural landscape, the CPRW/CDCW campaigns inside and outside Parliament in the cause of conservation. Fourteen local branches seek to influence the planning and development control decisions of local authorities. Concerns relate to the loss of landscape quality through farming and other management actions, as well as loss of land to development.

Country Landowners Association
16 Belgrave Square
London   SW1X 8PQ
071-235 0511

The CLA was founded in 1907 to promote and safeguard the interests of owners of agricultural and rural land in England and Wales. It is the only organisation completely dedicated to the cause of private ownership. Non-party political, its advisory services are available to members on legal, land use, tax and political issues.

Countryside Commission
John Dower House
Crescent Place
Cheltenham
Gloucestershire   GL50 3RA
0242 521381

A statutory national body charged with keeping under review all matters relating to the conservation and enhancement of landscape beauty and amenity in England and Wales, the provision and improvement of facilities for enjoyment of the countryside, including the need to secure public access for open-air recreation. The Commission designates National Parks and areas of outstanding natural beauty, and has grant funds for recreation and landscaping schemes.

Countryside Council for Wales
Plas Penrhos
Bangor
Gwynedd   LL57 2LQ
0248 370444

The Council is the government's statutory adviser on wildlife and countryside conservation matters in Wales. It is directly responsible for conserving geological features and wildlife, and promotes the protection of landscape and opportunities for access to the countryside.

Department of the Environment
2 Marsham Street
London   SW1P 3EB
071-276 3000

Regional offices

East Midlands Regional Office
Cranbrook House
Cranbrook Street
Nottingham   NG1 1EY
0602 476121

Eastern Regional Office
Heron House
49–51 Goldington Road
Bedford   MG40 3LL
0234 63161

North West Regional Office
Sunley Tower
Piccadilly Plaza
Manchester   M1 4BE
061-832 9111

Northern Regional Office
Wellbar House
Gallowgate
Newcastle upon Tyne   NE1 4TD
091-232 7575

South East Regional Office
Charles House
375 Kensington High Street
London   W14 8QH
071-605 9003

South West Regional Office
Tollgate House
Houlton Street
Bristol   BS2 9DJ
0602 476121

West Midlands Regional Office
Five Ways Tower
Frederick Road
Birmingham   B15 1SJ
021-631 4141

Yorkshire and Humberside Regional Office
City House
New Station Street
Leeds   LS1 4JD
0532 43232

The Department of the Environment is the central government department responsible for protecting the environment, administering the town and country planning system, managing inner city policies, and controlling the spending and activities of local government. It was created in 1970 from three ministries: Housing and Local Government; Public Buildings and Works; and Transport. Transport became a separate ministry once more in 1976 (The Department of Transport). In 1992 many powers relating to heritage and sport matters were transferred to the Department of National Heritage. The Department of the Environment is headed by a Secretary of State who assisted by a group of ministers and junior ministers (around five or six strong) each responsible for a particular field.

Department of National Heritage
2 Marsham Street
London   SW1P 3EB
071-270 3000

The DNH is responsible for the functions of the Office of Arts and Libraries, export licensing of antiques, broadcasting, the press, sport and sports-ground safety, tourism, the royal palaces, the National Lottery and the Millenium Fund. With regard to architectural heritage and ancient monuments, it has been given responsibility for listing, scheduling, repairs notices, urgent works notices and associated land acquisition, ecclesiastical exemption (save for demolition which stays with the DoE), and protection of wrecks.

Department of Trade and Industry
Ashdown House
1 Victoria Street
London   SW1H 0ET
071-215 5000

Regional offices

DTI East Midlands
Severns House
20 Middle Pavement
Nottingham   NG1 7DW
0602 506181

DTI East
Building A
Westbrook Research Centre
Milton Road
Cambridge   CB4 1YG
0223 461939

DTI North East
Stanegate House
2 Groat Market
Newcastle upon Tyne   NC1 1YN
091-232 4722

DTI North West
Sunley Tower
Piccadilly Plaza
Manchester   M1 4BA
061-236 2171

DTI South East
Bridge Place
88–89 Eccleston Square
London   SW1V 1PT
071-276 8083

DTI South West
The Pitay
Bristol   BS1 2PB
0272 272666

DTI West Midlands
Ladywood House
Stephenson Street
Birmingham   B2 4DT
021-631 6181

DTI Yorkshire and Humberside
Priestley House
Park Row
Leeds   LS1 5LF
0532 443171

The DTI aims to help UK businesses compete successfully at home, in the rest of Europe, and throughout the world. It promotes enterprise and competition, helping with the supply of business information and advice, and fosters the creation of new businesses and the expansion of existing companies. The DTI has responsibility for managing UK energy resources and ensuring the country's energy needs are properly met. Trade and industry issues in Wales are managed by the Welsh Office.

Department of Transport
2 Marsham Street
London   SW1P 3EB
071-276 3000

The DTp was created in 1976 by removing transport functions from the Department of the Environment. The DTp is responsible for strategies for road, rail and other forms of public transport; for civil aviation, shipping and ports, and for vehicle standards, driver and vehicle licensing, and safety. The Department oversees road-building and maintenance through allocation of transport funds to the various local highway authorities.

English Nature
Northminster House
Peterborough
Cambridgeshire
0733 340345

English Nature is the statutory advisor to the government on nature conservation in England. It promotes the conservation of England's wildlife and natural features. Its work includes the selection, establishment and management of national nature reserves, and the provision of advice and information on nature conservation. It conducts and supports research across the field of nature conservation, producing papers and other information.

English Tourist Board
Thames Tower
Black's Road
London   W6 9EL
071-846 9000

The ETB is responsible for the promotion both at home and abroad of tourism in England. It is assisted by regional boards throughout England.

European Commission
London Office
8 Storeys Gate
London   SW1P 3AT
071-973 1992

The UK office of the European Commission.

Friends of the Earth
26–28 Underwood Street
London   N1 7JQ
071-490 1555

FoE is a campaigning organisation promoting policies which protect the natural environment. It has particular interest in issues of energy, wildlife conservation, transport and pollution. It has a network of local groups throughout the country and links with similar campaigning organisations abroad.

Georgian Group
37 Spital Square
London   E1 6DY
071-377 1722

The Georgian Group was founded in 1937 to save and protect Georgian buildings, parks, gardens and monuments from destruction, and to encourage appropriate repairs or restoration. The Group is a statutory consultee of local planning authorities in cases where total or partial demolition of a listed building is proposed.

Health and Safety Commission
and
Health and Safety Executive
Baynards House
1 Chepstow Place
Westbourne Grove
London   W2 4TF
071-229 3456

The Commission was formed under the Health and Safety at Work Act 1974, with members being drawn from both sides of industry and from local authority organisations. The Executive is the operational arm formed from the five existing inspectorates: Factories, Mines and Quarries, Nuclear Installations, Hazardous Substances, and Agriculture.

Historic Buildings and Monuments Commission for England
(English Heritage)
Fortress House
23 Savile Row
London   W1X 2HE
071-973 3000

Set up 1984 under the National Heritage Act 1983, the HBMC is the largest independent body with statutory responsibility for conserving buildings and sites of architectural and historic importance, and is the single largest source of grant aid for such work. The Commission has responsibility for advising government on matters of conservation, listing and scheduling. It is also responsible for managing and maintaining around three hundred and fifty properties in care (although some of these may in the future be transferred to ownership of trusts, local authorities and other organisations). The greatest part of its funding comes from government. Details of grants are available on request.

Historic Churches Preservation Trust
Fulham Palace
London   SW6 6EA
071-736 3054

The HCPT, a charity, was established in 1952 with the sole object of making grants and loans towards the repair and maintenance of churches in use which are of architectural or historic importance.

Historic Houses Association
2 Chester Street
London   SW1X 7BB
071-259 5688

The HHA is an independent organisation representing private owners of historic houses. It has committees considering gardens, taxation and tourism, and acts as a watch-dog on legislative matters, lobbying for a fiscal regime allowing historic houses to be maintained for the future in private hands.

HM Inspectorate of Pollution
Romney House
43 Marsham Street
London   SW1 3PY
071-276 8083

Regional offices
HMIP East Division
Howard House
40–60 St Johns Street
Bedford   MK42 0DL
0234 272112

HMIP North Division
Stockdale House
Headingly Business Park
Victoria Road
Headingly
Leeds   LS6 1PF
0532 742642

HMIP West Division
Highwood Pavilion
Jupiter Road
Patchway
Bristol   BS12 5SN
0272 311211

The HMIP's regional offices deal with most regulation affairs in their area. The regions are supported by a central Regulatory Standards Division which co-ordinates technical standards and research and five specialised groups. These groups basically coincide with the industry groups specified in the 'prescribed processes' of the pollution control legislation.

House Builders' Federation
82 New Cavendish Street
London   W1M 8AD
071-580 5588

The HBF is the principal trade federation for the private housebuilding industry in the UK. It aims to work for the most favourable economic and political climate within which private housebuilders can operate. It acts as the representative body for the industry in dealing with local planning authorities over the release of land for housing development.

Housing Corporation
149 Tottenham Court Road
London   W1P 0BN
071-387 9466

The Corporation is a government agency responsible for funding and supervising registered housing associations to provide homes to rent and for sale by various methods. Since the demise of local authority council house building, the housing corporation has become the major provider of social housing. It has nine regional offices.

Institution of Civil Engineers
1–7 Great George Street
Westminster
London   SW1P 3AA
071-222 7722

The professional institution for civil engineers with defined standards of entry and a code of conduct.

Institution of Highways and Transportation
3 Lygon Place
Ebury Street
London   SW1W 0JS
071-730 5245

The professional institution for highways and transportation engineers with defined standards of entry and a code of conduct.

Institution of Structural Engineers
11 Upper Belgrave Street
London   SW1X 8BH
071-235 4535

The professional institution for structural engineers with defined standards of entry and a code of conduct.

Institution of Water and Environmental Management
15 John Street
London   WC1
071-831 3100

The IWEM is a learned society and examining body whose object is to advance the science and practice of water and environmental management. It publishes a journal and manuals on water supply and waste-water treatment and disposal.

Land Authority for Wales
Custom House
Customhouse Street
Cardiff   CF1 5AP
0222 223444

The LAW makes land available for development in the principality, particularly where the private sector experiences difficulties in acquiring land. It acts as an agent or consultant with all public bodies and local authorities in economic regeneration.

The Law Society
50–52 Chancery Lane
London   WC2A 1SX
071-141 1222

Ipsley Court
Benington Close
Redditch
Worcestershire   B98 0TD
0527 517141

The Law Society is the governing body for all solicitors practising in England and Wales, each of whom is required to belong to it. It has committees which review areas of law and lobby the government for change; it advises solicitors on professional ethics and can intervene in a solicitor's practice. It can discipline members, including striking a member off the roll and thereby preventing him from practising.

Landscape Institute
12 Carlton House Terrace
London   SW1 5AH
071-738 9166

The Institute is the professional body for the three landscape professions: landscape architects, landscape managers and landscape scientists. It has a code of conduct for members, enforced by disciplinary procedures. The Institute is active in attempting to influence government on environment matters.

London Docklands Development Corporation
Great Eastern Enterprise
Unit A, Millharbour
London E14 9TJ
071-512 3000

The LDDC came into existence in 1981, responsible for the regeneration of eight square miles in the London Boroughs of Newham, Southwark and Tower Hamlets. Funded by government, the Corporation is responsible for bringing about major private-sector investment and is assisted in this work by certain statutory planning powers.

Ministry of Agriculture, Fisheries and Food
Whitehall Place
London EC4Y 0BN
071-270 3000

The MAFF gives advice, through the Agricultural Development Advisory Service (ADAS), to planning authorities on the effects of development proposals on agriculture and publishes maps of agricultural land quality. ADAS also gives impartial advice to landowners, farmers and growers on a wide range of agricultural matters, including the design and appearance of farm buildings, farm waste disposal and the proper use of pesticides.

National Association of Estate Agents
Arbon House
21 Jury Street
Warwick CV34 4EH
0926 496800

Membership is open to persons practising as estate agents who accept the aims of the association and its rules. The association seeks to encourage standards of competitive practice combined with commercial experience. There are 9600 members.

National Heritage Memorial Fund
10 St James's Street
London   SW1A 1EF
071–930 0893

The NHMF was established by Parliament in 1980 and is controlled by independent trustees. It gives financial aid towards the cost of acquiring, maintaining or preserving land, buildings, works of art and other objects of outstanding interest and importance to the national heritage. NHMF is intended to operate as a safety net with grants offered only where other opportunities are exhausted.

National House-Building Council
Buildmark House
Chiltern Avenue
Amersham
Buckinghamshire   HP6 5AP
0494 434477

The NHBC consists of representatives of the building industry, building societies, professional bodies and consumer interests. It is an independent non-profit-making body providing owners of new houses with a ten-year warranty against defects. It applies only to houses built by NHBC members. The Council is also concerned with improving the standards of house-building generally. It offers, through a subsidiary company, an approved building control service.

National Rivers Authority
Rivers House
Waterside Drive
Aztec West
Almondsbury
Bristol   BS12 4UD
0454 624400

The NRA was established in 1989 with statutory responsibilities and powers in relation to pollution control, water resources, flood defence, fisheries, recreation, conservation and navigation in England and Wales. To ensure that the best ways of protecting, improving and managing the water environment are used, the NRA also undertakes an extensive research and development programme. The NRA has ten regional offices.

National Trust
36 Queen Anne's Gate
London   SW1H 9AS
071–222 9251

The National Trust was formed in 1895 and incorporated by Act of Parliament in 1907. It exists to promote the permanent preservation of land with outstanding natural features, and buildings of beauty or historic interest. The Trust is an independent charity. It is one of the major landowners in the country and has sixteen regional offices.

Ordnance Survey
Romsey Road
Maybush
Southampton   SD9 4DH
0703 972000

The agency responsible for preparing maps of the UK at all scales. Maps are available in a variety of forms including digitised for computer use, and special maps are produced including those with archaeological and geological information. Publications are supplied through OS agents and bookshops.

PSA Projects
and
PSA Building Management
2 Marsham Street
London   SW1P 3EB
071–276 3645

The Property Services Agency provided management, design and construction services to government departments, but, since 1 April 1990, the departments have had direct responsibility for their own works services. At the time of going to press, PSA is being split into two businesses: PSA Projects (the design and project management arm), which is being transferred to the private sector, and PSA Building Management (maintenance works) which is being offered for sale as five separate regional businesses.

Redundant Churches Fund
St Andrews-by-the-Wardrobe
Queen Victoria Street
London   EC4V 5DE
071–248 7461

The Fund was set up in 1969 to preserve Church of England churches which are no longer required for worship but which are of particular architectural, historic or archaeological interest. A charity, the Fund is assisted by the Department of the Environment, the Church Commissioners and public donations. A list of vested churches is available on request.

Rescue: The British Archaeological Trust
15a Bull Plain
Hertford
Hertfordshire   SG14 1DX
0992 553377

The Trust is an independent association which seeks to alert public opinion to the need to preserve or adequately to record important archaeological sites which are threatened. It arranges meetings and conferences, gives technical advice and offers publications.

Royal Commission on Ancient and Historical Monuments in Wales
Crown Buildings
Plas Crug
Aberystwyth
Dyfed   SY23 2HP
0970 624381

The RCAHMW was established in 1908 to make an inventory of monuments. Today its duties include maintenance of the Welsh section of the National Monuments Record. In most respects its powers are the same as the Royal Commission on Historical Monuments in England.

Royal Commission on Environmental Pollution
Church House
Great Smith Street
London   SW1P 3BL
071–276 2080

The Royal Commission is appointed to advise on matters both national and international concerning the pollution of the environment, on the adequacy of research in the field, and future possible dangers to the environment. It is a standing commission with wide powers of enquiry.

Royal Commission on Historical Monuments in England
Fortress House
23 Savile Row
London   W1X 2JQ
071–937 3500 (main switchboard)

National Archaeological Record, 071–973 3148 (Fortress House)
National Buildings Record, 071–973 3091 (Fortress House)
National Library of Air Photographs, 0793 414100 (Alexander House,
    Fleming Way, Swindon, SN1 2NG)

The RCHME was established in 1908. It is responsible for compiling, managing and promoting the national record of archaeological sites and historic buildings in England. The Commission has the right to make a record of any listed building prior to full or partial demolition. The National Monuments Record is divided into three sections: National Archaeological Record, National Buildings Record, and National Library of Air Photographs. Many millions of records are held, and all three sections are open to the public. Advice can be given on surveying historic sites and buildings.

Royal Fine Art Commission
7 St James's Square
London   SW1Y 4JU
071–839 6537

The RFAC was created in 1924 by royal warrant. It is concerned primarily with the architectural quality of proposed development schemes where they have a high profile or affect buildings or areas of special importance. Despite the RFAC's lack of statutory powers of intervention, its observations on proposed development schemes can have enormous impact, leading to radical redesign or even to abandonment.

Royal Institute of British Architects
66 Portland Place
London   W1N 4AD
071–580 5533

The RIBA is the professional institute for twenty-eight thousand architects and is funded by subscriptions and by activities such as publishing. Members are entitled to use the title 'Chartered Architect'. The Institute operates a strict code of conduct for members and may take disciplinary action for serious breaches. It comments on architectural and planning matters, seeking to influence the views of government and others. A range of conferences, seminars and other events is offered. A client advisory service gives guidance to the public and developers on the appointment of a suitable practice.

Royal Institution of Chartered Surveyors
12 Great George Street
Parliament Square
London   SW1P 3AD
071–222 7000

The RICS is the largest of the professions concerned with surveying and has the widest range of membership. Fellows and associates may use the title 'Chartered Surveyor'. The Institution is divided into seven divisions: building surveying; general practice; land and hydrographic surveying; minerals; planning and development; quantity surveying, and rural practice. A strict code of conduct is operated and disciplinary action may be taken against any member who is in breach. The RICS comments on property, development and construction matters, seeking to influence the views of government and others. A range of conferences, seminars and other events is offered.

Royal Town Planning Institute
26 Portland Place
London   W1N 4BE
071–636 9107

The RTPI is the primary professional body for town planners in the UK. Members may use the title 'Chartered Town Planner'. Most RTPI members are in local government service, but an increasing number are entering private practice. A strict code of conduct is operated and disciplinary action may be taken against any member who is in breach. The RTPI comments on planning, development and architectural matters, seeking to influence the views of government and others. A range of conferences, seminars and other events is offered.

Rural Development Commission
141 Castle Street
Salisbury
Wiltshire   SP1 3TP
0722 336255

The Commission (formerly CoSIRA) is charged by government with encouraging economic and social development within rural England. The Commission can provide loan capital for business ventures in certain circumstances and can give towards the cost of converting unused buildings into workshops. An important activity of the Commission is the provision of courses and other training to small businesses.

Save Britain's Heritage
68 Battersea High Street
London   SW11 3HX
071–228 3336

SAVE was formed in 1975 to campaign publicly to protect endangered buildings of historic interest. It emphasises the possibility of alternative uses for such buildings. The organisation is a statutory consultee in all cases where demolition of a listed building is proposed. A list of publications is available on request.

Society for the Protection of Ancient Buildings
37 Spital Square
London   E1 6DY
071–377 1644

Founded by William Morris, SPAB is the original building preservation organisation established to promote sympathetic repairs and oppose detrimental restoration. It is a statutory consultee in the case of applications for full or partial demolition of any listed building. A list of publications is available on request.

Solicitors Complaints Bureau
Portland House
Stage Place
Victoria
London   SW1E 6BL
071–834 2288

This independent body receives and investigates complaints about solicitors from the public or other professionals. It attempts to conciliate, may recommend the payment of compensation, and may recommend that disciplinary proceedings are followed.

Sports Council
16 Upper Woburn Place
London   WC1H 0QP
071–388 1277

The Council fosters the practice of sport and recreation among the public at large. There are nine regional sports councils and a separate council for Wales. Grants are offered towards activities and toward sports development.

The Twentieth Century Society
58 Crescent Lane
London   SW4 9PU
071–738 8480

The Society (formerly the Thirties Society) was founded in 1979 to promote the study of post-1914 buildings. It produces a newsletter and journal, and arranges study events.

Victorian Society
1 Priory Gardens
Bedford Park
London W4 1TT
081–994 1019

The Society was founded in 1958 as the national society responsible for the study and protection of Victorian and Edwardian architecture and decorative arts. Since 1971 the Society has been a statutory consultee in all cases in which demolition or partial demolition of a listed building has been sought. The Society is a charity.

Welsh Development Agency
Pearl House
Greyfriars Road
Cardiff CF1 3XX
0222 222666

The WDA was set up by government in 1976 to regenerate the economy and improve the environment of Wales. It has wide-ranging responsibilities in providing investment capital for industry, building factories, developing and managing industrial estates, reclaiming derelict land, improving the environment and promoting Wales as a location for economic growth. It provides investment finance for industrial and commercial projects by offering equity funds or loans (including from EC sources). An advisory service for small firms is available.

Welsh Office
Cathays Park
Cardiff CF1 3NQ
0222 825111

The Welsh Office is responsible for most matters affecting environmental protection, nature conservation, economic and physical development, planning, sport, housing policy, and local government funding in Wales.

APPENDIX 4

ABBREVIATIONS IN COMMON USAGE

ACA   Associate of the Institute of Chartered Accountants
ACIArb   Associate of the Chartered Institute of Arbitrators
ACO   Association of Conservation Officers
ADAS   Agricultural Development Advisory Service
AG   Attorney-General
AHF   Architectural Heritage Fund
ALI   Associate of the Landscape Institute
All ER   All England Law Reports
AMS   Ancient Monuments Society
ANAEA   Associate of the National Association of Estate Agents
AONB   Area of Outstanding Natural Beauty
APT   Association of Building Preservation Trusts
ARIBA   Associate of the Royal Institute of British Architects
ARICS   Associate of the Royal Institution of Chartered Surveyors
ARVA   Associate of the Rating and Valuation Association
ASVA   Associate of the Incorporated Society of Valuers and Auctioneers

BATNEEC Best available techniques not entailing excessive cost
BBA   British Board of Agrément
BCIS   Building Cost Information Service
BMCIS   Building Maintenance Cost Information Service
BPF   British Property Federation
BPN   Building Preservation Notices
BPT   Building Preservation Trust
BRE   Building Research Establishment
BSI   British Standards Institution
BWB   British Waterways Board

CAA   Civil Aviation Authority
CAD   Computer aided design
CADW   Welsh Historic Monuments
CBA   Council for British Archaeology
CBI   Confederation of British Industry

C.Eng	Chartered Engineer
CIC	Construction Industry Council
CIOB	Chartered Institute of Building
CIPFA	Chartered Institute of Public Finance and Accountancy
CIRIA	Construction Industry Research and Information Association
CLA	Country Landowners Association
CLEUD	Certificate of Lawful Existing Use or Development
CLOPUD	Certificate of Lawfulness of Proposed Use or Development
CNT	Commission for New Towns
CoSIRA	Council for Small Industries in Rural Areas (now part of the Rural Development Commission)
CPD	Continuing professional development
CPO	Compulsory purchase order
CPRE	Council for the Protection of Rural England
CPRW	Council for the Protection of Rural Wales
CTT	Capital transfer tax
DES	Department for Education and Science
DLO	Direct Labour Organisation (of a local authority)
DNH	Department of National Heritage
DoE	Department of the Environment
DPP	Director of Public Prosecutions
DSO	Direct Services Organisation [of a local authority]
DTI or DTi	Department of Trade and Industry
DTp	Department of Transport
DV	District Valuer (Inland Revenue)
EA	Environmental Assessment
EIP	Examination in Public
EPA	Environmental Protection Agency
ETB	English Tourist Board
EZ	Enterprise zone
FCA	Fellow of the Institute of Chartered Accountants
FCIArb	Fellow of the Chartered Institute of Arbitrators
FoE	Friends of the Earth
FR&I	Full repairing and insuring lease
FRIBA	Fellow of the Royal Institute of British Architects
FRICS	Fellow of the Royal Institution of Chartered Surveyors
FRTPI	Fellow of the Royal Town Planning Institute
FRVA	Fellow of the Rating and Valuation Association
FSVA	Fellow of the Incorporated Society of Valuers and Auctioneers
GDO	Town and Country Planning (General Development) Order (currently 1988)
GLC	Greater London Council (abolished 1986)
Ha	Hectare

HAT   Housing Action Trust
HBMCE   Historic Buildings and Monuments Commission for England (commonly referred to as
               English Heritage)
HCPT   Historic Churches Preservation Trust
HHA   Historic Houses Association
HIMO   House in multiple occupation
HMIP   Her Majesty's Inspectorate of Pollution
H&SE   Health and Safety Executive

IAAS   Incorporated Association of Architects and Surveyors
ICE   Institution of Civil Engineers
ICOMOS   International Council on Monuments and Sites
IStructE   Institution of Structural Engineers
ISVA   Incorporated Society of Valuers and Auctioneers

JPL   *Journal of Planning and Environment Law*

LAW   Land Authority for Wales
LDDC   London Docklands Development Corporation
LI   Landscape Institute
LNR   Local Nature Reserve
LPA   Local planning authority
LPA   Law of Property Act
LRT   London Regional Transport

MAFF   Ministry of Agriculture, Fisheries and Food
MCIOB   Member of the Chartered Institute of Building
MICE   Member of the Institution of Civil Engineers
MIStructE Member of the Institution of Structural Engineers
MLGD   Minister for Local Government and Development
MMC   Monopolies and Mergers Commission
MPG   Minerals Policy Guidance Note (see also PPG and RPG)
MRTPI   Member of the Royal Town Planning Institute

NAEA   National Association of Estate Agents
NHBC   National House-Building Council
NHMF   National Heritage Memorial Fund
NMR   National Monuments Record
NMRW   National Monuments Record for Wales
NNR   National Nature Reserve
NRA   National Rivers Authority
NT   National Trust

OS   Ordnance Survey

PD   Permitted development
POS   Public open space

PPG   Planning Policy Guidance Note (see also MPG and RPG)

QC   Queen's Counsel
QS   Quantity surveyor

RCHME   Royal Commission on Historical Monuments in England
RCAHMW   Royal Commission on Ancient and Historical Monuments in Wales
RFAC   Royal Fine Art Commission
RIBA   Royal Institute of British Architects
RIPA   Royal Institute of Public Administration
RICS   Royal Institution of Chartered Surveyors
RPG   Regional Policy Guidance Note (see also PPG and MPG)
RPI   Retail prices index
RTPI   Royal Town Planning Institute

SI   Statutory instrument
SPAB   Society for the Protection of Ancient Buildings
SPZ   Simplified planning zone
SSofE   Secretary of State for the Environment
SSSI   Site of Special Scientific Interest

TCPA   Town and Country Planning Association
TPO   Tree preservation order

UBR   Uniform business rate
UDC   Urban Development Corporation
UP   Urban Programme

Vic. Soc. Victorian Society

WDA   Welsh Development Agency
WO   Welsh Office

APPENDIX 5

GLOSSARY OF TERMS IN COMMON USAGE

Abandonment When a right or interest in land is relinquished. It applies equally to the giving up of an easement (a legal right) as to the giving up of a planning use of land (a statutory right).

Abatement notice Requests a person to cease carrying out some activity on his land. It may be served by a private individual who is affected by a nuisance from adjoining land or under the Environmental Protection Act 1990 in connection with a *statutory nuisance* (refer to Chapter 4).

Absolute title *See* Land registration.

Act of Parliament Formally, the legislative decree of the Queen in Parliament. Also known as a statute, an Act, unless stated otherwise, comes into force on the last moment of the day before it receives royal assent.

Adoption of highway The process by which the highway authority takes over responsibility on behalf of the public for the maintenance of a highway and its footpaths.

Advance Payments Code An arrangement under the Highways Act 1980 whereby a builder either makes a payment to the highway authority or enters into an indemnity bond at an early stage in the development of the site in anticipation of adoption of the roads. This is intended to cover the cost of the highway authority making up the roads if the builder defaults.

Advertising control Local planning authorities have wide powers of control over the advertisements which can be displayed in public (refer to Chapter 2).

Alternative use value An assessment of the value of land if it were used for a purpose different from its current use.

Amenity land In a planning context, land which is available for the enjoyment of the public, such as a park or other open space. *Amenity* simply means something which makes the environment more pleasant.

Ancient lights A window or other opening through which light is enjoyed, and has been enjoyed for a long period, is an ancient light. *See* Right to light.

Ancient monument *See* Scheduled monument.

Ancillary use A planning term which describes a use that is subsidiary, but related to, the main use. For example, a large factory may have offices; the main use would be as a factory and the office use, which is dependent on the main use, would be an ancillary use.

Appeal Any proceeding which is brought before a superior body to challenge a decision made by an inferior body. (Refer to Chapter 1 for methods of appeal.)

Appointed day The day which is specified for the coming into operation of an Act of Parliament. Most Acts do not take effect until some time after they have obtained royal assent. This ensures that the public has an opportunity to take steps for compliance and the government or other enforcement body has time to put in place any necessary new administrative machinery. Some sections of Acts come into operation at different times and these are specified in regulations.

Arbitration   A method of resolving disputes without recourse to the court system in that an independent person is appointed by the parties to the dispute to reach a decision on the dispute. The decision is binding, but can be challenged on the law by appeal to the High Court. The advantage is cheapness, speed and the opportunity of agreeing on the appointment of an arbitrator who is skilled in the area of dispute, perhaps a surveyor in a construction matter.

Architect   A person who designs buildings and is qualified to do so in accordance with the Architects Registration Acts 1934 and 1938.

Area of Archaeological Importance   An area designated by SofSE under s.33 of the Ancient Monuments and Archaeological Areas Act 1979 (refer to Chapter 3).

Area of Outstanding Natural Beauty   The Countryside Commission has responsibility for the designation of these areas under the Countryside Act 1968 (refer to Chapter 3).

Article 4 Direction   Under article 3 of the Town and Country Planning (General Development) Order 1988, rights are granted for certain types of development without the need for formal planning permission. In some circumstances, a local planning authority (LPA) might feel it is not appropriate for these rights to be exercised without formal planning control. The LPA can issue an Article 4 Direction which takes away all or some of those rights, thus making an application for planning permission necessary (refer to Chapter 2).

Assignment   When the owner of a leasehold interest in land wishes to sell that interest, the sale is done by way of assignment. Assignment is also used to describe the document which transfers the legal interest in a lease.

Backland   Land which has no frontage to a highway.

Bailiff   An officer of the court who is empowered to serve writs and other court documents and to enforce judgements. He may also levy distress (that is, take and sell property in satisfaction of unpaid rent) on behalf of a landlord.

Beneficial interest   The interest in property enjoyed by a beneficial owner (*see* Beneficial owner).

Beneficial owner   The person who enjoys the benefit of property, as opposed to a person who owns property as a trustee on behalf of beneficiaries.

Betterment   Usually an increase in value of property which results from action taken by a local authority or government body. For example, the building of a new road or the granting of planning permission.

Bill   Until an Act of Parliament receives royal assent, and whilst it is progressing through the Houses of Parliament, it is known as a Bill.

Bill of Quantities   The document which details the plant, materials and labour required to complete a project and estimates the costs involved. It is usually prepared by a quantity surveyor.

Blight   Also known as planning blight, blight is the decrease in value of property due to the proposals of a local or government body, which will usually include the compulsory purchase of part of the property.

Bona fide   Literally, in good faith.

Breach of contract   A person who does not fulfil his obligations under a contract is in breach of that contract and may be forced to complete the contract or compensate the aggrieved party.

Building control   Normally refers to the system of controls over building works under the Building Act 1984 which are enforced by the local authority (refer to Chapter 6).

Building Cost Information Service   A subscriber service which collates and distributes information on building construction costs (often referred to as BCIS).

Building Maintenance Cost Information Service   A subscriber service which collates and distributes information on building maintenance and property occupancy (often referred to as BMCIS).

Building Preservation Notice A notice issued by a local planning authority to protect an unlisted building for a limited period which it believes is worthy of inclusion in the statutory list (refer to Chapter 3).

Building regulations Produced in accordance with the Building Act 1984 (discussed in detail in Chapter 6).

Bye-law A law which operates only in the area of a local authority. It is made by the local authority, with the approval of the appropriate Secretary of State, and is enforced by it in the magistrates' court.

Caveat emptor Literally, let the buyer beware. At common law a buyer of goods or property has no remedy against a seller if the goods are faulty (unless the seller has acted fraudulently). There is some statutory protection.

Certificate of immunity Also known as a certificate of non-listing, it states that a building will not be included in the statutory list for a period of at least five years from the date of application for the certificate. Application can only be made after the building has been the subject of a planning application.

CLEUD (Certificate of Lawfulness of Existing Use or Development) The issue of a certificate by a local planning authority (LPA) determines that the current use or development of land is lawful and is immune from enforcement action. This certificate replaces the 'established use' procedure under the 1971 planning legislation (refer to Chapter 2).

CLOPUD (Certificate of Lawfulness of Proposed Use or Development) The issue of a certificate by a LPA determines that a proposed use or development of land will be lawful and immune from enforcement action. This certificate replaces the 's.54 determination' procedure in the 1971 planning legislation (refer to Chapter 2.)

Certiorari An order of the court which quashes the decision of an inferior court, a tribunal or other administrative body (refer to Chapter 1).

Chancery Division The division of the High Court which deal mainly with trusts, probate, company law and property.

Commercial court Comprised of judges from the Queen's Bench Division of the High Court which hears cases on banking, insurance and similar matters.

Common land Land over which the public (the common man) has rights often of access or for grazing animals or digging peat.

Compensation A payment made to an aggrieved person to make amends for the loss or injury which has been suffered.

Completion *See* Contract.

Compulsory purchase order An order made to enable a local or government body and others to purchase land against the will of the owner or occupier.

Conservation area An area designated in accordance with the Planning (Listed Buildings and Conservation Areas) Act 1990 (refer to Chapter 3).

Contract Any legally enforceable agreement between two or more parties, including verbal as well as written agreements. Contracts dealing with the sale or leasing of land must be in writing to be enforceable. With a land transfer, the agreement becomes binding when the contracts are exchanged, that is when each party has signed a copy of the contract and these have been exchanged so that each party holds the copy signed by the other. The contract is completed on the date specified in the contract for the final transfer of the purchase monies, known as the completion date.

Conveyance The document which legally transfers interest in property from one person to another.

County court The lowest tier of civil court (refer to Chapter 1).

Court of Appeal Hears appeals from the High Court, Crown Courts, some county courts and some administrative tribunals (refer to Chapter 1).

Covenant *See* Restrictive covenant.

Curtilage Any yard, garden, field or similar land which is used together with a house or building in such a way as to form an integral part of that house or building.

Damages The name given to the compensation which is awarded by a court for breach of contract or for the loss suffered as a result of a tort.

Definitive map County councils are responsible for the preparation and updating of definitive maps which show public paths and bridleways. Once paths, etc. appear on a definitive map, this is proof of their status as public rights of way.

De minimis Something which is of so little significance as to be ignored is *de minimis*. This is a shortened form of *de minimis non curat lex*, literally, the law does not concern itself with trifles.

Derelict Abandoned property or property which has been neglected is described as derelict.

Development For planning purposes, is defined by s.55 of the Town and Country Planning Act 1990 (refer to Chapter 2).

Development brief *See* Planning brief.

Development control The system of control which is used by local planning authorities over the development of land in its area (refer to Chapter 2).

Development Corporation A body set up to plan, develop and manage an area of land, such as a new town under the New Towns Act 1981.

Development plan The statutory documents prepared by planning authorities which set out proposals and policies for development. In shire areas, the development plan will usually consist of the structure plan (prepared by the district council) and the local plan. In metropolitan areas it comprises part 1 and part 2 of a unitary plan prepared by the single authority responsible for that area.

Discontinuance Order An order made by a local planning authority requiring the discontinuance of a lawful use of land. Compensation would normally be payable in such circumstances (refer to Chapter 2).

Divisional court Comprised of two or more judges from one of the divisions of the High Court who sit and hear appeals from lower courts.

Duty In the context of local authorities and other public bodies, a duty is an obligation which must be fulfilled. Failure to carry out that duty could lead to an aggrieved party successfully taking action against the public body in the High Court for an order of mandamus (*see* Mandamus and refer to Chapter 1).

Easement A right which belongs to a parcel of land and entitles the owners and occupiers of the land to exercise the right over an adjoining property, for example a right of way. An easement can be acquired by long user or by necessity, or it can be purchased by negotiation.

Enforcement notice A notice issued by a local planning authority when it believes that there has been a breach of planning control (refer to Chapter 2).

Equity A body of rules which developed alongside the common law, but which is founded on natural justice or fairness and supplements the rules and procedure of the common law.

Established use *See* CLEUD and CLOPUD, and refer to Chapter 2.

Exchange of contracts *See* Contract.

Fee simple An estate of freehold land, the best possible type of estate in that it is free of conditions or limitations with regard to inheritance.

Fire certificate   Issued by a fire officer to confirm that a building complies with the Fire Precautions Act 1971.

Flying freehold   An expression used to describe the situation when a freehold property extends over the top of a neighbouring property. For example, property A comprises three floors and also the third floor and attic of the adjoining property B. The part which extends over property B is the flying freehold.

Foreclosure   If a mortgagor defaults on his mortgage, the mortgagee can enforce his security by transferring the interest of the mortgagor to himself. This is known as foreclosure.

Forestry Commission   A government body responsible for the promotion of forest industries and the protection, development and improvement of forests.

Freehold   Originally, under the feudal system, land was held by free men in return for services which they performed. Freehold land is owned for an indeterminate period of time and is transmitted on death in accordance with the type of estate. There are three estates of freehold: fee simple, fee tail and life interest. *See above* for fee simple. Fee tail is an interest in land which is passed on to one's heirs, possibly only specified heirs, e.g. males. Since the Law of Property Act 1925, 'entailed' interests can no longer subsist as legal interests in land, although they can be created through the use of trusts. Life interests are interests which subsist only until the death of the person referred to in the interest.

General Development Order (GDO)   A statutory instrument made under the Town and Country Planning Acts which sets out the procedures for development control and grants permitted development rights for some classes of development (refer to Chapter 2).

Green belt   A planning term which describes a rural area surrounding a town or city and in which development is restricted.

Green field site   An undeveloped site, usually at the edge of a town or city which is now proposed for development (it may have previously formed part of the green belt).

Green Paper   A government document which sets out proposals for new legislation, prior to a consultation period.

Ground rent   The proportion of rent attributable to the site and disregarding the buildings on the site.

Hereditament   Usually refers to a unit of property which appears in its own right in the valuation list. Legally, it means 'real property' or property which is capable of being transferred on death.

High Court of Justice   The lowest tier of the Supreme Court of England and Wales (refer to Chapter 1).

Improvement line   A line on a map prepared in accordance with s.73 of the Highways Act 1980 and running alongside a street. The land between the improvement line and the street cannot be used for building and is usually being reserved for future highway widening purposes.

Industrial improvement area   An area declared by a local authority under the Inner Urban Area Act 1978 and within which the local authority is prepared to make loans and grants to secure the improvement or conversion of buildings and the area generally. The term usually applies to an old industrial or commercial area.

Infrastructure   Comprises the apparatus and structures which are required to provide essential services to a development, for example roads, sewers, gas, telephones.

Injunction   An order of the court which prohibits a person from doing something or, more rarely, which compels a person to do something (refer to Chapter 1).

Inns of Court   Every barrister must belong to one of the four Inns of Court: Gray's Inn, Inner Temple, Middle Temple and Lincoln's Inn. These have existed since the fourteenth century and impose their own form of control and discipline on their members. No Inn is superior to another.

Intensification of use   A planning concept which refers to an increase in the degree of use to which a site is put. There comes a point when the intensification becomes a material change of use and planning permission is required.

Joint tenancy   When two or more people own land together so that on the death of one joint owner the whole of the land vests in the survivors. Every joint tenant must own every part of the land, if this is not the case there is no joint tenancy. It is not possible for a joint tenant to dispose of the land by will unless he is the sole survivor.

Judicial review   The procedure whereby an application can be made to the High Court to challenge a decision made by a public body (refer to Chapter 1).

Lady Day   *See* Quarter-days

Land charge   Under the Land Charges Act 1972, records are kept at the Land Charges Registry of various charges against land. These charges, which fall into a number of classes, must be registered by the person who benefits from them to protect his interest in the land. If he does not lodge a land charge then he may lose any rights against a bona fide purchaser of the land. The types of charge which are registerable are mortgages which are not protected in any other way, restrictive covenants, options to purchase and writs affecting land.

Land registration   The Land Registry was first established in London as a result of the Land Registry Act 1862. It provided for the voluntary registration of the title to land. This was extended with compulsory registration affecting areas of the country. Since the Land Registration Act 1925, and in particular over the past ten years, compulsory registration has spread to almost the whole of England and Wales. On any transfer of land the title to the land must be registered at the appropriate district land registry. The title is then recorded in a *land certificate* which is used to prove the title in future. The land certificate is divided into three sections which describe the property, the proprietors and any charges against the land. If there is a mortgage on the land, the certificate is known as a *charge certificate*. Land registration avoids the problems of retaining many old deeds and the land certificate presents the title to land in a more easily digestible format.

Lands Tribunal   Established in 1949, the tribunal hears appeals from local valuation courts, as well as determining issues relating to compulsory purchase and restrictive covenants and other similar matters (refer to Chapter 8).

Lawful use   In a planning context, a use of land which was begun with the benefit of planning permission or with deemed permission is lawful. Uses and operations on land are also lawful if no enforcement action can be taken against them. (*See also* CLEUD and CLOPUD, and refer to Chapter 2).

Leasehold   An estate in land which is for a term certain (e.g. for ten years from 25 September 1992) or is on a periodic tenancy. The document granting the right is called a lease.

Legal charge   A form of security for the payment of a debt whereby land is 'charged' with the payment. If the debtor fails to pay, the land can be sold by the lender to discharge the debt.

Listed building   A building which is included in the List of Buildings of Special Architectural or Historic Interest and which is compiled by the Secretary of State for the Environment (refer to Chapter 3).

Local authority   Includes district councils, county councils, parish councils, London borough councils and metropolitan councils. All of these comprise elected members who administer public services in their area of responsibility.

Local land charge   Some charges against land are registerable with the local authority as local land charges. For example, listed buildings, tree preservation orders, road widening schemes are all registered against the properties affected by them. The local authority is obliged to keep a local land charges register for its district for this purpose.

Local plan   A written statement supported by plans showing the proposals of a district planning authority for the development and land use of an area (*see also* Development plan).

Locus standi   Literally, a place of standing. A person who has *locus standi* has a right to be heard in court or other proceedings.

Mandamus   An order of the High Court which commands someone to perform a public duty. Literally, we command.

Mesne profits   The profits which a landlord is entitled to when a tenant remains illegally in possession of land. If there is no legal agreement between the parties, rent is not applicable, so mesne profits are assessed on the basis of the rent which would have been paid had there been a legal agreement.

Mineral rights   The rights of an owner to extract minerals from the ground. Property may be sold with the mineral rights included or these may be reserved to the original owner. Some minerals are, in fact, now vested in the Crown, such as coal and gas.

Natural justice   An unwritten body of rules which are to be adhered to by any person or body which sits in judgement on others. The main rules are that each party should have equal opportunity to state his case; each party should see and comment on the evidence of the other; the judge must be impartial and act in good faith. Basically, the rules of natural justice are designed to ensure that justice not only is done, but is seen to be done.

Notice to treat   The notice which is served on the owner of land by a body which wishes to acquire that land by compulsory purchase. Persons with other interests in the land, such as tenants, are also entitled to receive a notice to treat (refer to Chapter 8).

Obiter dictum   Literally, a saying by the way. It is an observation made by a judge during his decision which does not directly affect the case before him and upon which he does not have to make a decision. This part of a judgement is not binding as precedent. *See also ratio decidendi*.

Option   A unilateral contract whereby one party has the right at a specified time in the future to require the other party to carry out some act, if the first party so wishes. A common example is the grant of an option by a landowner to sell land at a future date, but at the request of the buyer.

Outline planning consent   This is permission to carry out development subject to the approval by the local planning authority of 'reserved matters' (refer to Chapter 2).

Parcel (of land)   An area of land which is identifiable in itself and is usually in one ownership.

Periodic tenancy   A tenancy whereby the rent is paid by reference to a period of time, e.g. weekly, monthly. The tenancy can be terminated at common law by either party giving to the other one period's notice, but this must be construed in accordance with the appropriate statute law.

Permitted development   *See* General development order.

Planning appeal   This is an appeal to the Secretary of State for the Environment against a local planning authority's decision to refuse to grant planning permission, or against conditions attached to a permission, or against a failure to reach a decision (see Chapter 2).

Planning blight   *See* Blight.

Planning brief   A document produced by a local authority setting out for a particular site advice on how development might be carried out. It might refer, for example, to access, density or landscaping. Sometimes known as a development brief.

Planning gain   An informal term used to describe an advantage which is gained by the public as a result of the grant of planning consent to a developer. For example, a developer may agree to contribute to the cost of widening a road if he obtains consent for his proposals.

Planning permission   Also known as planning consent, this is the formal approval granted by the local planning authority for development in accordance with the Town and Country Planning Acts.

Possessory title   A person who has been in undisputed possession of land for over twelve years can claim title to that land against the true owner. He will obtain a possessory title which is not as conclusive as a freehold or leasehold estate.

Prima facie   Literally, of first appearance. It is used when referring to evidence in a case; *prima facie* evidence is not conclusive, but is sufficient to justify prosecution in criminal proceedings.

Primary use   In a planning context, is the main use to which a site is put.

Private Act   An Act of Parliament which is introduced to Parliament by a private individual.

Public nuisance   An act which adversely affects a body of people or a community. The Attorney-General can be asked to bring criminal proceedings on behalf of the public against someone who is creating a public nuisance.

Purchase notice   A notice which can be served by an owner on a local authority requiring it to purchase his land on the basis that the land is no longer of reasonably beneficial use, perhaps because planning consent has been refused.

Quarter-days   Christmas Day (25 December); Lady Day (25 March); Midsummer Day (24 June) and Michaelmas (29 September). Rent which is paid quarterly is historically paid on the quarter-days.

Queen's Bench Division   The division of the High Court which primarily hears disputes relating to contract and tort.

Rack-rent   The rent which represents the full letting value of a property.

Ratio decidendi   Literally, the reason for the decision. This is the vital part of a judgement which will form precedent for future cases (*see also Obiter dictum*).

Reasonably beneficial use   After an adverse planning decision (either a refusal or one with onerous conditions), the owner may be entitled to request the local planning authority to purchase the land on the basis that it is not capable of reasonably beneficial use in its present state nor with the benefit of any planning consent which might be granted. To ascertain whether land is capable of reasonably beneficial use, the Secretary of State for the Environment considers its physical characteristics, its location and its general use (refer to Chapter 8).

Redemption   The paying off of a mortgage or other debt.

Reserved matters   The matters which remain to be dealt with by the local planning authority after the grant of outline planning consent.

Restrictive covenant   A covenant is an obligation contained in a deed, usually a conveyance or lease, which imposes requirements on the occupier of land. A covenant may be either positive, requiring the doing of some action or payment of money, or negative (also known as 'restrictive'). Positive covenants do not pass on to new owners of land, but negative covenants can be enforced even after the original covenantor has sold the land. These covenants, in effect, attach themselves to the land rather than to the person affected by them.

Reversion   The part of the interest in property which is left after some other interest has been granted. For example, the interest which remains after the grant of a lease of land.

Riparian   A property which is riparian is along the side of a river or stream. Riparian rights are rights which belong to the land which adjoins the river or stream and may be rights in the water itself, such as for fishing.

Scheduled monument   A monument which is included in the schedule of monuments compiled under the Ancient Monuments and Archaeological Areas Act 1979 and given protection in accordance with that Act (refer to Chapter 3).

Section 18 agreement   An agreement under s.18 of the Public Health Act 1939 which is entered into by a developer and a water authority and which empowers the water authority to adopt drains and sewers after they have been constructed by the developer. This power is now found in s.104 of the Water Industry Act 1991.

Section 40 agreement   Under s.40 of the Highways Act 1959 it was possible for a developer to enter into an agreement with the highway authority for the adoption of roads. The developer would agree to construct highways to the authority's specification and then the authority would take them over for public maintenance. This power is now found in s.38 of the Highways Act 1980, but the agreements are still often referred to as section 40 agreements.

Section 106 obligation   An agreement under s.106 of the Town and Country Planning Act 1990 into which a developer or other interested party may enter with a local planning authority to control development either on or away from the development site. It is particularly used to impose conditions which cannot legally be attached to the planning consent because they relate to off-site matters, such as road-widening at a near-by junction. Under the previous planning legislation this power was found in a similar but not identical form (s.52). The agreements are still sometimes referred to as section 52 agreements (*see also* Unilateral undertaking).

Simplified planning zone   A local planning authority has the power to create simplified planning zones within which planning permission is not required for development of specified types, for example in an industrial area.

Specific performance   A remedy which is available to the court at its discretion. If one party is in breach of contract and the other party cannot be adequately compensated by the payment of damages, the court may order specific performance of the contract. This makes the party in breach fulfil his obligations under the contract.

Spot-listing   Normally buildings are added to the statutory list of buildings of special architectural or historic interest on a regular basis when the area is reviewed. A local planning authority or other interested person can apply to the Secretary of State for the Environment for an individual building to be listed, usually to protect it from threatened development. This is known as spot-listing.

Stamp duty   Payable to the Inland Revenue on the transfer of land by either a lease or conveyance in accordance with a scale in force at the time. It is also paid on some other transactions.

Statutory instruments   Delegated legislation in the form of orders or regulations which are promulgated by a government department in accordance with powers contained in an Act.

Stop notice   A notice which can be served under the Town and Country Planning Act 1990 at the same time as or following service of an enforcement notice. The aim is to stop development continuing whilst the enforcement notice is taking effect.

Structure plan   A written statement, supported by diagrammatic plans, of the county planning authority's proposals for the development and land use of its area (*see also* Development plan).

Term   The duration of a lease. A lease for a term of ten years from 29 September 1992 will expire on the 28 September 2002.

Title   The right to ownership of property or land. A proper title to land must be traceable for at least fifteen years and reveal all the covenants or other matters affecting the land. The document which shows the commencement of the title is called the 'root of title'.

Tort   Literally, wrong. Wrongful acts or omissions which are independent of contractual obligations are torts. Torts comprise, amongst others, negligence, nuisance and trespass.

Tree preservation order   Usually referred to as a TPO, an order which may be made under s.198 of the Town and Country Planning Act 1990 by a local planning authority to protect trees or woodlands in its area. Breach of a TPO is a criminal offence and may lead to prosecution as well as a requirement for replacement of any damaged tree (refer to Chapter 3).

Unilateral undertaking   S.106 of the Town and Country Planning Act 1990 enables an applicant for planning permission to give a unilateral undertaking to carry out additional (usually off-site) work or to do or refrain from doing something in the event that planning permission is granted. This is particularly useful on appeal as the inspector appointed to determine the appeal can accept the undertaking as binding and enforceable on the appellant even though the local planning authority has not consented to it.

Unitary plan   A two-part plan produced by a London Borough or metropolitan district council showing strategic development and policies (part 1) and specific proposals for particular sites and areas (part 2). (*See also* Development plan.)

Use classes order   The Town and Country Planning (Use Classes) Order 1987 divides many common types of use into classes. Planning permission is not required to change use within the class, for example from a hairdresser to a post office both of which fall within class A1 (refer to Chapter 2).

Vacant possession   On completion of the sale of a property with vacant possession, no-one except the new owner has any interest or rights in the occupation of the property.

Vicarious liability   A legal liability which results from a particular relationship between the persons concerned whereby one person is liable for the torts and crimes of the other. It applies in an employer–employee relationship where the employer is responsible for the actions of his employees whilst they are carrying out their employment.

Visibility splay   Also known as a 'sight line' or 'vision splay', this is a section of land, usually on two sides of a road junction, which remains undeveloped and otherwise unobstructed to ensure that visibility from the junction is unimpeded for a specified distance.

Void   When referring to a contract, this means that the contract has no legal effect, perhaps because it was entered into fraudulently.

Volenti non fit injuria   Literally, that to which a man consents cannot be considered an injury. A person who genuinely consents to run the risk of suffering some harm cannot later take action in connection with any resulting injury. In those circumstances, the defendant could successfully allege that the plaintiff had voluntarily waived or abandoned his rights. For example, a person who undertakes an intrinsically dangerous hobby such as boxing or parachuting by implication assents to run the risk of injury. Similarly, a person who submits to a surgical operation cannot sue the surgeon for assault because he has expressly consented to the act.

White land   Land which has no particular allocation in the development plan.

White Paper   An official government publication which sets out government policy and usually makes proposals for new legislation.

Without prejudice   When parties are negotiating either verbally or in writing the negotiations are often 'without prejudice'. This means that if an agreement is reached as a result of the negotiations, any letters or other documents can be used as evidence of the agreement. If agreement is not reached, however, those negotiations cannot be used as evidence in future court proceedings.

APPENDIX 6

RECOMMENDED FURTHER READING

Chapter 1
L. A. Rutherford, I. A. Todd and M. G. Woodley, *Introduction to the Law* (Sweet and Maxwell, 1982).

Chapters 2 and 3
Sir Desmond Heap (Gen. Ed.) and M. Grant (Ed.), *Encyclopaedia of Planning Law and Practice* (Sweet and Maxwell).

Chapter 4
J. F. Garner (Ed.), *Control of Pollution Encyclopaedia* (Butterworth).
C. Cross (Gen. Ed.) and N. Hawke (Asst Ed.), *Encyclopaedia of Environmental Health Law and Practice* (Sweet and Maxwell).

Chapter 5
J. Bates, *Water and Drainage Law* (Sweet and Maxwell).

Chapter 6
V. Powell-Smith and M. J. Billington, *The Building Regulations Explained and Illustrated* (Blackwell, 9th edn, 1992).

Chapter 7
M. J. Goodman (Gen. Ed.), *Encyclopaedia of Health and Safety at Work Law and Practice* (Sweet and Maxwell).
C. Cross (Gen. Ed.) and N. Hawke (Asst Ed.), *Encyclopaedia of Environmental Health Law and Practice* (Sweet and Maxwell).
C. Cross (Gen. Ed.) and S. Sauvain (Asst Ed.), *Encyclopaedia of Highway Law and Practice* (Sweet and Maxwell).

Chapter 8
C. Brand (Gen. Ed.), *Encyclopaedia of Compulsory Purchase and Compensation* (Sweet and Maxwell).
B. Denyer-Green, *Compulsory Purchase and Compensation* (Estates Gazette, 3rd edn, 1989).
D. J. Hawkins, *Boynton's Guide to Compulsory Purchase and Compensation* (Longman, 6th edn, 1990).

INDEX OF
STATUTES

INDEX OF STATUTORY INSTRUMENTS

INDEX OF CASES

Notes

1. The citations above refer to the following law reports:
    - All ER   All England Law Reports
    - AC   Appeal Cases
    - LT   Law Times

2. The use of (HL) after a case means that the case was heard and the decision made by the House of Lords.

3. Square brackets around a date in the case reference indicates that the date is an essential part of the citation, as the law reports are published annually and identified by reference to the year of publication. Round brackets indicate, by contrast, that the date is not significant because the reports are published on a volume-to-volume basis and the case could be found solely with the volume number.

INDEX